U.S. Foreign Policy
and the
United Nations System

CONTRIBUTORS

FREDERICK C. CUNY, INTERTECT

MICHAEL W. DOYLE, Princeton University

LEWIS A. DUNN, Science Applications International
Corporation

FELICE D. GAER, American Jewish Committee

CATHERINE GWIN, Overseas Development Council

EDWARD C. LUCK, United Nations Association of the USA

CHARLES WILLIAM MAYNES, *Foreign Policy*

DONALD J. PUCHALA, University of South Carolina

BRIAN URQUHART, Ford Foundation

MAURICE WILLIAMS, Overseas Development Council

RICHARD S. WILLIAMSON, Mayer Brown & Platt

THE AMERICAN ASSEMBLY
Columbia University

U.S. Foreign Policy and the United Nations System

CHARLES WILLIAM MAYNES
and
RICHARD S. WILLIAMSON
Editors

W. W. NORTON & COMPANY
New York   London

First Edition

For information about permission to reproduce selections from this book, write to
Permissions, W. W. Norton & Company, Inc., 500 Fifth Avenue, New York, NY
10110.

The text of this book is composed in Baskerville.
Composition and manufacturing by the Haddon Craftsmen, Inc.

Library of Congress Cataloging-in-Publication Data
U.S. Foreign policy and the United Nations system / edited by C.
   William Maynes and Richard S. Williamson.
      p.   cm.
   Includes bibliographical references and index.
      1. United Nations—United States.   I. Maynes, C. William.
   (Charles William)   II. Williamson, Richard S.
   JX1977.2.U5U15   1995
   327.73—dc20   95-37932

ISBN 0-393-03907-2

W. W. Norton & Company, Inc., 500 Fifth Avenue, New York, N.Y. 10110
W. W. Norton & Company Ltd., 10 Coptic Street, London WC1A 1PU

1 2 3 4 5 6 7 8 9 0

Contents

U.S. Foreign Policy
and the
United Nations System

Preface

This American Assembly volume was written not only because this year is the fiftieth anniversary of the signing of the United Nations Charter, but also because U.S. policy concerning the U.N. is in a state of crisis. The United States is moving in conflicting directions that are having a negative impact on the U.N. system. On the one hand, the United States is turning inward to deal with serious economic, social, racial, and other challenges. As part of that reorientation, there has been an increasing desire on the part of many of our citizens for the United States to withdraw from its global leadership role and not to be the world's police officer. At the same time, however, the United States appears to be withdrawing its support for the United Nations system, which, because of its security functions, is the only alternative world police officer, in the absence of the leadership of a single country.

In search of policy recommendations that might reconcile this apparent conflict, The American Assembly, in cooperation with the United Nations Association of the United States of America, sought bipartisan leadership for a group of representative experts to analyze the current situation and make policy recommendations. We were encouraged in this undertaking by senior officials of the U.S. government and of the United Nations Secretariat.

We were very fortunate in securing two co-editors who had occupied the same high government position concerning U.S. policy for the United Nations, namely assistant secretary of state for international organization affairs. Richard S. Williamson, who served under President Reagan, was recently the Republican candidate for the U.S. Senate from Illinois and is an attorney in practice with Mayer Brown & Platt. Charles William Maynes was the assistant secretary under President Carter and is now the editor of *Foreign Policy* magazine.

It is our hope and expectation that this volume will serve U.S. national interests by helping decision makers and the informed public to understand more fully the implications of our present policy directions and seek appropriate policies to assure that U.S. national interests are protected. It is also our hope that this volume will prove useful for years to come in American college and university courses, will help analysts in research, and will assist other nonprofit institutions and those in the media who help guide the understanding of the American public on critical foreign policy issues.

The American Assembly particularly wishes to thank those institutions and individuals who helped to make this program possible: The Carnegic Corporation of New York, The Hauser Fund of the New York Community Trust, The United States Institute of Peace, and an anonymous donor. These organizations as well as The American Assembly take no position on issues discussed in this volume.

The papers in this volume were commissioned to serve as background for an American Assembly held at Arden House, Harriman, New York, April 20–23, 1995. The forty-two men and women who attended that meeting represented a wide cross section of American leadership opinion on this subject. The report that they prepared together before they left Arden House is included in this volume as an appendix.

Daniel A. Sharp

President, ~~The New York Stock Exchange~~

(Error)   American Assembly

NYSE supported this Am. Assembl. Project.

Introduction

CHARLES WILLIAM MAYNES
AND RICHARD S. WILLIAMSON

It is time for the United States to get its act together regarding the United Nations.

It is traditional and appropriate to celebrate major anniversaries such as the U.N.'s fiftieth. It is a time to reflect upon the United

CHARLES WILLIAM MAYNES has served since 1980 as editor of *Foreign Policy*, one of the leading journals in the world on international affairs. Over the course of his career he has held positions in the Department of State, entering the foreign service in 1962; the U.S. Congress, where he served as senior legislative assistant in the office of Senator Fred R. Harris; and in the foundation world. He was named assistant secretary of state for international organization affairs by President Carter in 1977. RICHARD S. WILLIAMSON is a partner in Mayer Brown & Platt. He served as assistant secretary of state for international organization affairs in the Reagan administration. He had previously served as a member of President Reagan's White House senior staff, as a member of the U.S. delegations to U.S.–USSR bilateral negotiations on nuclear nonproliferation in 1983 and 1984, and as U.S. representative to the U.N. offices in Vienna from 1983–85. He is the author of *The United Nations: A Place of Promise and of Mischief* and of *Reagan's Federalism: His Efforts to Decentralize Government*.

Nations' history, to assess its accomplishments and disappointments. But there are more compelling reasons to look anew at U.S.
foreign policy and the U.N. system. We confront a new world, and
multilateral fora are more central than ever before to advancing
U.S. interests and managing global problems.

The United Nations was forged fifty years ago by the horrors of
World War II. After turning our back on the League of Nations
and fighting another world war, the United States embraced the
new world assembly with its idealism and hope. But concurrent
with its founding, the cold war began, which informed every aspect of U.N. activity and often dictated its action.

During the cold war, as the United States and the Soviet Union
faced off against one another, other nations aligned themselves
with one or the other driven by ideology, geography, economics,
or expediency. The framework to manage foreign affairs was
structured by the cold war realities. The United Nations became
another venue to wage cold war competition or to help contain
situations that threatened to spin out of control.

During this long period the U.N. was a valuable arena to develop international norms in many important areas such as human
rights and nuclear nonproliferation. It was an enormously helpful
vehicle to pool knowledge and resources in a number of areas such
as global health, civil aeronautics, and meteorological information. It launched a number of successful "peacekeeping" missions
to help to disengage from armed conflict belligerents exhausted by
warfare. And at times it was a political greenhouse where rhetoric
or ill-conceived political resolutions made problems worse.

And throughout this long period, all U.N. activity passed
through the cold war prism and was subsidiary to it. Now all that
has changed.

Today there is only one superpower. The bipolar ballast is gone.
The dominant, defining logic for old alliances has disappeared.
The immediate threat of nuclear holocaust has diminished, yet
very real threats to peace and security remain with the proliferation of weapons of mass destruction, especially the threat of a
renegade regime achieving nuclear breakout; with instability
caused by intense ethnic conflict; with centuries-old tribal hatred
in the Middle East; with massive, destabilizing migration of refu-

gees; with precarious supply lines for strategic supplies such as oil; and so on.

Also, in this new world the United States has a large number of other important interests and preferences such as advancing free trade, maintaining international monetary stability, protecting intellectual property, keeping order in the increasingly interconnected global marketplace, protecting universal human rights, containing and eventually eradicating dreaded diseases, advancing a cleaner global environment, promoting sustainable development, and so on.

For many of the aspects of these vital security issues, as well as these important national interests and preferences, traditional bilateral diplomacy is inadequate for the new challenges. They require attention by a broad range of nations. And nations, released from the discipline of the cold war, will no longer accept decisions made by Washington and Moscow alone. As sovereign states, albeit with wide ranges of economic and military power, they demand participation in deliberations. And while the strongest and most powerful nations can influence and lead, the capacity to dictate the terms of engagement, if it was ever there, today is gone.

The United States has its own constellation of security issues, national interests, and preferences, and the new world dictates that in many cases they be advanced through multilateral means.

There is a menu of multilateral institutions. Some such as the United Nations, the North Atlantic Treaty Organization, the World Bank, and the Organization of American States are old. Others such as the Group of Seven (G-7) have been around for decades. And some such as the Council for Security and Cooperation in Europe were launched at the cusp of the new world. Each of these multilateral institutions has a different mission and capacity, varying membership, and history that better equip it to address one international issue or another.

Among these international institutions, the United Nations has a particularly rich tradition and a number of unique characteristics such as universality that warrant reexamination during this time of transition. Furthermore, since the end of the Gulf War, large parts of U.S. foreign policy generally and in particular U.S. engagement in the United Nations have been wobbly.

As a great power with unique economic and military strength, a broad range of important national interests, and a tradition of international involvement, it is incumbent upon the United States to get its act together regarding the U.N. We can ill-afford to diminish this instrument to advance our foreign policy interests through wild inconsistency, thoughtlessness, or neglect.

Therefore, not only because it is the U.N.'s fiftieth anniversary but also because of the new international environment and the growing potential importance of the U.N. to U.S. foreign policy, this book was conceived. It has been executed with a deep appreciation of the valuable United States tradition of a bipartisan U.S. foreign policy, drawing upon Democratic and Republican authors. And it has sought to address most of the big issues U.S. foreign policy should reexamine in the U.N. system.

Edward Luck, a long-time student of U.S. policy toward the United Nations, points out that no American president has questioned the need for an active, high-profile American presence in the U.N. or suggested weakening the international body. What matters to national leaders is not the institution, but the specific policy tasks that can be accomplished there. Multilateralism is a series of quid pro quos, of supporting another nation's favorite programs in exchange for their support of yours.

The United States has a fundamental interest in the U.N. as an institution because it has an unquestioned stake in international law, order, and stability. The United States is a status quo power with a strong preference for change through peaceful means, and therefore has a strong interest in the U.N., in spite of the organization's many weaknesses and shortcomings.

The end of the cold war has produced a new set of circumstances that is still not fully understood by U.S. policy makers, Luck asserts. Confusion about our purpose in the U.N. is a sign of a far deeper malaise about our role in the world. Paradoxically, even as the U.N.'s political climate has become more favorable to America, our relations with the U.N. have deteriorated. There is more concern now, even among traditionally nonaligned countries, about a leadership vacuum than about the United States throwing its weight around.

Luck notes that everybody agrees that "national interest"

should be the determining factor in deciding which U.N. missions to support, but nobody has explained what those interests are. Luck identifies four basic schools of thought about U.S. relations' interests in the United Nations:

- isolationists who find multilateralism to be abhorrent to the protection of American values and interests;
- neo-isolationists who are skeptical about the value of the U.N. but who do not reject involvement in the world body outright;
- internationalists who tend to believe that a confluence of U.S. interests and those of other key U.N. members has laid the foundation for a reinvigoration of the U.N. and other multilateral institutions;
- world citizens who see the U.N. as a stepping stone on the route to world government.

Most Americans fall roughly into the internationalist or neo-isolationist camps, and it is their debate that will decide U.S. policy outcomes.

In his chapter, Michael Doyle, a professor at Princeton who has served as a consultant to the International Peace Academy, focuses on the ways in which the United Nations could better carry out its peacekeeping functions, which have become so controversial after setbacks in Bosnia and Somalia.

Doyle separates peacekeeping operations into three categories. In "first generation peacekeeping" U.N. forces interpose themselves between two warring factions who have agreed to a ceasefire while they pursue a permanent end to hostilities. "Second generation peacekeeping" (SGP) also involves the consent of the host country, but U.N. forces do more than simply separate the combatants. They play an active role in securing a peace treaty, and they assist in building the structures necessary to ensure that both the peace and the state they leave behind are durable. "Third generation peacekeeping" is defined by the absence of consent to the U.N. involvement. It is the last that has generated the most controversy, and Doyle concludes that such operations will be rare because the U.N. does not have the resources to fulfill the mission.

In Doyle's view the future of peacekeeping lies in SGP. "In these operations," he writes, "the U.N. is typically involved in implementing peace agreements that go to the roots of the conflict, helping to build a long-term foundation for stable, legitimate government." Successful SGP operations involve peacemaking, peacekeeping, and peacebuilding.

The problem, as with so many U.N. programs, is the cost. But according to Doyle, the alternatives to working with the U.N. are acting alone or "allowing human disasters to take their course." Such options make multilateralism much more appealing.

Another key area of security concern lies in the realm of arms control. Lewis Dunn, who held a senior position in the Arms Control and Disarmament Agency during the Reagan administration, believes that a more creative use of the United Nations can strengthen traditional nonproliferation efforts.

There are five categories of developments that seriously undermine traditional nonproliferation procedures:

- The accelerating erosion of technical constraints—The advancement of global industrialization and technological development has ensured that more countries can gain the capability to produce weaponry quicker than ever.
- New-style proliferators—The new style of proliferator, such as Iraq, Iran, or North Korea, may be motivated less by the need to feel secure than by actual aggressive intent. Possession of nuclear, chemical, and biological weapons is seen as an actual means to expand influence, rather than just to feel secure.
- Breakdown of the cold war security framework—The network of ties that maintained the cold war status quo is gone, and so are the informal influences that served to buttress security, constrain ambitions, and influence regional proliferation dynamics.
- Lack of credible responses to noncompliance—Both individual nations and the international community have failed to devise a credible and effective response to noncompliance with nonproliferation efforts, as shown by the case of Iraq.
- The danger of use—The greatest danger of all is that of the future physical use of nuclear, biological, or chemical weapons.

Dunn asserts that greater U.S. recourse to the U.N. can be beneficial to nonproliferation efforts and identifies five areas of nonproliferation in which the U.N. has the greatest potential. These are:

- nonproliferation norm building;
- institutionalizing attention and concern;
- security building;
- nuclear crisis management;
- buttressing nonproliferation compliance.

Could there be an eventual possibility of a complete global ban on any use of nuclear, chemical, or biological weapons? Only the prospect of "international outlawry" will deter some potential aggressors, he argues, and the U.N. Security Council is the best body to create and maintain such a taboo.

A first step in this direction would be a complete ban on at least chemical and biological weapons, while seeking to build consensus among the five declared nuclear weapon states on the principle of an enforceable nonuse ban. This could be followed by the passing of resolutions reflecting these principles. Although the eventual establishment of such a ban may be an illusory idea, a gradual evolution of attitudes is the only way to bring about such a momentous change.

An area of U.N. activity that has always attracted both strong support and vigorous criticism has been the overall development effort involving a host of U.N. agencies. Catherine Gwin, vice president of the Overseas Development Council, and Maurice Williams, who has had a long and distinguished career in international development institutions, underscore the role the United States played in the initial design, construction, and implementation of the U.N. system, including the various multilateral development institutions attached to it. Having "so actively helped to create" this system, they argue, the United States now has a major responsibility in "revising and reviving" it.

But there is, today, within the United Nations system a lack of international policy coherence, both across various sectors and across major institutions and programs. Another problem is "program sprawl": the agenda for development has broadened, funding has increased, and the expectations of both donor and recipient countries have grown, with no corresponding increase in

institutional capabilities. This has also led to a proliferation of
multilateral aid agencies, which all increasingly see themselves in
competition with one another. Meanwhile, administrative laxness
on the part of the U.N. itself exacerbates these problems.

The authors identify six areas of priority in U.N. reform, where
specific changes can make the working of the U.N. system more
effective:

- consolidation of central U.N. development funds and programs;
- creation of a single emergency relief organization;
- activating the institutional structure of the U.N. to implement
  the Earth Summit conclusions;
- reinventing the Economic and Social Council;
- across-the-board improvements in relations with nongovernmental organizations;
- eliminating unnecessary bureaucracy.

But here again, little can happen without adequate financing.
Reform is linked to financing. Significant changes in general funding are unlikely to take place until U.N. institutions provide better
accountability and transparency in their management and governance.

A growth area in U.N. activity has been the field of human
rights and democracy promotion. Felice Gaer, who is director of
the Jacob Blaustein Institute for the Advancement of Human
Rights of the American Jewish Committee, examines the roles of
the United States and the U.N. in the promotion and protection of
human rights, where there are tensions.

The U.S. preference is to attempt to protect people from violations of human rights by investigating abuses in particular countries and enacting sanctions, if necessary. The U.N., by contrast,
seeks consensus on norms and standards for human rights. The
U.N. then encourages nations to sign treaties in which they commit themselves to the maintenance of these standards.

This latter approach has its limitations. The United Nations has
no enforcement mechanisms, and its High Commissioner for
Human Rights currently lacks the power to link the human rights
agenda to other U.N. programs. Additionally, U.N. member states
disagree about what constitutes a universal human right and

whether the U.N. should condition aid to adherence to human rights treaties.

Gaer would correct this shortcoming by granting more power to the U.N. High Commissioner for Human Rights. The high commissioner would have the authority to inject a human rights agenda into all U.N. functions; he or she would enjoy close contact with the secretary-general and U.N. security and development organizations. He or she would advise the Security Council regularly on situations in which human rights violations might occur and should have the ability to act independently to order fact-finding missions and to publicize abuses. In order to protect human rights more effectively, the Centre for Human Rights would gain material and communications support and expert personnel for field missions.

Another crisis area for the United Nations and target for its critics is the treatment of refugees. A system designed by the Western powers during the cold war is now forced to confront problems that it was not designed to face. New problems from the religion of refugees to their location in the world have put an enormous stress on the international refugee regime. More and more refugees live in the Northern Hemisphere, where the colder weather increases the cost of caring for them. By 1990, 75 percent of the world's refugees were Muslim. The hierarchy of the internal refugee regime is unclear, and international law's definition of refugee status may be outdated.

Fred Cuny, president of INTERTECT, a Dallas based emergency management consulting firm, believes that the major deficiency in the international aid system in 1995 is that there is no U.N. agency specifically tasked with providing assistance to the internal refugees, or displaced persons, or others under attack by their own government. United Nations organizations must be invited to assist in a crisis to ensure that they do not interfere with sovereignty. The result is that internally displaced persons fall outside the realm of international law—they are not refugees unless they cross an international border, but they are often desperately in need of humanitarian assistance.

The increasingly Islamic nature of refugee crises, too, has proven difficult for the international refugee regime to handle.

The body of international refugee law is predicated on Western notions of law and morality, and Islamic scholars hold that law must be based upon the Holy Koran. The resultant culture clash often renders refugee advocacy groups irrelevant and unwelcome.

Four categories of preventive diplomacy, in Cuny's view, are needed:

- the prevention of conflict and humanitarian emergencies by international diplomacy and deterrence;
- mitigation and containment of crises through effective sanctions, military isolation, and arms embargoes; these methods must punish the guilty rather than the innocent;
- a review of aid strategies in conflicts to find measures that can alleviate suffering without exacerbating strife or increasing risks to aid providers;
- conflict resolution.

Sir Brian Urquhart, long-time senior U.N. civil servant who worked closely with the first five secretaries-general on peace and security matters and currently is scholar-in-residence at the Ford Foundation, examines the role of the secretary-general and calls for reforms of the appointment process. The U.N.'s founders were unsure of what they wanted in the secretary-general. However, they did want the U.N.'s senior international civil servant to go beyond just an administrative role and to encompass some political dimension vaguely defined.

The secretary-general is both an international civil servant answerable to all 185 member states and at the same time often asked to be a leader. His mandate is founded upon the idealism and global objectives of the U.N. Charter and constrained by the pragmatic national sovereignty of the member states.

Urquhart reviews how the nature of the job of the U.N. secretary-general has grown over the years by providing a summary of the six secretaries-general from Trygve Lie to Boutros Boutros-Ghali. Then he discusses the present scope of the job.

While Urquhart believes the secretary-general's role as a political intermediary may be less essential in the post–cold war world, the role as operational director of the U.N. will grow and become increasingly difficult. Furthermore, the U.N. is increasingly engaged in civil and ethnic crisis for which it was not originally designed. And in Urquhart's view, the greatest future challenges will come in the great global problems of poverty, environment, trade arrangements, responsible governance, and other problems in the economic and social area.

Therefore, Urquhart recommends that the U.N. members improve the process of selecting future secretaries-general. The members should define the essential qualifications necessary to determine the best person for the job. Individual campaigns for the job should be prohibited. A thorough, stringent, and wide-ranging search procedure should be initiated. And, Urquhart recommends, the secretary-general should be limited to a single seven-year term.

In Urquhart's view, the secretary-general's office and efforts are central to the strength and growth of the U.N. And the reforms he outlines are intended to better insure that success.

What if it proves impossible to make some of the reforms called for by the authors already discussed? Donald Puchala, professor of government at the University of South Carolina, has produced a highly provocative answer. A disappointed U.N. supporter, he has concluded that serious reform of the U.N. is impossible under current conditions. He therefore envisions a dramatic deconstruction of the United Nations system along "functionalist" lines: he would have the United States press for an even more decentralized system of agencies with individual specializations, rather than press for a single more centralized bureaucracy.

Puchala begins by reviewing four key areas in which the U.N. has drawn the most criticism—peacekeeping, development, financing, and management.

Peacekeeping in the post–cold war era is radically different and more complex than ever before; yet, according to Puchala, the U.N.'s failure to adjust to the new circumstances contributes to the confusion that plagues its peacekeeping operations. Enhancing the U.N.'s preventive diplomacy capabilities is one of the important steps toward reform.

Development, in Puchala's view, is perhaps the U.N.'s greatest failure, caused by a lack of coherent strategy, North-South political rivalries, and lack of administrative coordination among the plethora of U.N. assisted development agencies.

Finance is a major problem. Contributions are erratic and often

withheld altogether. Puchala calls for granting additional resources to the U.N. reassessing individual members' contributions
in order to reflect their capabilities, and authorizing the U.N. to
charge interest on outstanding balances.

Bureaucratic mismanagement at the U.N. has always been a
major concern of the United States. Here politicization of appointments has been a key reason for the lack of competent people.
Calls for reform have frequently included suggestions to create the
post of an inspector-general to press for transparency.

Finally, Puchala addresses Security Council reform, emphasizing that it is important for the Council to be more representative of
power distribution in the world today.

Regrettably, the prognosis for all these reforms is discouraging.
Ideological divides between North and South have replaced cold
war era superpower rivalry as a stumbling block to the smooth
functioning of the U.N. Meanwhile, the increasing hostility toward
the U.N. within the American political system, coupled with Third
World disenchantment, makes it even more difficult to reinstate
international faith in the U.N. system.

It may be, however, that even if all the reforms proposed could
be implemented, it would not be enough. Perhaps no single organization can accommodate the unique multilateral needs of the
post–cold war world. Puchala believes this is the case and calls for
a return to functionalism, which argues that multilateralism is better served by dismantling centralized bureaucracies and individually strengthening specialized agencies. Thus functionalism calls
for an efficient division of labor, with individual agencies specifically mandated, staffed, and budgeted to execute specific tasks.

Building on this approach, Puchala argues that the General
Assembly, as the only international forum for debate, should be
maintained, as should the U.N. Educational, Scientific, and Cultural Organization, while the various human rights agencies
should all be collapsed into the World Court. Puchala also recommends the creation of a world peacekeeping agency that could
fulfill the functions of the secretary-general's office, its Department
of Political Affairs, and the Security Council. Similarly, the U.N.
Development Programme could be collapsed into several specific
development agencies such as the Food and Agriculture Organization, the World Health Organization, etc.

These and other changes, Puchala argues, would eliminate much of the duplication that currently occurs among the various agencies of the U.N., conserve resources, and eliminate much of the bureaucratic red tape while enhancing efficiency and accountability. Thus Puchala looks to go much further than just simply calling for U.N. reform. Instead he seeks a decentralized, functionally focused system that he believes is the only viable hope for the future of multilateralism.

The Puchala chapter is perhaps the one to conclude this discussion because the alternative to reform is not paralysis. Governments do have a growing amount of international business to conduct. They ordinarily prefer to conduct this business in institutions that already exist, but the business must be done. If existing institutions are found wanting, there will at some point be a search for a different approach. Puchala's views suggest one direction that effort might take, but they also suggest the stakes involved for a U.N. that cannot be reformed.

The editors believe that reform is possible but that it is also difficult. Success requires a U.S. policy toward the U.N. that is both critical and engaged. While legitimate differences in perspective may exist, there also are large areas of common ground for Democrats and Republicans to build upon together.

It is the hope of the editors that this volume will lead to precisely such an approach by this administration and its successors.

1

The United Nations, Multilateralism, and U.S. Interests

EDWARD C. LUCK

At a time of great change in the world, it should come as no surprise that Americans are uncertain about the nature and scope of their global interests. Prevalent notions of interdependence, global markets, and humanity without borders coexist uneasily with a wariness of distant entanglements, a reluctance to serve as the world's police officer, and a preoccupation with domestic economic and social concerns. The certainties and rigidities of the cold war competition have given way to the dilemma of plotting a foreign policy strategy without either ideological or historical guideposts. Ambivalence may be the natural reaction to the ambiguities of a transition period in world politics, but it provides a shaky foundation for global leadership.

Nowhere are these confusions and hesitations more evident

EDWARD C. LUCK is president emeritus and senior policy advisor of the United Nations Association of the USA (UNA–USA) and a consultant to foundations, universities, and government agencies. A frequent media commentator, he has published and testified widely on arms control, national security, Russia, Japan, and the United Nations.

than in U.S. relations with the United Nations. As long as Americans are uncertain of their interests in the world, they are bound to be unsure of their place and their purposes in the world body. Policies toward the U.N. are caught in the intersection 1) of partisan bickering over the conception and management of U.S. foreign policy; 2) of struggles between the executive branch and Congress over the control of policy making; 3) of contention between internationalists and neo-isolationists about the wisdom and scope of foreign engagements; and 4) of longstanding debates regarding the relative advantages of unilateral versus multilateral approaches for dealing with major policy concerns. For symbolic as well as substantive reasons, the United Nations has become the handiest target for those critical of the current management of U.S. foreign policy.

At the heart of these debates, though rarely addressed squarely and openly, is the question of American national interests. What are we seeking to achieve, what are we willing to risk or sacrifice in the effort, and are our priorities shifting? What mix of unilateral, bilateral, and multilateral vehicles would most effectively further American interests and be most appropriate to changing conditions? The answers to these queries define the nature of U.S. interests in the U.N., the subject of this chapter. American national interests in the U.N. must derive from and be a subset of our global interests, for the United Nations is more than an ideal. From a day-to-day policy perspective it is a place in which to advance, and when necessary to defend, our national goals and purposes.

Yet do Americans also have a long-term interest in bolstering the U.N. as an institution, in giving it greater capabilities for addressing the world's problems, in making it a stronger organization? For example, are American national interests reflected more accurately by the near-record public support for the world body registered in public opinion polls, or in the congressional legislation to restrict U.S. funding for the U.N. and limit participation in its peacekeeping operations? In what specific ways does the U.N. serve to advance or undermine U.S. national interests, and how should those interests be defined (and defended) in a multilateral context in which decision making is shared with many other countries? In short, what are American national interests and priorities in the U.N. system, and what kind of a profile should the United States take in the world body to advance them more effectively?

In order to address these questions in a larger conceptual, historical, and strategic context, this chapter will first consider the nature of "national" interests in a broad based international body. It will then trace briefly the historical evolution of U.S. policies and attitudes toward the U.N., with particular attention to the unsteady and incomplete transition from cold war to post–cold war conditions. This discussion will lay the foundation for an analysis of the current American debate over U.N. peace operations and U.S. participation in and contribution to them.

On the Nature of National Interests

Does the United States as a nation have interests in the United Nations as an institution? The answer is more often assumed than articulated. Top U.S. policy makers rarely address the question of American national interests in the U.N. in a direct or comprehensive manner. Policy makers do enunciate our national interests in specific parts or activities of the U.N. from time to time, particularly when justifying specific budget outlays or program initiatives. The expression of American interests, however, is done in parts, reflecting the way policy toward the U.N. tends to be made: by different people in different bureaus and agencies working on different aspects of the U.N.'s vast agenda. From the top—the president or secretary of state—are heard mostly broad statements of the importance of multilateralism or international cooperation. No president has questioned the need for an active, high-profile American presence in the world body, though the tone and tactics of their approaches have varied significantly. None has suggested that the U.N. should be weakened instead of strengthened or that the U.S. should withhold payment of its legally assessed dues. For national officials, the U.N. is a functional and instrumental place, a place to carry out some portion of the nation's business, and a forum in which support can be gathered from other nations for one's own priorities or opposition can be generated to actions perceived to be antithetical to U.S. interests.

Support for the United Nations, therefore, tends to be broad more than deep, to be made up of many parts that are not embraced or even understood as a whole. The U.N. is a highly decentralized institution in which interests in one part or another may not be translated or transferred readily into a perceived interest in the fate of the confederated system. Sometimes different U.N. agencies even compete with each other for attention and funds from the U.S. government. Not only are interests in the United Nations disaggregated, they also tend to be instrumental. What matters to national leaders—in the short run at least—is not the institution, but the specific policy tasks that can be accomplished there. Since policy making is inherently a myopic enterprise, it is understandable that officials will evince much more interest in what happens at the U.N., whether in human rights, disarmament, sustainable development, refugees, conflict resolution, population, or peacekeeping, than in building the institution itself for the long haul.

This raises the murky, but parallel question of whether nations or just constituencies have interests. In an era of one-issue nongovernmental organizations and lobbying groups, the voices expressing an interest in a single aspect of the U.N.'s activities—farmers in the Food and Agriculture Organization, unions in the International Labor Organization, arms controllers in the International Atomic Energy Agency, relief workers in the U.N. High Commissioner for Refugees, human rights activists in the U.N. High Commissioner for Human Rights, pilots in the International Civil Aeronautics Organization, and bankers and investors in the World Bank and the International Monetary Fund—tend to be louder and more influential than those seeking a general strengthening of the world body and an expansion of multilateral cooperation as a way of handling the world's business. This factor partly explains why U.S. voluntary funding for specific U.N. programs and agencies continued at a high level, with broad congressional support, in the mid-to-late 1980s when the United States began withholding a substantial portion of its legally obligated assessments for the U.N.'s regular budget. U.S. interests—and U.N. performance—vary markedly from one agency or program to another, as have U.S. judgments about the value of supporting different parts of the whole.

Parts of the U.N. system may be handy from time to time, but are U.S. interests in the whole more than those in the sum of its parts? If not, is it possible to pick and choose among the programs and agencies, to select only a few for active U.S. participation? Some differentiation is inevitable, and priorities shift somewhat from one U.S. administration to the next, but given the range of American global involvements, it is hard to imagine the United States abandoning large stretches of the U.N. entirely. While the first Reagan administration conducted a sweeping review of U.S. participation in U.N. activities, it concluded that withdrawal from only one agency—the United Nations Educational, Scientific, and Cultural Organization (UNESCO)—was justified. (The Clinton administration determined that there had been sufficient changes in UNESCO to justify reentry, if funding could be found.) Small countries often have to limit the range of their U.N. participation, but the United States is too big, too important, and too visible to pursue such a highly selective strategy without doing real harm to the system as a whole. Likewise, while some parts would survive the demise of the whole—the Universal Postal Union and the International Labor Organization, among others, preceded the founding of the U.N.—many would not. The United Nations may be a decentralized system, but it still strives to be a system, one that is woven from the disparate, as well as the common, interests and priorities of its members.

Every member state has its pet projects and agencies. To make a multilateral system work in one's favor requires paying at least lip service to some of the favorite programs of other states whose support one needs for one's own priorities. Multilateralism is a process of quid pro quos, of trade-offs that are the substance of compromise and consensus. These trade-offs and compromises, of course, are the source of considerable worry to those skeptics who fear that the United States will give up too much for too little gain. But to others, this is a process of accumulating political savings for a rainy day when one will need others' support. In extremis, as in the war with Iraq, American power and leadership far transcend the day-to-day logrolling politics of the United Nations, but even the United States needs to play the game in terms of forwarding its regular agenda at the U.N.

The United States has a fundamental interest in the United Nations as an institution because it has an unquestioned stake in international law, order, and stability. However imperfectly the U.N. performs this function, the world body is, on balance, a net contributor to a more orderly, predictable, norm-abiding, and hence stable world. It provides a forum for developing, step-by-step, a legal and normative framework that defines standards for national behavior both toward other nations and toward one's own citizens. It provides as well an array of services and processes for resolving simmering disputes and for addressing, however superficially, their causes. In security terms, the United States is a status quo power with a strong preference for change through peaceful means. So it has an abiding interest in seeing the U.N.'s peacemaking, peacekeeping, and enforcement functions strengthened. To the extent that those functions succeed—and their record has been mixed—they tend to dampen the incentive for the further proliferation of weapons of mass destruction and to heal wounds that produce continuing instability and even terrorism.

The U.N.'s judicial processes are only slowly gaining teeth and more comprehensive jurisdiction, most recently through the establishment of war crimes tribunals for Rwanda and the former Yugoslavia. Its enforcement mechanisms, most graphically the Security Council, are selective, arbitrary, and frequently hollow instruments. Yet over time, the U.N. has helped the nations of the world to gain a much sharper consciousness of what kinds of actions—whether in terms of human rights, population, environment, arms control, decolonization, trade, or military adventurism—are considered acceptable and appropriate by international standards. With little supranational authority beyond peer pressure, media attention, public concern, and on rare occasions economic and military enforcement measures, the system lacks the ready muscle of national governments. But it certainly represents the boldest and most concerted step in this direction in human history.

The U.N.'s functional, development, financial, and humanitarian agencies and programs, moreover, help a world of almost 200 nation states to operate more smoothly, efficiently, and humanely. In this manner, the U.N. system contributes not only to global commerce and investments, but also to lessening frictions among fully sovereign nation states. It acts both to promote international economic interdependence and to reduce some of the stresses on a world of ever-growing demand and an uneven distribution of resources and wealth. It serves too as a voice to remind governments and peoples of the potential ecological damage of excessive population growth, explosive migration, or unbalanced industrial development. As the Charter proclaims, the U.N. was established "to be a centre for harmonizing the actions of nations."

To conservative critics, however, these propositions seem both empty and dangerous. It has been said, for instance, that multilateralism is the last refuge of isolationists, since multilateral bodies inevitably are much more likely to talk about problems than to do anything substantial about them. When it comes to operational activities, moreover, critics are quick to point to persistent inefficiencies and corruption in the U.N. system. The United Nations, it is said, promises much more than it can deliver in terms of security and stability, so there is real danger in depending too much on idealistic notions of collective security and multilateral cooperation. If support for U.N. peace operations saps U.S. military preparedness, for example, American national security would be lessened. In an earlier era, critics were concerned that the trend toward multilateralism could erode American values and boost statist notions that smack of world government. Today the U.N. is despaired of by the political left for being under the thumb of narrow-minded nation states, while to some on the right, even hollow steps toward building a more effective system of international norms and institutions raise the specter of global government (the ultimate nightmare of those who find government by its very nature threatening to individual liberties and initiative). The U.N., therefore, is disparaged for being so weak that it is useless and so strong in terms of promoting "un-American" norms that it is dangerous. One moment we are told that the U.N. is impotent and the next that it is dictating American foreign policy.

In my view, these fears are grounded in a misconception of the U.N.'s role in the historical evolution of international relations. The U.N. is not a threat to nation states or to their sovereign integrity (and especially not to America's). It is a mechanism created by states to serve their needs. It does so 1) by helping to avoid, manage, and resolve conflicts between nations (or within nations when the situation threatens international peace and security); 2) by identifying areas of potential cooperation among states and organizing a collective response where possible; and 3) by providing humanitarian, development, functional, or technical assistance to those in need. The U.N.'s primary function is to provide services to its members across the growing range of policy problems that neither individual nor small groups of states can resolve without broader international cooperation. The U.N., in short, has become a necessity. It is, moreover, firmly in the control of its member states. The Security Council, of course, does have unprecedented enforcement powers, but they can only be invoked by a vote of nation states—not by international civil servants—when there is unanimity among the five permanent members and agreement among a supermajority of Council members. For the United States, its interests are protected by its veto power in the Council—including over the choice of secretary-general—and its considerable influence throughout the U.N. system.

The U.N. is a long way from being a world government, and there are no signs that it is getting any closer. Even as conceptions of sovereignty have evolved, countries have been quick to reassert the primacy of the nation state as *the* unit of decision making in international bodies. By helping states to address problems that would otherwise be well beyond their control individually, the U.N. system has actually reinforced the basis for national sovereignty and extended the life of the nation state era in the expanse of human history. In this way, the U.N. serves a fundamental interest of the United States and other countries: the perpetuation of the nation state as a relatively effective level of governance. For those of the right or left who would like to see the role of national governments diminished in favor of local or global forms of government, this is not a comforting conclusion. Perhaps this is an underlying reason why both political flanks are uncomfortable with the U.N. and its intergovernmental structure.

Historical Evolution

The last president to have reason to address directly the question of whether participation in the U.N. serves U.S. national interests was Harry Truman. Having inherited President Franklin Roosevelt's vision of a new world order, to which the U.N. was central, President Truman had to sell it to Congress and the American people. Roosevelt and Truman were determined not to repeat President Wilson's failure to persuade the Senate to approve America's participation in the League of Nations, seen as one of the principal reasons for the League's futility. In marketing the new world organization to the American people, the Truman administration was quick to contrast its considerable powers and potential with the weakness of the League. Some scholars have concluded that this high-powered sales campaign tended to exaggerate the U.N.'s capabilities to such a degree that the American people came to have overly high expectations of what was really an experiment in international cooperation. Whatever their expectations, Americans were clearly disappointed by the degree to which the rapidly unfolding cold war immobilized the vaunted Security Council and turned most U.N. deliberative bodies into polarized debating societies. Some of the most negative results ever recorded in surveys of American public opinion about the U.N. were in the late 1940s and early 1950s.

Despite these early disappointments, U.S. membership in the U.N.—an organization largely molded from American ideas and ideals, and headquartered in New York City—has been favored by the vast majority of Americans consistently in every national poll over the past fifty years. These margins have varied little as approval ratings for U.N. performance have ebbed and flowed. Even with the controversies engulfing the U.N. operations in Bosnia and Somalia, recent surveys have shown remarkably resilient support among the American people for the U.N. in general and for peacekeeping in particular. The public seems to have been saying consistently through the years: if the U.N. has flaws, fix them; but do not abandon the institution.

Initially a World War II victors' club of fifty-one member states, the U.N. took on a universal character in the 1950s and 1960s, through decolonization and the acceptance of Germany and Japan into the fold. With stubbornly neutral Switzerland as the only significant holdout, membership in the U.N. has become a symbol of sovereignty and nation state status for 185 countries. Membership, in essence, has become an existential matter. For the United States, as architect, host, founding member, permanent member of the Security Council, and the world's leading power, participation in the U.N. has been a given for half a century. It is simply part of our world, part of the landscape of international politics. The question has not been whether to exercise leadership in the U.N., but how to do it and for what ends.

During the cold war years, support for and interest in the United Nations was buttressed by a broad bipartisan consensus on the need to contain Soviet expansionism and to deter Soviet military threats to the United States or its allies. There were lively debates over tactics and mechanisms—especially over the wisdom and morality of the war in Vietnam—but relatively little dissent on the fundamental goals and interests of American foreign policy. The Soviets, in essence, defined the case for active American engagement with the world in military, economic, and political terms. While the East-West competition insured that the United Nations would usually remain on the sidelines when important politico-military issues were being addressed, U.S. interests were unambiguous in using the U.N. as a forum for making its case before the world community, for rebutting Soviet propaganda, and for employing international peacemaking and peacekeeping as stabilizing elements in regions where instability served Soviet ambitions. These considerations insured active, though sometimes selective, American engagement with the U.N. during four decades of cold war. American attitudes, both public and official, toward the U.N. soured when a combination of North-South and East-West tensions made the U.N. appear to be a less friendly place to do business in the mid-1970s and early 1980s. Yet on the whole, the politics of the cold war compelled active U.S. participation in the U.N. even as it limited the areas for consensus in and actions by the world body. As obnoxious as many found the politics and procedures of the U.N. to be, there was little question that it was an important arena in which to promote and defend vociferously American values and interests on the one hand, and to pursue the search for common ground on the other.

As long as the Soviet Union remained (or was perceived to be) a global threat, the United States had little choice but to define itself as a global power with interests throughout the world. And the U.N. was *the* universal body in which decisions were made and norms were shaped of global proportions. America, moreover, defined its global interests in largely geopolitical or strategic terms. U.N. peacekeeping missions in the Middle East, Cyprus, Kashmir, and the Congo thus were readily accepted in the United States, with little partisan rancor, as a logical extension of a global containment strategy. The blue helmets promised to defuse terrorism and to contain local conflicts that threatened to open the door for Communist influences, to escalate into East-West confrontations, to weaken Western alliance structures, or to divert U.S. forces from the central fronts. Since America tended to perceive itself in those years as an essentially status quo power, at least in geopolitical terms, peacekeeping was attractive as a stabilizing element in the global equation.

For the Soviet Union, however, whose ideology called for global change, by peaceful means if possible and by violence and wars of national liberation if necessary, U.N. mediation and peacekeeping efforts were more often hindrances than assets. The two enforcement operations in those years—Korea, which was undertaken under Chapter VII, and Congo, which was not—moreover so favored Western strategic interests that they threatened to shred the organization's political fabric. These experiences reinforced the Soviet tendency to be strict constructionists about the Charter, emphasizing the unique role of the Security Council in which Moscow was accorded both a veto and a sense of equality and occasional partnership with the United States. Soviet policy remained skeptical of most U.N. peace operations until a major reassessment under President Gorbachev concluded that a sweeping reform campaign at home required a more stable and predictable environment abroad.

American humanitarian impulses, such as those behind the Somalia mission, were much less in evidence in the cold war days. Nor would anyone have suggested then that the United Nations should be conducting elections, writing constitutions, or encouraging more democratic governments, especially since the term "democracy" was not used even once in the U.N. Charter or its eloquent Preamble. While the Congo operation took on many of the elements of contemporary nation-building efforts, that was not the mission's original intention and no one would have given it such an audacious label or mandate. Peacekeeping by and large was seen as a step to give diplomacy a chance to work or to reinforce the status quo, not as the security midwife to a political and social metamorphosis within troubled nations. The U.N., reinforced by Soviet and Third World attachment to a strict interpretation of sovereignty, simply was not in the business of delving too deeply into the social, political, and economic roots of conflict and instability within its member states.

Yet while a status quo power in geopolitical terms, the United States repeatedly employed the United Nations as a vehicle to promote its core values and principles in a strikingly dynamic and eventually successful manner. Breaking with its allies, in the early years the United States encouraged the U.N. to take the lead in assisting the decolonization movement, which led to the creation of scores of newly independent countries. This, in turn, changed the geopolitical map of the U.N., as well as much of the Southern Hemisphere. When the cold war prevented the U.N. from making much progress on the political-security front, the United States championed an enormous but largely unheralded expansion of humanitarian, development, technical, and functional agencies within the growing U.N. family. From Eleanor Roosevelt's early days with the U.N. Human Rights Commission, American representatives persistently worked for codification of civil and political rights. In these areas, as well as in disarmament, population, and environment, the U.N. became the center for global norm setting to a degree unanticipated in its Charter.

Debates over values and norms in the U.N. were never easy. The influx of large numbers of developing countries with divergent interests and often authoritarian regimes tended to put Western democracies on the defensive in General Assembly debates. By the 1970s and early 1980s, a marriage of convenience between socialist and developing countries sparked a heated series of

North-South debates over economic, social, and security issues. Much of the rhetoric took on a decidedly statist tone, while Western countries managed to maintain control over most U.N. programs and activities. During these difficult years, questions of human rights were left to codification rather than enforcement. The Carter administration's emphasis on human rights as one of the determining factors in U.S. policy choices was substantially modified by the Reagan administration, which tended to differentiate between authoritarian friends and totalitarian foes. While tactics varied from administration to administration, American diplomats, much more than their Western European or Japanese partners, have consistently sought to use the U.N.'s bully pulpit to advance these and other normative concerns. The relatively activist stance of the United States has derived both from its core values and from its interest in winning the East-West (and then North-South) struggle for influence inside and outside the U.N. The competition with the Soviet Union dealt not only with military matters beyond the U.N.'s reach and competence. It also revolved around fundamental economic, social, political, and ideological questions for which U.N. forums provided an important, if not always friendly, battleground for verbal jousting and seeking to disseminate American values.

With the collapse of the Soviet Union and the end of the cold war, the U.N. underwent a political (though not structural) metamorphosis. The changes, while enormously favorable to American interests and perspectives, have still not been fully understood or digested by U.S. policy makers, nor reflected in American strategies and policies. Readjustment, even to good news, is rarely easy. Because policies toward the U.N. are, in essence, policies toward the world, new departures in the U.S. approach to the U.N. should follow and reflect a redefinition of American interests and strategies on a global scale. Confusion about our purpose in the U.N. is a sign of a far deeper, and more troubling, malaise about our role in the world. There is still no consensus on the nature, depth, and extent of U.S. interests in the world, much less in the U.N. All is in limbo until partisan wounds heal or unfavorable international events force a congealing of policy perspectives. The United Nations, like the League of Nations before it, is a tool forged out of the ashes of a global catastrophe. Hopefully it will not require another trauma of such magnitude to convince national leaders of the need to sharpen and renovate the existing tools for bolstering international security.

It is paradoxical, but as the U.N.'s political climate has become more positive and more favorable for American interests, U.S. relations with the U.N. have become increasingly problematic. It is partly a matter of expectations, and partly an action-reaction phenomenon. Public support and official rhetoric soared after American military and political muscle and U.N. political authority and legitimacy teamed up to expel Iraqi forces from Kuwait and to impose a far-reaching arms monitoring and economic sanctions regime on the defeated aggressor following the Gulf War. With the demise of the Soviet Union and the rise of multilateralism, not to mention President George Bush's call for a "new world order," few prominent voices initially challenged the apparent marriage between U.S. global interests and a born-again United Nations. At the same time, the growing trend toward multilateralism itself stimulated a strong negative reaction from those Americans who mistrusted the U.N. or were skeptical of its capabilities. When a Democrat was elected in the White House, especially one espousing "assertive multilateralism," these concerns coalesced into partisan political debate, largely focused on Capitol Hill. U.S.–U.N. relations, as in the early days, took on a "two-step forward, one-step back" appearance.

Where the U.N. had relatively few opportunities to demonstrate its capabilities in previous years, all of a sudden it was deluged with too many opportunities. This was especially evident in the Security Council. Vetoes all but disappeared as Council members put a premium on consensus, and on getting along in public. The Council, literally working overtime, launched more peacekeeping missions than it had in the previous forty years, quadrupling the costs and number of blue helmets in just one year. Building on a highly successful mission in Namibia, complex and expensive new nation-building operations were undertaken in Cambodia and El Salvador, places long torn by vicious civil warfare and foreign interference. More ominously and less successfully, the Council authorized operations in Somalia and Bosnia-Herzegovina that mixed peacekeeping and enforcement functions, lacked the full consent of the parties, and had only limited commitments from key member states. Expectations had clearly outstripped capabilities, leaving lots of room for second guessing as things got rough in Somalia and Bosnia.

While there was more to like about the "new" U.N., there was more to criticize and to be apprehensive about as well. The failures of will and foresight by the international community could no longer be blamed on the cold war, and the U.N. became a handy scapegoat when things went wrong. In all the celebrating over the end of the cold war, no one had cautioned the public, the media, or Congress about the complexities of assembling and managing international enforcement operations, something on which no one had much experience in any case. Instead of the anticipated peace dividend, the United States was faced with the task of leading international efforts to police an increasingly unruly world in which global peace was accompanied by local havoc in many parts of the world. At a time when many people longed for a cost-free, risk-free foreign policy, the U.N. secretary-general—like an unwelcome voice of conscience in the night—pointedly reminded them of the obligations and responsibilities of wealth, power, and leadership. A new modus vivendi is needed between the U.N. and its most important member, and it will not happen overnight.

Ironically, American policy makers seem least certain of their interests in the U.N. just at the historic point when American values are most welcome at the U.N., and international conditions seem ripest for successful multilateralism. In theory, at least, multilateral mechanisms like the U.N. should have been out of place during the predominantly bipolar era of the cold war. Yet, as discussed above, the organization adapted, coped, and displayed remarkable agility and flexibility in unpromising times. In the essentially multipolar world that has followed, however, multilateral decision making should be a natural fit. The U.N. would appear to be far better suited for the current geopolitical situation than for that which prevailed for its first four and a half decades. These should be salad days for the United Nations, and for the United States; one survived the cold war and the other won it.

Instead, neither the United Nations nor the United States has adapted well to the new conditions. In a multilateral system, of course, it is awkward when one country is much stronger than the rest. In theory, if the distribution of power is highly skewed and the system is imbalanced, there will be a tendency for other players to use multilateralism as a way of constraining the leading power, reducing its unilateral impulses, and in the end creating resentment all around. Ironically, however, the United States has shown little desire to dominate international politics, now that it might conceivably have the capacity to do so. It certainly is not exercising consistent leadership in the U.N. and other multilateral decision-making bodies. There seems to be more concern at the U.N. these days, even among traditionally nonaligned countries, about a perceived leadership vacuum than about the United States throwing its weight around. Critics charge that American foreign policy, with its ambivalence and hesitancy, has come to resemble that of a middle, not a great, power. Persistent congressional efforts to cut back on U.S. funding for the U.N., moreover, give the impression that America cannot afford even one of the less expensive attributes of leadership. The highly partisan and largely incoherent rancor in Washington, D.C. about the nature of American interests in the rest of the world adds to the sense that America is no longer capable of exercising global leadership.

On a purely functional level, the need for improved forms of multilateral cooperation is becoming increasingly evident in a number of fields. Problem solving necessarily entails substantial cooperation in areas as diverse as weapons proliferation, population, environment, health, refugees and migration, trade, humanitarian relief, finance and capital flows, terrorism, narcotics, human rights, AIDS, communications, peacekeeping, and conflict resolution. Only through activating, orchestrating, and harnessing a number of power centers toward common ends can these problems be resolved or even substantially ameliorated. Whether the U.N. is sufficiently well structured, funded, or led to get the job done remains to be seen, but the challenges to practical multilateralism are not going away. And in quiet ways, beyond the rhetorical combat, international cooperation grows year by year in an inevitable progression. In most cases, multilateral cooperation is a necessary but not sufficient condition for addressing such tough transnational issues. It is not a miracle cure. Usually a mix of policy tools—unilateral, bilateral, regional, and multilateral—is required in the final analysis. The advancement of American national interests in such a complex and demanding environment will require flexibility, agility, and the ability to move on several levels simultaneously, as well as a very clear conception of where one wants to go and how one wants to get there. Interests cannot be ambiguous nor commitments ambivalent if decisive action is needed or desired. Fuzzy thinking, lack of resolve, and indecision—the products of divided or uncertain leadership—are especially dangerous when military force is involved.

At the same time, successful outcomes also presume that there is a substantial degree of overlap between U.S. interests and those of other countries whose cooperation is essential. In the peacekeeping realm, leading Republicans in Congress, including Senate Majority Leader Bob Dole and Speaker of the House Newt Gingrich, have stated repeatedly and emphatically that a number of U.N. operations—such as in Haiti, Somalia, Rwanda, and Angola— reflect "U.N.," not U.S., interests. (In Bosnia, apparently they believe that America has sufficient interest to send arms but not enough to deploy U.S. troops on the ground.) President Clinton and his administration, which approved and often helped initiate these missions, obviously believe that they advance American foreign policy and national security objectives. Yet they have been remarkably feeble and ineffective in making the case to Congress and the public for these undertakings, especially in terms of a core conception of American interests and strategies for the new era.

The ensuing debate—more a dialogue of the deaf—has been as partisan as it has been vague, producing no basis for a domestic consensus on the nature of national interests in a changing world. In fact, neither side in the debate has sought to clarify the boundaries, scope, or content of American national interests. The Republicans in Congress have not given a clue to who the "U.N." is other than Secretary-General Boutros Boutros-Ghali, who is accused of running American foreign policy. The implication is that other countries, or perhaps international civil servants, have somehow hoodwinked or coopted the Clinton administration for the purpose of forwarding some secret agenda that is contrary to America's best interests. The themes here have a decidedly isolationist ring, and phrases like "entangling alliances" come to mind. It is ironic, in any case, that most observers in the U.N. community traditionally have decried U.S. influence over the U.N., not vice versa. The question of who influences whom in a multilateral system is likely to be a bit murky, but in this case the opposing stereotypes about whose tail is wagging whose dog have gone too far in both directions, for multilateralism entails some give and take over competing agendas in the search for common good.

The Clinton administration, for its part, struggled for months to produce a weighty interagency peacekeeping policy review (PDD 25) that refers repeatedly to national security interests as key criteria for deciding which operations to support without once even hinting what those interests might be. In arguing against proposed congressional restrictions on U.N. peacekeeping, administration spokespeople have put much more emphasis on the need to preserve presidential prerogatives and flexibility than on how these U.N. missions have served specific U.S. national interests. Both points should be underlined. The very pace of authorizing new U.N. operations, moreover, has left the administration voting first in the Council and then explaining breathlessly and incompletely to Congress and the public how American interests would be forwarded. The consensus building—at home as much as in the Security Council—should come first. So while international political developments would seem to have spurred a convergence of interests among major powers on a number of issues and conflicts, relatively little progress has been made in producing a parallel convergence at home: a prerequisite for the international system to work properly.

U.S. Interests and U.N. Peace Operations

In the ongoing debate about U.S. participation in and support of U.N. peace operations, several important distinctions tend to be overlooked. As discussed above, interests rarely appear in black and white, unambiguous ways. In most situations there is a range of choices that would each advance some interests, but sacrifice others. There is a temptation, moreover, to see interests everywhere if there are no price tags attached. If the true measure of a national interest is found in a willingness to make real sacrifices to advance it, then U.S. interests abroad would seem to be much narrower than the rhetoric sometimes suggests. Short-term and long-term considerations may suggest different responses, while some interests may be worth much deeper sacrifices than others. Some interests are purely national and others transnational in scope. Likewise, strategic interests might call for one kind of response and humanitarian interests another.

While short-run concerns necessarily dominate foreign policy decision making, it would be a serious mistake to act in a way that undermines longer-term options, norms, and institutions. For example, even if one decides that current U.N. peace operations are addressing conflicts of only marginal interest to the United States—a contention I would dispute—it still would be in the U.S. national interest to work with other countries to build U.N. capabilities for responding to future contingencies that might be of greater interest and strategic concern to the United States. The U.N., like a muscle, has to be exercised and strengthened step by step if it is to be strong and reliable when needed most. U.S. policy makers, moreover, should avoid taking unilateral steps, such as breaking Security Council–imposed arms or economic embargoes or failing to pay peacekeeping assessments. American interests could be harmed if other countries follow our example when and where it suited them. Precedents can be dangerous things. When a permanent member that voted for Security Council enforcement steps later decides to flaunt them unilaterally, it can only reduce the credibility of the Council and of the permanent member itself. As the United States and its allies successfully argued before the International Court of Justice when the Soviet Union failed to pay its assessed contributions for the Congo operation, to permit member states to withhold legally assessed contributions at will could only lead to financial and legal chaos.

At the risk of oversimplification, one can think in geographic terms of U.S. security interests falling in two concentric circles of inner and outer interests. The inner circle might include the Western Hemisphere, Western and Central Europe, Israel, Japan, Korea, Australia, New Zealand, and friendly Persian Gulf states;

in other words, our traditional allies and neighbors, those countries with which the United States has security pacts and to whose defense U.S. troops, with a fairly high degree of probability, would likely be committed. These relationships, of course, were largely based on cold war assumptions, alliances, and circumstances, but there remains a broad consensus in the United States today that these places are strategically and politically important. For those whose world view was largely defined by cold war requirements, interests in these regions are still easily understandable and strategic in nature.

The United States would not expect to depend on the U.N. to play a major role in organizing defense efforts or deploying peacekeeping forces in most of these places following a conflict (possibly with a veto-bearing permanent member of the Security Council). But there have been some important exceptions, such as the Chapter VII action in Korea (where the facade of a U.N. command remains), in Cyprus (where U.N. peacekeepers for three decades have helped to prevent the destruction of NATO's southern flank), and on the Golan Heights and in southern Lebanon (where U.N. peacekeepers add a bit of stability to two of Israel's troubled borders). For all of its shortcomings, the United Nations Protection Force (UNPROFOR) in the former Yugoslavia has helped to keep the virulent conflict there from spreading throughout the Balkans and perhaps elsewhere in southern Europe, as well as to support a massive humanitarian effort. While historically peacekeeping has been thought of as a crutch to unstable countries in the developing world, today a full 70 percent of the U.N.'s blue helmets are deployed in Europe.

Once the Yugoslav mission is completed—one way or another—the chief demand for U.N. peace operations, however, will likely again come from places in the Southern Hemisphere. These contingencies in all likelihood either will fit into the outer circle of U.S. interests or will fall altogether beyond the circles of traditional interests, out where humanitarian impulses have replaced strategic ones. The nature and extent of U.S. interests in these parts of the world—in the gray areas—are subject to greater controversy and domestic debate. It is here that partisan differences emerge most sharply. In these areas, U.S. strategic interests are less clear, less direct, or longer term. Other countries may well have as large or larger a stake in the resolution of conflicts in those places as does the United States.

Where a number of significant countries have overlapping interests, but none of them has an overwhelming need or urge to act unilaterally, the politics should be promising for some type of multilateral action, whether under Chapter VI or VII. With the end of the cold war, the geographic bounds of these gray areas are expanding. Places like Somalia—considered by some to be a prime strategic asset in the East-West competition—have lost their strategic meaning (even as they have gained a humanitarian one). Shared interests should be translated into a sharing of burdens and responsibilities. Deciding how this can be done equitably and efficiently is a primary task of the Security Council, which in some cases can delegate this responsibility to regional organizations.

However sensible this system sounds on paper, it still faces the recurring problem of a divided and uncertain American body politic. For the purpose of analysis, and with considerable risk of oversimplification, one can sketch four basic schools of thought about U.S. relations with and interests in the United Nations.

- *Isolationists* tend to be rejectionists when it comes to the U.N., as they were in keeping the United States out of the League of Nations. They have zero interest in the U.N., seeing it as an imposition on U.S. sovereignty and a vehicle for other countries to get Americans ensnared in solving their problems for them. They find the notion of multilateralism to be abhorrent to the protection of American values and interests. Their rallying cry is "to get the United States out of the U.N., and the U.N. out of the United States." (Presumably their favorite musical would be "Stop the World, I Want to Get Off.") If their group is roughly defined by those who favor "giving up the U.S. seat in the U.N." in public opinion surveys, then they comprise at most 10 to 15 percent of the population—a determined and persistent stream in American thinking, but consistently a small one.
- *Neo-isolationists* are skeptical about the value of the U.N. and cognizant of the dangers that multilateralism can pose for the United States, but they are far from rejecting active involvement

in the world body outright. They would embrace the spirit of the Contract with America provisions that would restrict U.S. participation in U.N. peacekeeping, while doubting both the feasibility and the desirability of U.N. military capabilities for enforcement purposes. Their approach to the U.N. could be described as selective engagement. On the one hand, they recognize that multilateral support for U.S. initiatives can be helpful at times and that the humanitarian and technical agencies do much good work. On the other hand, they fear imperial overstretch should U.N. obligations lead the United States into too many far-flung military and economic commitments in places of relatively little strategic value since the demise of the Soviet Union and of the East-West competition for influence in the developing world. In their view, many of the U.S. interests in the U.N. are essentially negative ones, requiring damage limitation strategies to insure that bad things do not happen to U.S. interests there and that American values do not get diluted in the compromise oriented politics of multilateral decision making. They would tend to subscribe to Senator Daniel Patrick Moynihan's phrase when he represented the United States at the U.N. in the mid-1970s and called the U.N. "a dangerous place," even if the end of the cold war has eased the downside dangers and opened new possibilities for cooperative outcomes.

- *Internationalists* tend to believe that a confluence of U.S. interests and those of other key U.N. member states with the end of the cold war has laid the political foundation for a reinvigoration of the U.N. and other multilateral institutions. As hard-core opposition to American values and interests has tended to fade in the U.N., it is argued that today U.S. purposes would be well served by the strengthening of U.N. structures and capabilities. The United States, in their view, has a central stake in bolstering international law and institutions in a world that is chaotic, interdependent, and heavily armed. Multilateral cooperation, moreover, is seen as essential to the growing number of policy areas in which one or a few countries cannot get the job done. Their approach, which could be described as active engagement, does not foresee multilateral solutions for all problems, but it does argue that the U.N. and other multilateral institutions can (and will) carry a heavier burden than they did (or were allowed to do) in the past. Internationalists conceive of American national interests in relatively broad terms both geographically and substantively, with a preference for intervening earlier rather than later and with partners if possible rather than alone.

• *World citizens* see the U.N. as a stepping stone on the route to world government. Because it is ruled by the narrow preferences of national governments and tainted by their cynical manipulations, the U.N. has lost its moral and political compass according to this group. These people, pledging their loyalties more to humanity than to nations, like to think in terms of human interests rather than national interests. The U.N., they believe, should be opened up to civil society—to the voices of private citizens—on a transnational basis, rather than being kept prisoner by its nation state members. In their minds, since unilateral action tends to have unfair and unstable consequences, inviting retribution, multilateralism provides a less damaging alternative until true global government is achieved and the root evil of nationalism is extinguished. While it is hard to estimate how many Americans identify with this viewpoint, public opinion surveys and the size of membership rolls for organizations espousing this perspective suggest that they comprise an even smaller number than the 10 to 15 percent who can be considered to be hard-core isolationists.

The views of most Americans fall roughly into the internationalist or neo-isolationist camps, and it is their debate that will decide U.S. policy outcomes. The more extreme groups, in any case, do not show much interest in U.S. policies within the U.N. since their priorities are elsewhere. Those who would like to see the United States less engaged with the rest of the world necessarily have little use for the U.N., which epitomizes and facilitates the kind of global involvements they perceive as distracting and draining. Such isolationism, however tempting to those who would like the world's problems to disappear, is utterly unrealistic in a world characterized by financial and commercial interdependence, by a host of transnational challenges that demand multilateral solutions, by a global communications revolution, and by rapid and massive movements of people, technology, and ideas. When the security of millions of Americans—living in the one nation long protected by a combination of geographic distance and military strength—is necessarily held hostage to decisions by foreign leaders or even terrorists half a world away, isolationism is no more than an empty promise and a dangerous mirage.

Neo-isolationists are more realistic, and their arguments need to be addressed seriously. Their vision, however, is too limited and their policy prescriptions too narrow. While their critiques of U.N. weaknesses are often on target, their policy responses tend to be unilateral and to penalize the world body for the failings of its members. They advocate policies that end up weakening the U.N. further, contributing to a vicious cycle rather than to the rebuilding and strengthening of the institution. In their acute concern about short-run costs and risks, they invite much greater ones in the future. Their perception of the U.N. is as a glass half empty, yet they do not seem prepared to help fill it up with additional resources, powers, or people. They know better what they do not like about the world body than what they do.

While my sympathies tend to lie with the internationalists, their perspective also has some serious shortcomings. They have a tendency to expect too much from the U.N. and to overload its agenda with far more of the world's problems than it can handle. For example, while neo-isolationists need to clarify when and where they believe that intervention is warranted, internationalists need to specify when and where they believe this is not feasible or desirable. One side needs to locate the accelerator, and the other the brakes. Even internationalism has to have limits given inevitable shortages of resources, finances, and patience. Some problems do not have solutions, others do not have U.N. solutions. It is better, in any case, for the U.N. to manage a few conflict situations well than to do many poorly.

Neo-isolationists tend to focus on the U.N.'s current performance, to apply impossibly high standards, and to find it wanting. Internationalists, on the other hand, like to point to the organization's potential, and to remind us that there is really no alternative in many cases. In terms of long-term American interests, however, the key point is not whether the U.N. is doing a good or bad job at the moment, nor even whether the members of the Security Council are giving it sensible mandates to carry out, but rather whether the United States has a stake in the future success of the world body. Neo-isolationists should favor a stronger U.N. to help ease some of the burdens on the United States (even though burden sharing requires American sacrifices as well). For internationalists, a more capable U.N. will build American confidence in global problem solving even as it reinforces patterns and norms of international cooperation. While neo-isolationists tend to be skeptics, and internationalists enthusiasts, about today's U.N., they should find common ground in the desire to see the U.N. be more effective and efficient in the future.

As the U.N. becomes a more capable organization—doing a better job of what it does now—it will serve a range of important American interests. Among these would be the following:

- containing local conflicts so that they do not spill across borders and threaten American interests and allies;
- deterring potential aggressors by demonstrating the possibilities for collective action, whether through economic and political sanctions or military enforcement;
- dampening incentives for further proliferation of weapons of mass destruction by boosting regional security and providing some sense of credible security assurances, as well as through the monitoring efforts of the International Atomic Energy Agency, the United Nations Special Commission, and the new chemical weapons agency;
- resolving ongoing conflicts through the wide range of mediation, fact finding, and conciliation services provided by the secretary-general under Chapter VI of the Charter;
- addressing the sources of terrorism by these conflict resolution efforts as well as by assisting refugees and facilitating their repatriation through the work of the United Nations High Commissioner for Refugees and other humanitarian agencies;
- advancing democratic principles and pluralistic practices around the world through election monitoring, constitution writing, judiciary and police reform, and encouraging press freedoms;
- codifying international human rights norms, establishing war

crimes tribunals, and using rapporteurs, truth commissions, and reporting mechanisms to bring the light of international publicity to bear on gross human rights abuses;
* setting international labor rights standards through the International Labor Organization that can both help transform rigid societies and improve the competitive position of U.S. based corporations in the global economy;
* expanding markets for U.S. products by organizing and carrying out a wide variety of development, technical, humanitarian, and financial programs in developing countries;
* helping to preserve the environment while promoting sustainable development through international dialogue, norm setting, and population programs;
* facilitating international commerce and communication through the work of a range of functional agencies such as the Universal Postal Union, the International Civil Aviation Organization, the International Telecommunications Union, the World Meteorological Organization, the International Maritime Organization, and the World Intellectual Property Organization;
* coordinating global responses to illegal narcotics trafficking through the work of several U.N. programs; and
* combatting AIDS and other scourges through the World Health Organization's efforts.

Certainly these programs cost money and certainly they serve the interests of other nations as well as the United States. But peace is a lot less expensive than war, and U.S. assessments for U.N. peacekeeping at their peak in 1994 were still less than one-half of 1 percent of U.S. defense expenditures. The United States, moreover, with its global economic reach, democratic institutions, and preference for change by peaceful means, has as large a stake as any country in the success of U.N. peace operations, and in getting other potentially competitive powers enmeshed in the web of multilateral arrangements and institutions. Prosperity and stability in other nations around the world tend to contribute to economic growth and political tranquility back home as well.

As President Bush recognized in Kuwait and President Clinton in Haiti, the blessing of the Security Council is an important asset in gaining the support both of the American people and of the international community for forceful, American led action abroad. For all of the controversies swirling about the U.N., numerous public opinion surveys suggest that it remains a remarkably popular institution, whose political legitimacy often outstrips its ability to deliver. Even when its performance ratings dip, the U.N. stands in public eyes for all-American values and ideals, including the humanitarian impulses that led both the United States and the United Nations into Somalia and Haiti. In an era when idealism is in short supply in political discourse, the United Nations continues to represent—however imperfectly—purposes that transcend the ugliness and cynicism of politics-as-usual and that move the American people today as in 1945.

If all of its programs, agencies, and peace operations were stripped away, the U.N. would remain an unparalleled stage on which international politics are played out year after year. Americans have worked hard and sacrificed much to gain, and then retain, a position of unquestioned global leadership. It is not something that should be relinquished easily and without good cause. For if the United States falters, if it fails to exercise leadership in the U.N. and other world bodies, then other nations will be tempted to flex their political, economic, and perhaps even military muscles in ways that assuredly would not serve U.S. strategic interests. The scenario of the 1930s is not bound to repeat itself, but the parallels are troubling. Should Americans fail to recognize, much less to exert and protect, their global interests, then they will—over time, step-by-step—lose them. So the bottom line is simple: America's first interest in the U.N. is to solidify its rightful position of global leadership. Its second, and related, interest is to lead a concerted international campaign to reform, rebuild, and revitalize the United Nations to meet the challenges of a new century and new era in international politics.

2

Managing Global Security: The United Nations Not a War Maker, a Peace Maker

MICHAEL W. DOYLE

S ince the end of the cold war, the community of nations has
experienced a revolution in the relation between what is in
the legitimate realm of state sovereignty and what is subject to
legitimate international intervention.[1] Employing a strikingly intrusive interpretation of Chapter VII provisions concerning international peace and security, from 1991 through 1993 the U.N.'s
member states endorsed a radical expansion in the scope of collec-

MICHAEL W. DOYLE is professor of politics and international affairs
in the Politics Department and Woodrow Wilson School of Princeton
University. He is currently a senior fellow and was formerly vice president
of the International Peace Academy. His publications include *Empires,*
two other books, numerous articles, chapters in books, and occasional
essays including "Kant, Liberal Legacies, and Foreign Affairs: Parts I and
II," in *Philosophy and Public Affairs.* He is a faculty associate of the Center of
International Studies of Princeton, North American editor of *International
Peacekeeping,* and a member of the Committee of Editors of *World Politics.*
His current areas of special interest are in philosophies of world politics
and new developments in U.N. peacekeeping. His most recent publica-
tion is *U.N. Peacekeeping in Cambodia: UNTAC's Civil Mandate* in the IPA
Occasional Paper Series.

tive intervention just as a series of ethnic and civil wars erupted across the globe. Unfulfilled commitments, on the one hand, and escalating use of force, on the other, soon provoked a severe crisis in U.N. Chapter VII based "peace enforcement." In Bosnia and Somalia "peace enforcement" amounted to "war making" as the United Nations threatened to impose by force outcomes—ranging from disarmament to safe havens, "no fly zones," and national borders—on armed factions that recognized no political authority superior to their own.[2] Current evidence suggests that the United Nations has proven to be a very ineffective war maker, which raises the question of whether we can reduce the consequent burden on limited U.N. resources while still protecting global human rights and respecting national self-determination. Drawing on the examples of the U.N. operations in Cambodia and El Salvador, I argue that the U.N. can succeed in fostering peace through a political engagement with national sovereignty, an internationalist alternative based on an enhancement of Chapter VI based consent. The U.N.'s future as peace maker, however, is now under challenge in the U.S. Congress and elsewhere from those who fail to understand how successful the U.N. has been and can continue to be in a "peacemaking" role.[3] The theme of this chapter is simple: we should avoid throwing the "baby" out with the bathwater.

A Crisis in War Making, or "Peace Enforcement"

The U.N. peace enforcement effort in the large part of Somalia outside of General Aidid's stronghold in southern Mogadishu proceeded according to plan. By mid-1993, starvation was not an issue in the areas within the reach of U.N. protection. In contrast, 300,-000 Somalis died in 1991–92 in a famine induced by the murderous competition of the Somali warlords. In 1993, with the protection of the United Nations Operation in Somalia (UNOSOM II), the United Nations International Children's Emergency Fund (UNICEF) was assisting 40,000 pupils. Thirty-two hospitals and 103 mobile vaccination teams were active (75 percent of the children under five received measles vaccine). Seventy thousand refugees returned from Kenya. Thirty-nine district councils and six regional councils were formed. UNOSOM had begun to recruit 5,000 former Somali police officers to perform basic police functions.

Nonetheless, the October 3, 1993 disaster involving the killing of eighteen U.S. soldiers (in which about 300 Somalis also died), the earlier crisis on June 5 in which twenty-four Pakistani peacekeepers were killed after they fired on a Somali crowd, and the fruitless effort to capture General Aidid over the previous summer together exposed what had become a politically bankrupt attempt to enforce law and order on an increasingly resistant population.

With the advantage of hindsight, we can identify policy mistakes, without which Somalia might look very different today.[4] A more thorough partnership with Somalia's regional neighbors in a mediation effort in 1991,[5] a more extensive mandate for the U.S. led Unified Task Force (UNITAF) in December 1992 (when controlling the heavy and light weapons of the clans would have been easier), and above all a smoother political transition from UNITAF's partial successes in negotiating with the warlords to UNOSOM's more ambitious state-building agenda might have made a difference.

The fundamental problem was a famine induced by drought, by the ravages of the civil war that followed on the collapse of Siad Barre's dictatorship, and by the rapacious extortion of the Somali warlords who taxed relief convoys in order to fund their competition for power. Only a Somali "leviathan" with a monopoly of violence or a "super-warlord" capable of playing warlord against warlord could restore order and end the famine. UNOSOM I (with 500 Pakistani troops holed up in the port of Mogadishu) could do very little, not even prevent grain ships from being shelled from shore. U.N. Special Representative Mohammed Sahnoun valiantly tried to negotiate a peace, appealing to the humanity of the very warlords who ran the famine. In December 1992, the U.S. led UNITAF became the Somali "leviathan," and the roads were opened and the famine broken.[6] UNITAF met almost no opposition because the mass of the people welcomed the relief, and the warlords knew it was temporary—no threat to their power.

In May 1993 UNOSOM II came face to face with the fundamental problems. Its mandate included the authority to disarm the factions—a disarmament to which, we should note, the faction leaders had agreed at the Addis Ababa Conference in March 1993. But this mandate, unlike UNITAF's, threatened the political existence of the warlords. It proposed the establishment of a Somali national authority that would be elected by the people and sustained by a police force trained by the U.N. UNOSOM, however, was a paper tiger, lacking the capacity to enforce (or even bargain for compliance with) the agreement. The bulk of its troops were lightly armed, vulnerable to the weapons the warlords withdrew from the temporary UNITAF cantonment. UNOSOM's logistics were immobile, dependent on Mogadishu port facilities, which made the U.N. too dependent on Aidid to threaten a credible withdrawal from his zone. The rank-and-file faction fighters were required to disarm in May 1993; UNOSOM established an alternative employment program in January 1994. The entire force relied too much on the military and logistic backbone of the U.S. contingent, which was poorly coordinated with the overall UNOSOM force. UNOSOM survived casualties inflicted on the Pakistanis in June, but when Aidid attacked the Americans in October he struck UNOSOM's Achilles heel.

The opposite problem to UNOSOM's aggressiveness emerged in the United Nations Protection Force (UNPROFOR) operation in the former Yugoslavia. There the U.N. is not doing what it has been criticized for doing in Somalia. The U.N. is committed to protecting the humanitarian convoys and the safe areas as well as maintaining an arms embargo over the entire area and an economic embargo against Serbia. But the failure to protect the Bosnian Muslims (but also the Croats and Serbs), the relief convoys, and even the peacekeepers themselves left the U.N. force in a most equivocal position. In Bosnia alone, after the establishment of UN-PROFOR, tens (perhaps even hundreds) of thousands of Muslims and thousands of Serbs and Croats have died, and more than a million Muslims and 250,000 Serbs have had to flee their homes, according to the estimates of Thorvald Stoltenberg, the U.N. mediator.[7]

The protection dilemma is real. With more than half the population in the U.N. designated Bosnian "safe areas" directly dependent on U.N. convoys for food and medicine, military action against the predominantly Serb aggressors would be met by a complete cutoff of humanitarian assistance by those same Serbian forces, which control the access roads.[8]

None of UNPROFOR's military forces are prepared to undertake a massive military campaign designed to defeat the Bosnian Serb forces. The United States limits its contribution to air forces. The United States' once preferred strategy—"lift (the 1991 U.N. arms embargo) and strike (by air, against Serb gunners)"—was designed to level the playing field between Serb forces and the poorly equipped Bosnian forces. But the United States was never prepared to invest its own soldiers on the ground in a peace enforcement operation, nor even to ship heavy weapons to Bosnia (presumably by airlift over the Croat and Serb lines) and train the Bosnians in their use.[9] Radical Muslim forces from Iran and the Palestine Liberation Organization (PLO) were ready to come to Bosnia's aid but they were rejected by Russia and would, it seemed to many observers, merely widen the fighting to Kosovo, Macedonia, and even beyond. The resulting UNPROFOR strategy— "constrict (the level of violence) and contain"—is not without costs to its European proponents. At this writing, UNPROFOR, with large contingents of British, French, and Canadian troops, has already sustained seventy fatalities. But the strategy has two great advantages: it has been tolerated by the Russians, and the killing so far has been contained within Croatia and Bosnia.

Again, with the advantage of hindsight, we can see what appear to be mistakes, most of them occasioned by the Security Council's foisting mandates (without the means to implement them) on the U.N. forces in the field. Resolutions are issued that bear upon the Bosnian Serbs, yet the international community may only now be discovering a way to exert pressure on them. What pressure there was came from the indirect effects of the misery that the international economic embargo inflicted on the Serbian public. In retrospect, we can see that the U.N. protected areas in Croatia lacked adequate buffer zones and sufficient peacekeepers, providing the Serbs with excuses not to disarm and the Croats with opportunity to engage in incursions.[10] In Bosnia, the declared safe havens were never adequately provided with U.N. forces. They were too small, militarily vulnerable, economically nonviable, and they lacked wide enough connecting corridors.

The taproot of error was identified in Cyrus Vance's warnings in December 1991 not to recognize the independence of Croatia and Bosnia outside of the framework of an overall settlement of Yugoslavia. The only separable parts of Yugoslavia immediately recognizable as independent, sovereign nation states were Slovenia and (arguably) Macedonia. For Serbs, the federal unity of "Yugoslavia" was what made "small" Serbia tolerable and the non-Serb governments of Croatia and Bosnia safe for their Serbs. For Croats, the inclusion of Bosnia in Yugoslavia was what made Bosnia safe for its Croats. For Bosnian Muslims, the inclusion of Croatia in Yugoslavia was what made the Bosnian republic safe in Yugoslavia, which otherwise would have been dominated by the Serbs. Croatia, some suggest, might have been partitioned between Croats and Serbs, but the ethnic mix was too intimate in Bosnia to allow a peaceable partition.

The peace on offer to the Bosnian Muslims is now (spring 1995) the only game in town. Accepted by the Croat-Muslim state of Bosnia, it has been rejected by an overwhelming vote in the Bosnian Serb Assembly. By dividing Bosnia into Serb and Muslim-Croat entities and implicitly condoning ethnic cleansing, it has been well-described by Lord Owen, the European Community mediator, as "the peace made in hell."

The operations in Somalia and Bosnia saved hundreds of thousands of lives. The starvation probably would have continued in Somalia, resulting in the loss of 110,000 to perhaps 250,000 lives.[11] Only UNPROFOR prevented the complete ethnic cleansing of Bosnia by the Serbs. Yet the political costs of strategic failure were high.

Both failures soon claimed victims elsewhere. Following the October 3, 1993 crisis in Somalia, U.S. senators clamored for immediate withdrawal of all U.S. forces from UNOSOM. The Clinton administration barely succeeded in holding out for a March 31, 1994 withdrawal date. Emboldened by the prospective U.S. withdrawal from Somalia, associates of the *attachés* terrorizing Haiti chased U.S.–U.N. advisers from the harbor of Port-au-Prince, wrecking the Governors Island peace plan and eventually forcing the administration to pursue the very risky decision (from the standpoint of domestic U.S. politics) to invade Haiti. Learning to say "no," the United States led the Security Council's rejection of the request to protect thousands of displaced persons in Burundi fleeing the coup and slaughter of the government in October 1993. It also sought to limit the scope of the U.N.'s engagement in massacre-torn Rwanda in May 1994. In Bosnia, General Francois Briquemont, the former commander of UNPROFOR, denounced "the fantastic gap between the resolutions of the Security Council, the will to execute those resolutions and the means available to commanders in the field." The "fantastic gap" now stimulates irredentist claims across Eastern Europe. It signals to some that borders are up for grabs and ethnic cleansing will go unpunished. (Leaders of the Abkhaz, who constituted 18 percent of the prewar population of the "Abkhaz" region of Georgia, were reported to be planning the establishment of an Abkhaz nation state.)

Generations of U.N. Peace Operations

Following on the costly and frustrating experiences of Chapter VII peace enforcement in Somalia and Bosnia, old precepts, painfully learned, from the early days of U.N. peacekeeping seem newly relevant. The emergence of a working consensus on the Security Council in favor of a more interventionist international order, however impartial those actions may now be, does not remove the other reasons to be wary of intervention.

In order to explore those reasons in a U.N. context, it is helpful to think in terms of three categories of peace support operations. In traditional peacekeeping, sometimes called "first generation peacekeeping," unarmed or lightly armed U.N. forces were stationed between hostile parties to monitor a truce, troop withdrawal, and/or buffer zone while political negotiations went forward.[12] They provided transparency—an impartial assurance that the other party was not violating the truce. They also raised the costs of defecting from and the benefits of abiding with the agreement by the threat of exposure, the potential resistance of the peacekeeping force (if it were attacked), and the legitimacy of U.N.

mandates.[13] The virtues were obvious; their costs, as in the long Cyprus operation, were often paid in conflicts delayed rather than resolved.

"Second generation" operations involve the implementation of complex, multidimensional peace agreements. In addition to the traditional military functions, the peacekeepers are often engaged in various police and civilian tasks, the goal of which is a long-term settlement of the underlying conflict. I will return to this rapidly growing category below.

"Peace-enforcing"—that is, war-making—missions are the "third generation," which extend from low-level military operations to protect the delivery of humanitarian assistance to the en-

TABLE 1.   The Expanding U.N. Role in Peacemaking and War Making, 1988–1994[14]

	31 January 1988	31 January 1992	16 December 1994
Security Council Resolutions in prev. 12 mos.	15	53	78
sanctions imposed by SC	1	2	7
preventive diplomacy and peacemaking	11	13	28
electoral activities		6	21
peacekeeping ops. deployed, total	5	11	17
first generation	5	7	9
second and third		4	8
military personnel	9,570	11,495	73,393
civilian police	35	155	2,130
civilian personnel	1,516	1,206	2,260
countries contributing personnel	26	56	76
U.N. budget for peacekeeping, $mil.	230.4	1,689.6	3,610

forcement of ceasefires and, when necessary, assistance in the rebuilding of so-called failed states. Like Chapter VII U.N. enforcement action to roll back aggression, as in Korea in 1950 and
against Iraq in the Gulf War, the defining characteristic of "third
generation" operations is the lack of consent to some or all of a
U.N. mandate.[15]

With all of Minerva's usual sense of timing, insightful doctrine
for these peace-enforcing operations appeared just as Somalia and
Bosnia exposed their limitations. Recent studies have thoughtfully
mapped out the logic of the strategic terrain between traditional
U.N. peacekeeping and traditional U.N. enforcement action.[16]
Militarily these operations seek to *deter, dissuade, and deny*. By pre-
cluding an outcome based on the use of force by the parties, the
United Nations instead uses collective force (if necessary) to persuade the parties to settle the conflict by negotiation. In the former
Yugoslavia, for example, the U.N., following this strategy, could
have established strong points to deter attacks on key humanitarian corridors. (It did but the Serbs by-passed them.) Or it could
threaten air strikes, as was done successfully around Sarajevo in
February 1994, to dissuade a continuation of the Serb shelling of
the city. Or it could have denied (but did not) the Serb forces their
attack on Dubrovnik in 1992 by counter-shelling from the sea or
bombing from the air of the batteries in the hills above the city.

This terrain is murky. Forcing a peace depends on achieving a
complicated preponderance in which the forces (U.N. and local)
supporting a settlement acceptable to the international community hold both a military predominance and a predominance of
popular support, which together permit them to impose a peace
on the recalcitrant local military forces and their popular supporters.

This strategy, however, is likely to encounter many of the problems interventionist and imperial strategies have faced in the past
and discover fresh problems peculiar to the U.N.'s global character. The U.N. showed itself to be ineffective in imposing order by
force, whether to disarm factions in Somalia or provide humanitarian protection in Bosnia. Instead it became complicit in a record of inadequate protection, mission creep, seemingly unnecessary casualties, and Vietnam-like escalation, on the one hand, and

1930s-style appeasement on the other. It is difficult to disagree with the conclusion that the U.N. is remarkably ill-suited to war making. Indeed, Clausewitz's famous principles, ranging from the tactical to the political, seem to have been consistently honored in the breech.[17]

• Tactically, even at the high point of the violence associated with UNOSOM, U.N. forces lacked the heavy equipment, including in particular tanks, that would have been needed to dominate the battlefield. UNPROFOR suffered from a lack of operationally relevant military information. Despite the escalating levels of violence, the missions in both Somalia and Bosnia remained defined as peacekeeping, not war fighting. The war that did occur was supposed to occur in the midst of a civilian population whose protection was the first purpose of the operation. All this gave rise to what has become known as the Force Commander's Complaint: "If you order me to fight a war I will, but not in vehicles painted white!"

• Strategically, force commanders lacked command and control, the classic requirement of unity of command. The first act of every peacekeeping battalion was to establish a communications and command link with its national command authority. Any proposed action involving the threat of violence would be referred to national authorities for approval.[18] Force commanders, by consequence, negotiated rather than directed their forces, which was part of the reason for the lack of support on both June 24, when the Pakistanis took twenty-four casualties, and October 3, when the U.S. Rangers (who operated independently of the UNOSOM command) experienced disaster.

• At the grand strategic, or political command, level, the U.N. suffers from an irresponsible divorce between the Security Council and the U.N. operation in the field. At times, the Security Council issued mandates, for example for Bosnian safe havens, without providing the forces that military experts had argued were necessary to implement the mandates.[19] Delays also erode the effectiveness of U.N. peace operations. The outline of a Cambodian peace agreement was in place in the late summer of 1991, but the U.N. Transitional Authority in Cambodia

(UNTAC) was not fully operational until a full year later (and even then some units were not complete).

• At the political policy level that shapes all strategic implementation, U.N. war making suffers from severe disabilities: some a product of the incapacity of the organization, others a product of the kind of wars the U.N. has tried to address.

1) Although the U.N. seems to have the advantage of global impartiality, which should and often does win it more local acceptance when it intervenes, this is not universally the case. Israel maintains a suspicion of U.N. involvement dating back to the U.N. General Assembly's notorious anti-Zionism resolutions of the 1970s. In Somalia, Egypt's support for Siad Barre seems to have tainted the role Boutros-Ghali, a former Egyptian minister of state for foreign affairs, sought to play as impartial secretary-general. And there is lingering distrust of the U.N. in other parts of Africa due to its role in the Congo.[20]

2) The United Nations is particularly poorly suited to interventionist strategies involving the strategic employment of coercive force. The political roots of the U.N.'s "command and control" problems are twofold. On the one hand, countries with battalions in U.N. peace operations are reluctant to see their (often lightly armed) troops engaged in combat under U.N. direction, distrusting that a U.N. force commander of any nationality other than their own will take due care to minimize risks. Countries with seats on the Security Council, on the other hand, pressured to achieve a response to civil war crises and unwilling to confront the U.N.'s ongoing resource crisis, assign missions to U.N. peace operations without providing adequate means to achieve those missions. On top of this, the U.N.'s traditional ideology (despite recent practice) is highly protective of national sovereignty, and (to its credit) it lacks the callousness or psychological distance required to inflict coercive punishment on political movements with even the smallest of popular support.[21]

3) "Peace-forcing fatigue" is afflicting the U.N.'s contributing countries, whether new or old. States are rarely willing to invest their resources or the lives of their soldiers in war other than for a vital interest (such as oil in the Persian Gulf). But if states have

a vital national interest in a dispute, they are not likely to exercise the impartiality a U.N. peace operation requires. Nor are they likely to cede decision-making control over or command of their forces to the United Nations.

4) The very act of intervention, even by the U.N., can mobilize nationalist opposition against the foreign forces. In Somalia, it contributed to a significant growth of support for Aidid's Somali National Alliance. Aidid's supporters soon roundly condemned U.N. "colonialism."[22] The strategic balance is not static. Military intervention tilts two local balances, improving the military correlation of forces but often at the cost of undermining the more important political balance.

5) Coercively intervening for eventual self-determination, as J.S. Mill noted over a century ago, is very often a self-contradictory enterprise. If the local forces of freedom, self-determination, and human rights cannot achieve sovereignty without a foreign military intervention, then they are very unlikely to be able to hold on to power after the intervention force leaves. Either the installed forces of freedom will collapse, or they themselves will employ those very coercive methods that provoked and justified the initial intervention. The Kurds, for example, won widespread sympathy for their resistance to Saddam Hussein and benefited from a U.N. endorsed U.S.-French-British intervention in the aftermath of the war against Iraq. Now the Kurdish factions are so divided that they appear incapable of establishing law and order in their territory. Instead, three factions have divided the region. None appears capable of sustaining themselves against whatever attempts to reincorporate Kurdistan that Saddam Hussein may make. The international community has thus placed itself in the awkward position of either adopting Kurdistan as a long-term ward or returning it to the not-so-tender mercies of Saddam Hussein.[23]

The United Nations presents an almost textbook case of multiple strategic incapacity. But encountering strategic problems while intervening in ethnic and civil wars is not unique to the United Nations. The multinational force in Lebanon created even larger catastrophes of misdirected, overly violent, and intrusive intervention in 1983. Even with national-quality command and control, the United States failed to impose peace in Vietnam in the 1960s; the Soviets also failed in Afghanistan. Moreover, the United Nations is nothing more than the collective agent of its member states. Many of the U.N.'s organizational incapacities could be cured by additional resources from its members states, who devote but a tiny fraction of the resources they spend on national security to collective action under the United Nations.

Peacemaking: Strategies of Enhanced Consent

The U.N.'s deficiencies as a war maker suggest the value of innovating within U.N. traditions, developing a superior form of "peacemaking" that recognizes the continuing political significance of national sovereignty. The U.N. should seek out a consensual basis for a restoration of law and order in domestic crises and try to implement its global human rights agenda in a way that produces less friction and more support.

Taking a substantial step beyond "first generation" operations in which the U.N. monitors a truce, and keeping a significant step short of the third generation "peace-enforcing" operations in which the U.N. uses force to impose a peace, *"second generation" multidimensional operations* are based on consent of the parties. But the nature of and purposes for which consent is granted are qualitatively different from traditional peacekeeping. In these operations, the U.N. is typically involved in implementing peace agreements that go to the roots of the conflict, helping to build a long-term foundation for stable, legitimate government. As Secretary-General Boutros-Ghali observed in *An Agenda for Peace:*

> peace-making and peace-keeping operations, to be truly successful, must come to include comprehensive efforts to identify and support structures which will tend to consolidate peace. . . . These may include disarming the previously warring parties and the restoration of order, the custody and possible destruction of weapons, repatriating refugees, advisory and training support for security personnel, monitoring elections, advancing efforts to protect human rights, reforming or strengthening governmental institutions and promoting formal and informal processes of political participation.

UNTAC in Cambodia, for example, was based on the consent of the parties, as expressed in the Paris Agreements, but it moved beyond monitoring the actions of the parties to the establishment of a transitional authority that actually implemented directly crucial components of the mandate. Moreover, its scale was vastly larger than all but the enforcement mandates, and it found itself operating without the continuous (in the case of the Khmer Rouge) or complete (in the case of the other factions) cooperation of the factions.

The U.N. has a commendable record of success in second generation, multidimensional peacekeeping operations as diverse as those in Namibia, El Salvador, and Cambodia.[24] The U.N.'s role in helping settle those conflicts has been threefold. It served as a *peace maker,* facilitating a peace treaty among the parties; as a *peacekeeper,* monitoring the cantonment and demobilization of military forces, resettling refugees, and supervising transitional civilian authorities; and as a *peacebuilder,* monitoring and in some cases organizing the implementation of human rights, national democratic elections, and economic rehabilitation.

Though nonenforcing and consent based, these operations are far from harmonious. Consent is not a simple "bright line" demarcating the safe and acceptable from the dangerous and illegitimate. Each function will require an enhanced form of consent if the U.N. is to help make a peace in the contentious environment of civil strife. We need, therefore, to focus on new ways to design peace operations if the U.N., in the face of likely resistance, is to avoid having to choose between either force or withdrawal.

Peacemaking

Achieving the peace treaty itself will often require heavy persuasion by outside actors. In Cambodia, the USSR and China are said to have let their respective clients in Phnom Penh and the Khmer Rouge know that ongoing levels of financial and military support would not be forthcoming if they resisted the terms of a peace treaty that their patrons found acceptable. Peace treaties may themselves depend on prior sanctions, threats of sanctions, or loss of aid, imposed by the international community.[25]

The construction of an agreed peace is more than worth the

effort. The process of negotiation among the contending factions can discover the acceptable parameters of peace that are particular to the conflict. Going beyond an agreed truce or disarmament, a comprehensive peace treaty addresses grievances and establishes new institutions that test the true willingness of the parties to reconcile. Peace negotiations, furthermore, can mobilize the support of local factions and of the international community in support of implementing the peace. And a negotiated peace treaty can establish new entities committed to furthering peacekeeping and peacebuilding.

The U.N. has developed a set of crucially important innovations that help manage the making of peace on a consensual basis. First among them is the diplomatic device that has come to be called the "Friends of the Secretary General." This brings together multinational leverage for U.N. diplomacy to help make and manage peace. Composed of ad hoc, informal, multilateral, diplomatic mechanisms that join together states in support of initiatives of the secretary-general, it legitimates with the stamp of U.N. approval and supervision the pressures interested states can bring to bear to further the purposes of peace and the U.N.

For Cambodia, the "core group" in New York and "extended P5" in Phnom Penh played a "friends" role in the negotiation and the management of the peace process. Composed of the Security Council "permanent five"—the United States, France, USSR, China, and the United Kingdom—and "extended" to include Australia, Indonesia, Japan, and other concerned states, it took the lead in the construction of the Paris Agreements. It provided key support to UNTAC, both political and financial, and, led by Japan, it helped organize the International Committee on the Reconstruction of Cambodia, which raised pledges for almost $1 billion, while providing special funds for various projects. But the extended P5 lacked a fixed composition. It, of course, included the P5 but then included or excluded others on an ad hoc basis, depending on the issue and topic covered and the "message" the group wished to send. For example, Thailand was excluded from certain meetings in order to send a signal of concern about its lack of support for the restrictions imposed on the Khmer Rouge. In Cambodia, moreover, there was not a sovereign government to monitor or support. Much of the extended P5's diplomacy was therefore directed at UNTAC itself, protecting, for example, the interests of national battalions. It also served as a back channel for the UNTAC special representative to communicate directly with the Security Council.[26]

In El Salvador, the "four friends" of the secretary-general were Venezuela, Mexico, Spain, and Colombia. Frequently joined by a "fifth friend"—the United States—they together played a crucial role in negotiating and implementing the peace accords. So too did the core group in Mozambique. Hopes for the former Yugoslavia now center on the "contact group" including Russia, the United States, France, Germany, and the United Kingdom. Informal diplomatic support groups have also been active in Haiti, Namibia, Nicaragua, Georgia, Afghanistan, and Guatemala.[27]

Playing a crucial role in the secretary-general's peacemaking and preventive diplomacy functions, these groupings serve four key functions. First, the limited influence of the secretary-general can be leveraged, multiplied, and complemented by the "friends." The U.N.'s scarce attention and even scarcer resources can be supplemented by the diplomacy, finances, and clout of powerful, interested actors. The second value is legitimization. The very act of constituting themselves as a group, with the formal support of the secretary-general, lends legitimacy to the diplomatic activities of interested states that they might not otherwise have.[28] It allows for constructive diplomacy when accusations of special and particular national interest could taint bilateral efforts. The third value is coordination. The friends mechanism provides transparency among the interested external parties, assuring them that they are all working for the same purposes, and when they are doing so, allowing them to pursue a division of labor that enhances their joint effort. It ensures that diplomats are not working at cross purposes because they regularly meet and inform each other of their activities and encourage each other to undertake special tasks. And fourth, the friends mechanism provides a politically balanced approach to the resolution of civil wars through negotiation. It often turns out that one particular "friend" can associate with one faction just as another associates with a second. In the Cambodian peace process, China backstopped the Khmer Rouge, just as France did Prince Sihanouk and Russia (with Vietnam) did the state of Cambodia. The friends open more flexible channels of communication than a single U.N. mediator can provide. They also advise and guide the U.N. intermediaries in the peacekeeping and peacebuilding discussed below, although the process tends to work best when they support rather than move out in front of the U.N.

Multidimensional Peacekeeping

Even consent based peace agreements fall apart. In the circumstances of partisan violence and "failed states," agreements tend to be fluid. In the new civil conflicts, parties cannot force policy on their followers and often lack the capacity or will to maintain a difficult process of reconciliation leading to a reestablishment of national sovereignty.[29]

Peace treaties and their peacekeeping mandates thus tend to be affected by two sets of contradictory tensions. First, in order to get an agreement, diplomats assume all parties are in good faith; they cannot question the intentions of their diplomatic partners. But to implement a peacekeeping and peacebuilding operation, planners must assume the opposite—that the parties will not or cannot fulfill the agreement made. Moreover, diplomats who design the peace treaty tend to think in legal (authority, precedent), not strategic (power, incentives) categories. Treaties thus describe obligations; they tend to be unclear about incentives and capacities.

All these militate against clear and implementable mandates. Diplomats seek to incorporate in the treaty the most complete peace to which the parties will agree. U.N. officials seek to clarify the U.N.'s obligations. Knowing that much of what was agreed to in the peace treaty will not be implementable in the field, the officials who write the secretary-general's report (which outlines the implementation of the agreement) contract or expand the mandate of the peace operation. Confused mandates are an inevitable result of this tension.

A second tension also shapes the peacekeeping mandate. The mandate, like a natural resource contract, is an obsolescing bargain. When a country begins a negotiation with an oil company for the exploration of its territory, the company holds all the advantages. The costs of exploration are large, while the possibility of oil is uncertain. The country must therefore cede generous terms. As soon as oil is discovered, the bargain shifts as discovered oil is easy to pump and any oil company can do it. The old bargain has suddenly obsolesced. So it is with a U.N. peacekeeping operation: the spirit of agreement is never more exalted than at the moment of the signing of the peace treaty; the authority of the United Nations is never again greater. Then the parties assume that the agreement will be achieved and that all are cooperating in good faith. They depend upon the United Nations to achieve their various hopes. Although the U.N. has put some of its diplomatic prestige on the line, it as yet has no investment in material resources. The U.N., in short, holds most of the cards. But as soon as the U.N. begins its investment of money, personnel, and operational prestige, then the bargaining relationship alters its balance. The larger the U.N. investment—these multibillion operations represent multibillion dollar investments—the greater is the independent U.N. interest in success and the greater the influence of the parties becomes. Since the parties control an essential element in the success of the mandate, their bargaining power rapidly rises. So, in the late spring of 1993 as the crucial elections approached, UNTAC chief Yusushi Akashi acknowledged, "I cannot afford not to succeed."

This dual tension in designing peacekeeping operations emphasizes that time is critical. The U.N. should be ready to implement the mandate as soon after the signing of a peace treaty as is practicable. UNTAC suffered a large decrease in authority in early 1992 as time passed and expectations of the factions and the Cambodian people were disappointed.

These tensions also explain how the ideal framework (both legal and political) of a treaty can dissolve in days or months, as the Cambodian peace agreements did. The provisions of peace accords become so general, ambiguous, or unworkable that many of the details have to be worked out in the implementation process. To be minimally effective under those circumstances, the U.N. must innovate.

The United Nations needs a flexible political strategy to win and keep popular support and create (not just enjoy) the support of local forces of order. In a failed state, as was the case in a society subject to colonial rule, what is most often missing is modern organization. This was what colonial metropoles supplied, in their own self-interest, as they mobilized local resources to combat local opposition. Over the longer run, indigenous forces such as the political Zamindars and the King's Own African Rifles and other locally recruited military battalions (not metropolitan troops) were the forces that made imperial rule effective, that preserved a balance of local power in favor of metropolitan influence—and that kept it cheap. Learning from the history of imperial institution building (while avoiding imperial exploitation and coercion), an effective and affordable strategy for U.N. peace operations faces a greater challenge. It needs to discover ways to generate *voluntary* cooperation from divided local political actors and mobilize existing local resources for *locally legitimate,* collective purposes.[30] And it must do so *rapidly.*

Recent peacekeeping experience has suggested a second peacekeeping innovation: an ad hoc, semisovereign mechanism designed to address those new challenges by dynamically managing a peace process and mobilizing local cooperation. Examples of these ad hoc, semisovereign mechanisms include the Supreme National Council (SNC) in Cambodia and the Commission on the Peace (COPAZ) in El Salvador.

It has often been remarked that Chapter VI presents the United Nations with too little authority and Chapter VII offers too much; and that Chapter VI is associated with too little use of force and Chapter VII with too much. The value of these ad hoc, semisovereign artificial bodies is that they provide a potentially powerful, political means of encouraging and influencing the shape of consent. Indeed, these semisovereign artificial bodies can help contain the erosion of consent and even manufacture it where it is missing. Created by a peace treaty, they permit the temporary consensus of the parties to be formally incorporated in an institution with regular consultation and even, as in the Cambodian Supreme National Council, a semiautonomous sovereign will. These mechanisms have proved crucial in a number of recent U.N. missions. They can represent the once-warring parties and act in the name of a preponderance of the "nation" without the continuous or complete consent of all the factions. They can both build political support and adjust—in a legitimate way, with the consent of the parties—the mandate in order to respond to unanticipated changes in local circumstances.

In Cambodia, the Supreme National Council, constructed by the Paris Peace Agreements, "enshrined" Cambodian sovereignty. The council, composed of the four factions and chaired by Prince Sihanouk, offered a chance for these parties to consult together on a regular basis and endorse the peace process. It also lent special authority to Prince Sihanouk, who was authorized to act if the SNC failed to achieve a consensus. Beyond that, it empowered the United Nations, represented by Special Representative Yasushi Akashi, to act in the interests of the peace process, if Sihanouk failed to do so. Artificially created, the SNC thus established a semisovereign legal personality designed to be responsive to the general interests of Cambodia (even when a complete consensus was lacking among all the factions) and to the authority of the United Nations special representative. Acting in the name of Cambodia—as a step in the implementation of the Paris Agreements—the SNC acceded to all the major human rights conventions (including the first and second Covenants on Human Rights), and it authorized the trade embargo against illegal exports of logs and gems. The SNC was the forum that endorsed the protracted and sensitive negotiations over the franchise. It legitimated the enforcement of certain elements of the peace, absent the unanimous consent of the parties and without the necessity of a contentious debate at the Security Council. It could have exercised greater authority, perhaps even designing an acceptable scheme for rehabilitation, if Prince Sihanouk or Akashi had been both willing and able to lead it in that direction.

The Commission on the Peace in El Salvador played a related, although much less authoritative, role in the Salvadoran peace process, serving as a forum for consultation among the Frente Farabundo Marti para la Liberacion Nacional (FMLN), the government, and the other political parties. Designed to monitor and establish a forum for the participation of civilian society in the peace process, it was the only political institution that embodied the full scope of Salvadoran politics, the only institution that could legitimately speak for "El Salvador." That its role in the peace process proved to be minimal was unfortunate. And in Somalia, the "Transitional National Council" was designed to perform a similar function, but its failure to obtain support from the leading actors was perhaps the single most disturbing problem in the peacemaking process, one that seriously eroded the attempt to create a peace.

In designing these semisovereign artificial bodies, the U.N. should try (to the extent that its freedom of negotiation allows) to "preview" the peace that the parties and the international community seek. For the Paris Peace Agreements for Cambodia, seeking a "pluralist democracy" should have meant supplementing the Supreme National Council with other bodies, such as one for civil society. It might have included Buddhist monks, nongovernmental organizations, and other representatives of society outside the state. These supplementary bodies need not perform executive or legislative functions. The important point is that civil society participate in the decision-making process, at a minimum through formally recognized consultative channels.

The U.N. must avoid the trade-offs between too much force and too little. The dangers of Chapter VII enforcement operations, whether in Somalia or Bosnia, leave many observers to think that it is extremely unlikely that troop-contributing countries will actually sign up for such operations. The risks are far more costly than the member states are willing to bear for humanitarian purposes. But when we look at Chapter VI operations, we see that consent by parties easily dissolves under the difficult processes of peace. U.N. operations in the midst of civil strife have often been rescued by the timely use of force by the United Nations, as were the operations in the Congo, when Katanga's secession was forcibly halted, and as was the operation in Namibia, when the South-West Africa People's Organization's violation of the peace agreement was countered with the aid of South African forces. But both nearly derailed the peace process by eroding local, regional, or global support. Given those options, the semisovereign artificial bodies offer the possibility of midcourse adjustments and "nationally" legitimated enforcement (should it be needed). In Cambodia, for example, UNTAC appealed through the SNC to all the factions to protect the election. The result was that the armies cooperating with the peace plan pushed the Khmer Rouge back from the population centers, permitting a safer vote in the last week of May 1993. Ad hoc, semisovereign entities systematize and artificially (but usefully) enhance the process of consent in the direction of the promotion of peace while avoiding the dangers associated with attempts to implement an externally forced peace.

Peacebuilding

Multidimensional, second generation peacekeeping pierces the shell of national autonomy by bringing international involvement to areas long thought to be the exclusive domain of domestic jurisdiction. If a peacekeeping operation is to leave behind a legitimate and independently viable political sovereign, it must help transform the political landscape by building a new basis for domestic peace.

Traditional strategies of conflict resolution, when successful, were designed to resolve a dispute between conflicting parties. Successful resolution could be measured by 1) the stated reconciliation of the parties; 2) the duration of the reconciliation; and 3) changes in the way parties behaved toward each other.[31] But successful contemporary peacebuilding changes not merely behavior but, more importantly, it transforms identities and institutional context. More than reforming play in an old game, it changes the game.

This is the grand strategy Lt. Gen. John Sanderson, UNTAC force commander, invoked when he spoke of forging an alliance with the Cambodian people, by-passing the factions. Reginald Austin, electoral chief of UNTAC, probed the same issue when he asked what are the "true objectives [of UNTAC]: Is it a political operation seeking a solution to the immediate problem of an armed conflict by all means possible? Or does it have a wider objective: to implant democracy, change values and establish a new pattern of governance based on multi-partisan and free and fair elections?"

UNTAC helped create new actors on the Cambodian political

scene: the electors, a fledgling civil society, a free press, a continuing international and transnational presence. The Cambodian voters gave Prince Ranariddh institutional power, and the Khmer Rouge was transformed from an internationally recognized claimant on Cambodian sovereignty to a domestic guerrilla insurgency. The peacebuilding process, particularly the election, became the politically tolerable *substitute* for the inability of the factions to reconcile their conflicts.

The U.N.'s role, mandated by these complex agreements rather than Chapter VII, includes monitoring, substituting for, renovating, and in some cases helping to build the basic structures of the state. The U.N. is called in to demobilize and sometimes to restructure and reform once-warring armies; to monitor or to organize national elections; to promote human rights; to supervise public security and help create a new civilian police force; to control civil administration in order to establish a transitional politically neutral environment; to begin the economic rehabilitation of devastated countries; and, as in the case of Cambodia, to address directly the values of the citizens, with a view to promoting democratic education.

The parties to these agreements, in effect, consent to limitation of their sovereignty for the life of the U.N. sponsored peace process. They do so because they need the help of the international community to achieve peace. But acceptance of U.N. involvement in implementing these agreements is less straightforward than, for example, consenting to observance of a ceasefire. Even when genuine consent is achieved, it is impossible to provide for every contingency in complex peace accords. Problems of interpretation arise, unforeseen gaps in the accords materialize, and circumstances change. The original consent, as the Salvadoran peace process suggests, can become open-ended and, in part, a gesture of faith that later problems can be worked out on a consensual basis. In the process, the international community, represented by the United Nations, exercises a monitoring pressure to encourage progress on the reform of the judiciary, the expansion of the electoral rolls, and the operation of free press.

But authentic and firm consent in the aftermath of severe civil strife, such as that Cambodia endured, is rare. The first clear

implication is the consequent importance of risk-spreading mul-
tidimensionality. The U.N. should design in as many routes to
peace—institutional reform, elections, international monitoring,
economic rehabilitation—as the parties will tolerate.

Second, the international negotiators of a peace treaty and the
U.N. designers of a mandate should, therefore, attempt to design
in bargaining advantages for the U.N. authority. Even seemingly
extraneous bargaining chips will become useful as the spirit of
cooperation erodes under the pressure of misunderstandings and
separating interests. The U.N. counted upon the financial needs of
the Cambodian factions to ensure their cooperation and designed
an extensive rehabilitation component to guarantee steady rewards for cooperative behavior.[32] But the Khmer Rouge's access
to illicit trade (with the apparent connivance of elements of the
Thai military along the western border) eliminated this bargaining
chip. And the suspicion of the dominant faction's (SOC, the "state
of Cambodia") rivals prevented a full implementation of rehabilitation in the 80 percent of the country it controlled.

Third, the architects of the U.N. operation should therefore also
design into the mandate as much independent implementation as
the parties will agree to in the peace treaty. In Cambodia, the
electoral component and refugee repatriation seem to have succeeded simply because they did not depend on the steady and
continuous positive support of the four factions. Each had an independent sphere of authority and organizational capacity that allowed it to proceed against everything short of active military opposition. Civil administrative control and the cantonment of the
factions failed because they relied on the continuous direct and
positive cooperation of each of the factions. Each of the factions, at
one time or another, had reason to expect that the balance of
advantages was tilting against itself, and so refused to cooperate. A
significant source of the success of the election was Radio
UNTAC's ability to speak directly to the potential Cambodian
voters, by-passing the propaganda of the four factions and invok-
ing a new Cambodian actor, the voting citizen. But voters are only
powerful for the five minutes it takes them to vote, if there is not an
institutional mechanism to transfer democratic authority to
bureaucratic practice. Now, lacking such a mechanism in Cam-

bodia, the voters are vulnerable to the armies, police, and corruption that dominate after the votes are tallied.

In these circumstances, the U.N. should try to create new institutions to assure that votes in U.N. sponsored elections "count" more. The U.N. needs to leave behind a larger institutional legacy, drawing, for example, upon the existing personnel of domestic factions, adding to them a portion of authentic independents, and training a new army, a new civil service, a new police force, and a new judiciary. These are the institutions that can be decisive in ensuring that the voice of the people, as represented by their elected representatives, shapes the future. This is exactly the task that lies ahead in Haiti, following the permissive takeover by the United States negotiated in September 1994.

Improving Peace Management

Peacekeeping and peacebuilding can be expensive. In El Salvador the costs have been about $111 million (at an average $29 million per year for three and one-half years, 1991–94). In Cambodia estimates suggest that at least $1 billion in additional costs would have been incurred beyond the official budget of $1.5 billion if the plans for economic rehabilitation could have been implemented. (Expenditures in this range are still required if Cambodia is to be put on its feet economically.) The April 1993 NATO estimates of the cost of implementing an agreed peace in Bosnia indicated a requirement for 50,000 soldiers and $10 billion per year, without including the civilian peacebuilding costs.[33]

Both the U.N. and the U.S. need to improve the management of peace operations. The U.N. is in the process of making improvements in the financial management of peacekeeping operations, but considerable attention still needs to be paid to the coordination of the U.N. multilateral aid system as a whole.[34] Equally important are changes in the way the United States funds the U.N. Taking peacekeeping expenses from either the Defense Department "operations and maintenance" or the State Department regular budget, depending on whether U.S. troops are used or not, makes little sense. Instead, and in addition to promoting the Presidential Decision Directive 25 (PDD 25) reforms concerning U.N.

planning, the United States should establish a consolidated budget for U.N. peace operations, including an annual estimate for peace operations. If the choices for U.S. foreign policy today are standing by while allowing human disasters to take their course, going it alone, or cooperating with others through the U.N. or other multinational arrangements, it seems time to recognize that there are going to be times when the United States will want to act through the U.N. The U.S. Senate bill for a "Peace Powers Act" cosponsored by Senators Robert Dole, Jesse Helms, and Strom Thurmond requires the president to provide two weeks prior notice to a U.N. Security Council vote that would dispatch U.N. troops to a crisis, and a certification that the peace operation is "in the national security interests of the United States," even for a mission involving only the military forces of other countries.[35] To the extent the U.S. Congress wants to increase its role in these decisions, including budgetary approval for U.S. participation in U.N. operations, and improve the quality of its oversight, it should consider a better option: establishing a joint committee on U.N. operations and making provision for some of its members to be regularly involved in the U.S. delegation in New York. Large deployments over the annual appropriation involving U.S. soldiers should be funded with a supplemental budget request that fully reimburses Defense Department direct costs and preserves military readiness and training. In-kind contributions outside the U.N. budget should be maintained. Charging the U.N. budget for these contributions (which are often two or three times the budgeted costs) will bankrupt the organization, as other states adopt the same policy, and cede too much authority to the U.N. Secretariat in the management of these operations that currently benefit from the multiple sources of funding and policy input that voluntary contributions offer.[36]

Difficult choices concerning U.N. financing need to be made with a better comparative perspective. For every $1,000 spent by member countries on their own military forces, they spend, on average, $1.40 on the U.N. peacekeeping budget. In 1994 the United States budgeted $267 billion on the Defense Department, about $28 billion on the intelligence community, and $1 billion for U.N. peacekeeping (our current 30 percent of the $3.2 billion total). Nor is the United States discriminated against in the assessment of U.N. costs. The 25 percent U.S. assessment to the U.N. regular budget (and the peacekeeping rate proposed by the Clinton administration) is .0076 percent of U.S. national income. The Netherlands, Austria, and Sweden pay 135 percent of the U.S. rate relative to their national income. Ministates, like Sao Tome, pay 330 percent of the U.S. rate relative to their income.[37]

In the end, however, the United States and other large contributors will have to ask whether U.N. peace operations are worth the cost. Today, for example, although no one calls Cambodia or El Salvador models of growth oriented, stable democracies, nonetheless, both governments were chosen in U.N. supervised elections that were the freest and fairest in their histories. Salvador's police were reformed; Cambodia enjoys an effective coalition government determined to resist the remaining and dwindling Khmer Rouge guerrillas. When we consider that some in the U.S. government once thought peace, pro-American states, and democratic development in Southeast Asia were worth more than 50,000 U.S. lives and about $179 billion (1990 dollars), and that as late as the 1980s the U.S. government thought that promoting a friendly regime, peace, and democracy was worth $6.01 billion (FY 1981–1990, in 1994 dollars) in El Salvador, both the U.N.'s Cambodian and Salvadoran operations look remarkably cheap and successful, even when measured solely in terms of U.S. national interests. Today, a successful operation in Haiti should preclude the U.S. having to spend what might have been even larger amounts to resettle Haitian refugees in the U.S. More importantly, the Haitians now have the opportunity to establish an independent democratic government in their own land.

Alternatives

When the United Nations cannot negotiate a peace, should the international community abandon the cause? What responses should have been made to acts of overt aggression, such as Iraq's invasion of Kuwait, or to the looming humanitarian disasters in Bosnia and Somalia in 1992, or Rwanda in the spring of 1994?

Delegation to national action has become, as it was in Korea in

1950, the U.N.'s answer to extreme emergencies—international aggression and humanitarian catastrophe. It offers a traditional national solution to the U.N.'s typical command and control problems. Now it is becoming so widespread that it is being designated "fourth generation" peacekeeping. Stimulated by the temporary success of UNITAF and by the delegations to Russia in Georgia, to France in Rwanda, and to the United States in Haiti, the U.N. is surmounting contributors' fatigue by assigning mandates to the national states willing to accept and perhaps enforce them. This, indeed, may be the best compromise available in difficult circumstances.[38] In itself, however, it does little to address the longer-run problems of leaving behind a stable form of locally legitimate government. Here there remains an important "hand-off" role for the U.N. Imposing a scheme of public order should be avoided in favor of mobilizing the peacemaking, peacekeeping, and peacebuilding strategies of enhanced consent that the U.N. exercises well. The UNITAF to UNOSOM II hand-off failed because peacemaking stopped short of negotiating a comprehensive, implementable agreement that included both the warlords and civil society. Instead, the U.N. attempted to impose law and order from New York and Washington, with all the consequences. In these cases, the U.N. should try to recruit the beginnings of a "friends" coalition of interested states to assist and help monitor the intervenor. These "friends" will also be needed to help negotiate, fund, and manage a peace on a multilateral basis.

Delegation raises difficult issues of U.N. responsibility. Can the Security Council be confident that the mandate it assigns will be implemented in ways that fulfill multilateral principles and serve the interests of the United Nations as a whole? Security Council "licenses" to intervene with preordained but renewable expiration clauses should address some of these concerns. But in our dangerous times, will states volunteer in reliably large enough numbers for international public service?

Another alternative centers about a new attention to the possibilities of regional peacekeeping—a multilateral, burden-sharing strategy recommended in the secretary-general's *Agenda for Peace*. A regional approach appears designed to elicit a more locally sensitive approach to political disputes. But the lack of institutional, military, and financial capacity of the regional organizations (with the exception perhaps of NATO) remains a considerable hurdle. As yet another alternative, Sir Brian Urquhart has issued an eloquent manifesto in favor of a U.N. rapid reaction force of 5,000–10,000. Small and centrally controlled, it would be suited for overcoming delays occasioned by the recruiting of peacekeeping forces, enabling the U.N. to engage in rapid interventions that can sometimes prevent an escalating crisis. Had they been available, these forces might have been decisive in Somalia in early 1992 or Rwanda in the spring of 1994. Very few countries, however, have expressed a willingness to establish such a force. Current discussions center on a less global but still valuable ready reaction force consisting of designated national units, trained in peacekeeping, and available at short notice.

When no state, group of states, or organization will volunteer to intervene, then sometimes the best that can be done is to try to mitigate the consequences of natural disaster or war. Humanitarian assistance from "above"—state efforts to establish "humanitarian corridors," as has been done in the Sudan, or protected convoys, and even, at the minimum, airdrops as was essayed in Bosnia—can make a valuable difference. Assistance from "below" by nongovernmental organizations, taking all the considerable risks of independent action, can also provide relief, as the voluntary agencies did in Somalia until they were overwhelmed in late 1992. In these circumstances, the U.N. should continue to attempt to recruit coalitions of states—"friends"—who will dedicate their energies to negotiating and managing a peace. UNPROFOR, to its credit, has remained committed to negotiating, rather than imposing, a peace. But the Security Council should avoid making promises—such as the Bosnian "safe havens" or the Croatian disarmed and protected "protected areas"—unless it either has the consent of all the parties and plans to provide adequate forces to implement the agreement against likely slippage, or, irrespective of consent, is prepared to enforce the pledges against opposition. As the secretary-general noted in 1995, there are often other areas of the world where—if the U.N.'s resources are fixed—those U.N. resources can sometimes be put to better use saving more people in situations closer to a negotiable solution.[39]

Neither U.N. peacemaking nor these alternative strategies will eliminate the formidable challenges of making, keeping, and building peace in the midst of protracted civil wars. Some crises will not find their solution. But today, as the United Nations is under attack in the United States and elsewhere, we should not neglect its authentic peacemaking potential. Employing strategies of enhanced consent, the United Nations can play a constructive role in the forging of peace and reconstruction in those areas of the world in need of assistance. Avoiding the dangerous and often counterproductive effects of armed imposition, whether unilateral or multilateral, the United Nations can be the legitimating broker in the making, keeping, and building of a stable peace that takes the first steps toward the opening of political space for human rights and participatory communal self-expression.

Notes

[1] This chapter draws on research supported by Princeton's Liechtenstein Research Program on Self-Determination, The Ford Foundation, and the International Peace Academy, and on "Forcing Peace," *Dissent,* Spring 1994, and *The U.N. in Cambodia: UNTAC's Civil Mandate.* I would like to thank Mr. Yasushi Akashi and Dr. Ramirez-Ocampo and many members of UNTAC and ONUSAL. Ambassador Emilio Cardenas, Ambassador Ibrahim Gambari, Professor Jeffrey Herbst, Mr. Ian Johnstone, Mr. Jeffrey Laurenti, Mr. F.T. Liu, Mr. C. William Maynes, Professor Clovis Maksoud, Professor Ali Mazrui, Ambassador Hisashi Owada, Mr. Laurence Pearl, Mr. Michael Switow, and Professor John Waterbury offered valuable advice. But none of them bears responsibility for the views advocated in this chapter.

[2] I realize that the United Nations regarded these activities as "peacekeeping" or "peace enforcement," not war making. The parties, however, can have reason to see them differently. Imagine, for example, how the U.S. federal government would have viewed a decision of the European Concert in 1864 to establish Washington, Baltimore, Atlanta, Mobile, and New Orleans as "safe havens" and to ban all interference with American commerce in American territorial waters—a "no sail zone"—by either the federal government or the Confederacy. None of this questions whether the UNPROFOR measures were justified.

[3] The U.S. Congress, National Security Revitalization Act (H.R. 7) includes provisions for charging the U.N. for a wide range of indirect as well as direct costs of U.S. participation in peacekeeping. If adopted, this legislation (in the eyes of many expert witnesses) would bankrupt U.N. peacekeeping as the United States and other states proceeded to charge the U.N. for what have been extensive voluntary commitments in support of U.N. peacekeeping efforts. See the testimony of Secretary Warren Christopher (January 26, 1995) and C. William Maynes (January 19, 1995) before the House International Relations Committee.

⁴ See Stevenson (1993), Clark (1993), and Jane Perlez, "Somalia Self-Destructs and the World Looks On," *New York Times,* December 29, 1991, p. 1.

⁵ For this argument see Sahnoun (1994).

⁶ For President Bush's rationale, see Michael Wines, "Bush Outlines Somalia Mission to Save Thousands," *New York Times,* December 5, 1992.

⁷ The figures are controversial. See Rieff (1995) and Kenney (1995), pp. 49–52.

⁸ Higgins (1993), pp. 468–470; Steinberg (1993); Ramet, (1992), pp. 79–98; and Glenny (1995).

⁹ Michael Gordon, "Pentagon is Wary of Role in Bosnia," *New York Times,* March 13, 1994.

¹⁰ Bair (1994), pp. 340–49, p. 345.

¹¹ Eric Schmitt, "Somalia's First Lesson for Military is Caution," *New York Times,* March 5, 1995.

¹² Traditional peacekeeping is a shorthand term that describes many but by no means all cold war peacekeeping missions—the most notable exception being the Congo operation of 1960–64. For a cogent analysis of different types of peacekeeping, see Goulding (1993).

¹³ In game theoretic terms, they solved variable sum, "coordination" problems, where both parties have the same best outcome, and will reach it if they can trust each other, and "prisoner's dilemma" problems, where the parties have an incentive to cheat. The peacekeepers provide the missing transparency in the first and alter the payoffs in the second, making the prisoner's dilemma into a coordination game. First generation operations include both sorts of games.

¹⁴ *Supplement to An Agenda for Peace: Position Paper of the Secretary-general on the Occasion of the Fiftieth Anniversary of the United Nations,* A/50/60;S/1995/1, 3 January 1995, p.4.

¹⁵ Other recent categories include "preventive deployments" deployed with the intention of deterring a possible attack, as in Macedonia today. There the credibility of the deterring force must ensure that the potential aggressor knows that there will be no easy victory. In the event of an armed challenge, the result will be an international war that involves costs so grave as to outweigh the temptations of conquest. Enforcement action against aggression (Korea or the Gulf), conversely, is a matter of achieving victory—"the decisive, comprehensive and synchronized application of preponderant military forces to shock, disrupt, demoralize and defeat opponents"—the traditional zero sum terrain of military strategy. See Ruggie (1993), who draws on "A Doctrinal Statement of Selected Joint Operational Concepts," Office of the JCS, DoD, Wash., D.C., 23 November 1992.

¹⁶ Categories of action are comprehensively set forth in Mackinlay and Chopra (1993), and Ruggie (1993), pp. 1–11. Also see Mackinlay's update (1993), pp. 29–50.

¹⁷ von Clausewitz (1976). See especially Book Eight: "War Plans." For a discussion of strategic categories applied to the Cambodian operation see Lieutenant General John Sanderson, "Consensus Without Objectivity: Problems of Command and Control for United Nations Peacekeeping," for the International Peace Academy, Vienna Seminar, March 2–4, 1995.

¹⁸ Doll and Metz (1993), p. 14. The problem of field command and control was less severe in first generation peacekeeping because it did not usually involve the use of force.

¹⁹ The safe havens were said to require 34,000 troops; the Security Council authorized 7,600.

²⁰ Recently this distrust has given way to a sense of urgency about Africa's conflicts, in which U.N. involvement is seen as necessary.

[21] An added problem is that the use of force in civil wars frequently causes casualties among civilians, opening the U.N. and its members to accusations of neocolonialism and brutality.

[22] Adbi Hassan Awale, an Aidid advisor in Mogadishu, complained, "The UN wants to rule this country. They do not want a Somali government to be established. The UN wants to stay and colonize us." *New York Times,* March 2, 1994.

[23] Chris Hedges, "Quarrels of Kurdish Leaders Sour Dreams of a Homeland," *New York Times,* June 18, 1994, p. A 1.

[24] Before the U.N. became involved, during the cold war when action by the Security Council was stymied by the lack of consensus among its five permanent members, the international community allowed Cambodia to suffer an auto-geno-cide and El Salvador, a brutal civil war. Indeed the great powers were involved in supporting factions who inflicted some of the worst aspects of violence the two countries suffered. We should keep this in mind when we consider the U.N.'s difficulties in Somalia and Bosnia.

[25] The Governors Island Accord, which produced the first (ineffective) settlement of the Haitian conflict, resulted from the economic sanctions on arms and oil imposed by the U.N. and the Organization of American States on Haiti as a whole. Sanctions targeted on perpetrators (the military elite and their supporters) might have been much more effective (and were later imposed in the summer of 1994). Restrictions on the overseas private bank accounts and air travel of the ruling elite would have been both more just and perhaps more effective than general economic sanctions, whose impact was most severe on the most vulnerable and from which the elite may actually have benefited.

[26] Yasushi Akashi, "UNTAC in Cambodia: Lessons for UN Peace-keeping," The Charles Rostow Annual Lecture (Washington, DC; SAIS October 1993), and Doyle interviews in Phnom Penh, March 1993, and New York, November 1993.

[27] The group of "friends" for Haiti consisted of France, the United States, Canada, and Venezuela.

[28] For a good discussion of the U.N.'s and especially the secretary-general's potential strength as a diplomatic legitimator, see Picco (1994), pp. 14–18. The "friends" mechanism seems to answer many of the objections to U.N. mediation expressed by Touval (1994), pp. 44–57.

[29] See Roberts (1993); Durch (1993); Berdal (1993); and Weiss (1993).

[30] It is interesting to note that some key, early U.N. experts in peacekeeping were eminent decolonization experts, deeply familiar with the politics of colonial rule, as was Ralph Bunche from the U.N. Trusteeship Division. See Urquhart (1993), chapter 5, and for a discussion of imperial strategy, Doyle (1986), chapter 12. But there are key differences. Empires were governed primarily in the interests of the metropole; U.N. peace operations explicitly promote the interests of the host country. And what made imperial strategy work was the possibility of coercive violence, the over-the-horizon gunboats that could be and often were offshore. That, for good and bad, is what the U.N. usually lacks, unless it calls in the enforcement capacity of the major powers. Rehabilitation assistance is sometimes an effective carrot, but not the equivalent of the Royal Navy.

[31] For a good account of traditional views of reconciliation see Fetherston (1994), p. 11, discussing a paper by Marc Ross.

[32] This link was drawn explicitly by Deputy Secretary of State Lawrence Eagleburger at the Conference on the Reconstruction of Cambodia, June 22, 1992, Tokyo, where he proposed that assistance to Cambodia be "through the SNC—to

areas controlled by those Cambodian parties cooperating with UNTAC in implementing the peace accords—and only those parties which are so cooperating." Disbursing aid through the SNC, however, gave the Khmer Rouge a voice, as a member of the SNC, in the potential disbursement of the aid.

[33] For Cambodia, these figures include the cost of refugee repatriation and the $800 million pledged by the International Commission on the Reconstruction of Cambodia. Bosnian costs are found in Bair (1994), p. 349. The Clinton administration pledged a U.S. contingent of 25,000 soldiers, drawn primarily from the 1st Armored Division and 3rd Infantry Division.

[34] Precontracting for peacekeeping logistics is helping. More needs to be done in system-wide coordination, as has been noted by de Soto and del Castillo (1994), pp. 69–84.

[35] The same bill, however, repeals the restrictions on U.S. unilateral deployments embodied in the 1973 War Powers Act. See the commentary in Jeffrey Laurenti, "Subverting Security," *Boston Globe*, February 16, 1995.

[36] It is difficult to overemphasize how important the combination of voluntary contributions were to the success of the Cambodian election, where U.S. assistance in the funding of human rights activities and the UNTAC Radio and Japanese donations of tens of thousands of radios to the Cambodian people made it possible for the Cambodian people to become informed about the significance and security of their act of voting.

[37] Some countries, such as some of the rapidly developing countries, are paying less than their full share because the U.N. budget is too slow to adjust to rapid changes in GNP. The United States will be able to shrink its share of the peacekeeping budget from 30 percent to 25 percent with little cost to the U.N. if Japan and Germany join the Security Council as permanent members, paying at the higher rate permanent members have traditionally accepted for their greater privileges and responsibilities in the direction of U.N. peace operations.

[38] For a case for an opinion similar to this, called "benign spheres of influence," see Maynes (1993–94).

[39] Barbara Crossette, "U.N. Chief Ponders Future of Peacekeepers," *New York Times*, March 3, 1995. The secretary-general referred specifically to transferring resources from UNPROFOR to possible operations in Afghanistan or Tajikistan.

3

Meeting the Proliferation Challenge: What Role for the United Nations?

LEWIS A. DUNN

The proliferation of nuclear, chemical, and biological weapons is widely acknowledged to be one of the most daunting challenges to regional security and global order in the post–cold war world.[1] As the fiftieth anniversary of the creation of the United Nations approaches—as well as the fiftieth anniversary of the first test of a nuclear weapon—it is especially timely to reflect on the potential role of the United Nations in meeting the future challenge of proliferation. From an American perspective, national

LEWIS A. DUNN is vice president and manager of the Weapons Proliferation and Strategic Planning Operation of Science Applications International Corporation. He is a former assistant director of the U.S. Arms Control and Disarmament Agency and served as ambassador to the 1985 Nuclear Non-Proliferation Treaty Review Conference and as ambassador to the 1987 United Nations Conference on the Peaceful Uses of Nuclear Energy. He is a member of the Director of Central Intelligence's Non-Proliferation Advisory Panel. Mr. Dunn is the author of *Controlling the Bomb* and of *Containing Nuclear Proliferation*, Adelphi Paper No. 263. He also is the coeditor (with Sharon A. Squassoni) of *Arms Control: What Next?* and (with Amy Gordan) of *Arms Control Verification and the New Role of On-Site Inspection*.

action and multilateral undertakings will remain the core of our response to this challenge. But creative use of the United Nations could strengthen more traditional nonproliferation efforts.

This chapter first briefly considers the main dimensions of the emerging proliferation challenge, including a growing threat of additional uses of nuclear, chemical, or biological weapons. The past role of the United Nations is then very briefly considered, with prime emphasis on what is revealed about the constraints to greater U.N. involvement. A number of potential near-term contributions of the United Nations to the achievement of U.S. nonproliferation objectives are then set out and assessed—norm building, institutionalizing international concern, fact finding, strengthening global security, and backstopping treaty compliance. Looking "over the horizon," the potential use of the U.N. Security Council to help create an enforceable taboo against the further use of nuclear, chemical, and biological weapons is considered.

The Changing Proliferation Challenge

The proliferation challenge is not new. For over four decades, since the Soviet detonation of an atomic bomb in 1949, the United States and other countries have wrestled with the dangers posed by the spread of nuclear weapons. Efforts to contain the use of chemical and bacteriological weapons go back even further to the 1895 Hague Protocol and the 1925 Geneva Convention Banning the Use in War of Chemical and Bacteriological Weapons.

But the proliferation challenge today is changing in fundamental ways. Traditional nonproliferation procedures, institutions, and measures put in place over the past decades are at best being seriously stressed and at worst increasingly undermined by at least five developments: the accelerating erosion of technical constraints; the emergence of a new style of proliferator; the breakdown of the cold war political-military order; lack of a credible response to noncompliance with nonproliferation obligations; and a growing danger of additional use of nuclear, biological or chemical (NBC) weaponry and missile delivery systems.

Accelerating Erosion of Technical Constraints

Multilateral actions to buttress the technical obstacles that confront countries seeking to produce or acquire NBC weaponry or missile delivery systems have long been the first line of defense of traditional nonproliferation efforts. Over the past decades, national export control regulations have been passed, multilateral suppliers' regimes established, and at least in the nuclear arena, a system of international inspections to detect misuse of peaceful facilities has been put in place. (Assuming entry into force of the Chemical Weapons Convention, that treaty will provide for an even more rigorous set of inspections. Attempts are underway, as well, to increase transparency under the Biological and Toxin Weapons Convention.) Not able to block proliferation, these attempts at technology denial have slowed proliferators' programs and bought time for other nonproliferation actions to be taken.

Looking ahead, the continuing global process of industrialization and technological development will further erode the effectiveness of technology constraints. As is already evident, a steadily growing number of countries will possess the capability to produce NBC weaponry should they make the political decision to do so. Dual-use chemical industries provide a ready stepping stone to chemical weapons production. Revolutionary developments in the biological sciences have made it far easier to produce rapidly significant quantities of biological agents. Perhaps most important, the collapse of the Soviet Union—and continuing political, economic, and social instability in Russia—have created a potential reservoir of nuclear weapons, nuclear weapons materials, technology, and personnel to be tapped by aspiring proliferators. For the first time, there is a real danger that a country or subnational group could vault rapidly into possession of at least a few nuclear weapons.

New-Style Proliferators

In varying degrees, a mixture of security concerns and a desire for status was the primary motivation behind pursuit of nuclear weapons in the cold war era. This holds, for example, for the former Soviet Union (perceiving itself threatened by a U.S. monopoly of atomic weaponry), China (confronting both the United States and the Soviet Union), Israel (facing several Arab armies and fearful of being overwhelmed by conventional attack), and Pakistan (fearful of Indian conventional military superiority and nuclear domination). Security concerns, not least fear of use by another country, also appear to have been a dominant driving force behind countries' research, development, or acquisition of chemical and biological weapons options.

By contrast, a new style of proliferator may be emerging. For some countries pursuit of NBC weaponry may be increasingly motivated not simply by perceived security needs, but possibly by more aggressive intentions. For them, possession of nuclear, chemical, or biological weapons may well be viewed increasingly as a means to expand their influence, dominate their neighbors, and deter distant outsiders from coming to the aid of threatened neighbors. This could be so, for example, for an Iraq seeking to dominate the Gulf, for an Iran that views nuclear weapons as a means to deter U.S. involvement in that same region, or a North Korea seeking chemical weapons as a means to enhance offensive force capabilities and missiles armed with NBC warheads as a means to blackmail its neighbors.

The bombing of the World Trade Center as well as the release of the chemical weapon agent Sarin in the Tokyo subway system suggest that the terrorist threat also has new dimensions. Future acts of terrorism may not be carried out only by well-organized, established organizations, with or without the backing of a state. Instead, terrorist acts may be perpetrated by handfuls of individuals whose primary concern may be to inflict death and destruction—not to make a political point or influence the public's "hearts and minds."

The Breakdown of the
Cold War Security Framework

The cold war alliance structure was one of the most effective measures for restraining horizontal proliferation in the past decades, though that structure clearly had its origins in other concerns and its nonproliferation contributions were a largely unintended by-product. By providing a framework of security on both sides of the dividing line in Europe, both the North Atlantic Treaty Organization and the Warsaw Treaty Organization dampened proliferation incentives. Outside Europe, U.S. and Soviet ties with key countries in other regions served frequently to buttress security, constrain ambitions, and influence regional proliferation dynamics.

Without its cold war rationale, NATO continues to search for a future role. Its potential contribution in helping prevent proliferation by providing a security structure for all of Europe, however, will need to be paid for in its own right and can no longer be counted as a free good for nonproliferation. Similarly, despite recent U.S. policy pronouncements, longer-term pressures to reduce the U.S. presence in Asia will continue to grow, again with nonproliferation implications. More generally, the uncertainty of the post–cold war political order provides not only greater freedom of action for certain countries but enhances pressures to step up pursuit of NBC options in others.

Lack of Credible Responses to Noncompliance

Events over the past decade have undermined the presumption of good faith compliance by parties to nonproliferation treaties and other undertakings. Iraq's repeated use of chemical weapons in the Iran-Iraq war, Saddam Hussein's decision to violate Iraq's obligations under the Nuclear Non-Proliferation Treaty (NPT), Soviet violation of the Biological and Toxin Weapons Convention, and North Korea's noncompliance with its NPT and International Atomic Energy Agency (IAEA) obligations stand out. Still other countries today may be pursuing NBC options in violation of their nonproliferation obligations.

Equally if not more important, both individual nations and the international community have so far failed to devise a credible and effective response to nonproliferation noncompliance. Excepting the special case of United Nations action against Iraq *after* that country lost the Gulf War, a strong signal has not been sent to potential proliferators that there is a significant price to pay for treaty noncompliance. Indeed, Iraq's earlier use of chemical weaponry against Iran went essentially unpunished. Though perhaps the best attainable in the situation, the U.S.–North Korea Framework Agreement (which sets out a pathway to the rollback of that country's nuclear weapons program) defers North Korea's return to full compliance with its NPT and IAEA obligations for at least five years.

The Danger of Use

Over the past decades, international efforts to prevent proliferation have succeeded beyond virtually all expectations. With strengthened nonproliferation institutions, prospects are good for containing the scope of further NBC proliferation. But even now, it is necessary to acknowledge that some proliferation has occurred and that more may be unavoidable. This poses the greatest challenge: the danger of future physical use of NBC weapons, possibly leading over time to their coming to be regarded as little different from the most powerful conventional weapons.

Past precedents are mixed. Chemical weapons were used on the battlefield on a number of occasions during the Iran-Iraq War of the mid-1980s. Use of ballistic missiles figured prominently not only in the "war of the cities" between Iraq and Iran in the closing stages of that war but also during the later Gulf War, as well as in the conflict in Afghanistan during which the Soviet forces used SCUD missiles. So far, neither nuclear nor biological weapons have been used since World War II (though controversy still persists about whether Soviet supplied toxins were used in Southeast Asia in the early 1980s).

In future regional confrontations, a mixture of elements—deep-seated political enmities; technical weaknesses of command, control, and weapon safety; lack of reliable second-strike capabilities; and political-military miscalculations—could fuel a process of escalation resulting in the first use of a nuclear weapon since Nagasaki. Or use of nuclear or biological weapons could be a coldly calculated move to disrupt military operations or shatter morale, an act of desperation by a regime seeking to avoid defeat, or a revenge blow by a defeated leader.

Further, though the most extreme, actual physical use of NBC weaponry is not the only use to be feared. Regardless of proliferators' actions, possession of NBC weaponry will cast a shadow both within and beyond a region. Neighbors will trim their political sails out of fear of NBC rivals; outsiders will adapt their policies and actions as well. Increasingly implicit and explicit threats of NBC use also may characterize future regional confrontations— whether between neighboring countries or between aspiring regional hegemons and coalitions of outsiders.

Some Aspects and Lessons of Past U.N. Activities

With the exception of the activities of the International Atomic Energy Agency, the past role of the United Nations and its associated organizations is often overlooked in tallying up the global response to the proliferation challenge. Since its creation, the United Nations has been involved in a wide range of nonproliferation activities. This record includes, moreover, both successes and failures. A brief review of this experience not only provides a context for thinking about possible ways to use the United Nations to help meet the future proliferation challenge, but also some useful lessons about the conditions for success.

From the UNAEC to UNSCOM

Throughout its first five decades, the United Nations, either directly or via its subsidiary and associated organizations, has served as a forum for negotiation and debate on nonproliferation. Created in 1946, the United Nations Atomic Energy Commission (UNAEC) provided a forum for the first, if unsuccessful, efforts to grapple with the threat posed by the new phenomenon of atomic weaponry. Two decades later, the eighteen-nation Committee on Disarmament was the venue for successful negotiations leading to the 1968 Nuclear Non-Proliferation Treaty. More recent negotiation of the Chemical Weapons Convention in the Conference on Disarmament in the 1980s and early 1990s typify this dimension as well.

At the same time, a continuing process of debate about nonproliferation has served to focus attention on issues, today exemplified by the annual discussions within the U.N. First Committee and the U.N. General Assembly on establishment of nuclear weapon-free zones in Africa, the Middle East, and other regions. More broadly, this process of continuing debate has probably contributed to a broader process of nonproliferation norm building by putting the international community on record in opposing the legitimacy of production of NBC weaponry.

Closely related, the Secretariat, at the request of the General Assembly, has periodically prepared reports and studies on selected nonproliferation issues. With use of outside experts, reports were prepared, for example, on the nuclear programs of Israel and of South Africa, as well as on steps that might be taken toward a nuclear weapon-free zone in the Middle East. Though triggered by specific countries' concerns and policy objectives, these studies at least have served to keep issues on the international agenda. In some instances, exemplified by the study on a Middle East nuclear-free zone (NFZ), new ideas emerged and the study itself helped to shape wider thinking about nonproliferation strategy for the region.

At times, the Security Council has also been used as an endorsing or legitimizing body for selected nonproliferation actions by the nuclear weapon states. When the NPT was opened for signature in 1968, for instance, Security Council Resolution 255 gave added political weight to the assurances provided by the United States, the Soviet Union, and the United Kingdom to come to the assistance of NPT nonnuclear weapon states should they be threatened with nuclear blackmail or victims of attack. More recently, the Security Council in Resolution 984 (April 1, 1995) recognized the intentions of all five nuclear weapon state NPT parties to provide such assistance. This new resolution updated SC 255 to reflect the adherence of France and China to the NPT.

The implementation of nonproliferation treaties, especially dealing with noncompliance, has also been at least indirectly a matter of concern of the United Nations. Though once removed from the United Nations, the IAEA is responsible for implementing safeguards under the NPT, and the director general reports annually to the General Assembly. The IAEA Statute, the Biological and Toxin Weapons Convention, and the new Chemical Weapons Convention all provide for access to the Security Council in responses to instances of treaty noncompliance. For its part, the 1992 Security Council Summit affirmed the readiness of its parties to respond to violations of IAEA safeguards. Over the past several years, moreover, closer working ties have developed between the IAEA, the secretary-general, and the Security Council, typified by the existence now of secure communications between the IAEA director general and the secretary-general.

For the most part, actual U.N. experience with regard to noncompliance, however, is not encouraging. The Secretariat did undertake important fact-finding activities in response to allegations of Iraqi use of chemical weapons during its war with Iran. But despite compelling evidence of such use, the Council proved unwilling, in the mid-1980s, to take action in response. More recently, difficulties in building a coalition to respond to North Korea's refusal to permit IAEA special inspections partly explain the U.S. decision to work bilaterally with North Korea.

In this regard, whether the United Nations Special Commission (UNSCOM) is a special case or a precedent remains an open question. Created after the 1991 Gulf War, UNSCOM reports directly to the Security Council. Its purpose has been to implement the nonproliferation aspects of United Nations Resolutions 687 and 715, including especially steps to ensure the destruction, elimination, or rendering harmless of Iraq's NBC and missile capabilities. Relying on the expertise of the IAEA in the nuclear field and independently otherwise, UNSCOM has steadfastly pursued this mission, though some hidden capabilities are presumed still to exist. In the future, UNSCOM (again relying on the IAEA in the nuclear field) will undertake long-term monitoring to make it technically more difficult for Iraq to reconstitute those capabilities.

A Few Lessons for the Future

One important, if not surprising, lesson for thinking about how the United States could make use of the U.N. system in helping to confront the future proliferation challenge bears reiterating. Cooperation among the United States, Russia, France, the United Kingdom, and China—the Perm 5—is critical. Absent that cooperation, action by the Security Council will not be possible, debates in the General Assembly will have little practical impact, and efforts by the secretary-general and Secretariat to raise issues will lead nowhere. In thinking about that cooperation in the nonproliferation arena, moreover, past experience suggests not simply the importance of a shared perspective by the United States and now Russia, but especially the increasingly critical and uncertain role of China. Moreover, winning such cooperation does not necessarily come easily. Instead, experience is that cooperation in the nonproliferation arena, as elsewhere, calls for a readiness to invest political and other resources to make something happen.

Nearly five decades of U.N. debates and discussions also reveal a continuing tension reflected in the work of the General Assembly about how to define the most important proliferation problem. For the United States, concern about proliferation has mostly focused on so-called horizontal proliferation, the pursuit or acquisition of NBC weaponry by additional countries; for developing countries, their attention has been primarily directed to vertical proliferation, the quantitative and qualitative expansion of great power capabilities, especially those of the five nuclear powers. Though this tension may be lessening as the cold war nuclear arsenals of the United States and Russia steadily draw down, it still persists.

Again not surprisingly, past experience demonstrates that other countries have their own proliferation agendas, some consistent with U.S. interests, others less so. For many years, this was best reflected in the controversy between the United States and virtually all other countries over a comprehensive nuclear test ban treaty. But resolutions and debates over Israel's nuclear program, South Africa's nuclear program, and nuclear weapon-free zones are other instances. Greater recourse to the United Nations in support of nonproliferation objectives means, therefore, greater recourse not only by the United States but also by other countries for their own purposes.

The United Nations and the
Future Proliferation Challenge

Successful efforts to meet the future proliferation challenge call for intensified activities by the United States and like-minded countries along many different tracks. More vigorous national nonproliferation efforts, new regional security and confidence-building undertakings, heightened multilateral cooperation and institution building, and prudent defense planning to deal with new threats of use will all be required. Greater recourse by the United States to the U.N. system can buttress these efforts.

Specifically, the United States could leverage the United Nations' potential in each of the following nonproliferation areas:

- norm building;
- consciousness raising and institutionalizing attention;
- global security building;
- crisis management; and
- backstopping treaty compliance.

In addition, over the longer term, U.S. interests would be served by making use of the United Nations to build toward an enforceable global taboo against threats or use of nuclear, chemical, or biological weaponry.

Nonproliferation Norm Building

Over the past decades, a norm of nonproliferation has developed. Increasingly, the acquisition of nuclear, chemical, or biological weaponry has come to be regarded as illegitimate and a matter of international concern. Though soft and illusive, this nonproliferation norm contributes to global nonproliferation efforts in several ways. In the midst of post–cold war political uncertainty, it comprises yet another brake on countries that might be weighing the payoffs and risks of seeking an NBC option. By isolating the unacknowledged NBC proliferators, moreover, this norm helps cap the further expansion of their programs and makes open NBC arms racing less likely. It reinforces, in turn, domestic political pressures in key suppliers to implement more effective export controls.

Debates and resolutions within the General Assembly have been—and remain—one way to express and reinforce this non-proliferation norm. In addition, the January 31, 1992 statement of the U.N. Security Council Summit for the first time records the participants' belief that proliferation per se constitutes a threat to peace. Building on that statement, U.S. policy makers should seek passage of a Security Council resolution that would express the Council's endorsement of the summit's conclusion and give its norm of nonproliferation further legal status.

Institutionalizing Attention and Concern

In many countries, attention to the issue of the proliferation of NBC weaponry is at best limited and sporadic. Foreign policy bureaucrats, energy planners, and political officials have traditionally been more concerned with other matters. When proliferation does rise toward the top of the official agenda, it frequently is because of outside events—from requests from the United States to stop a particular export of proliferation concern to the need to take a position at an upcoming international event such as the NPT Review and Extension Conference. For the most part, these countries agree rhetorically that international action to strengthen nonproliferation institutions is needed. But in practice, many questions arise about the extent to which such rhetoric reflects more deeply held beliefs and political instincts. This is especially so in such key countries as China, the newly independent states, and increasingly the new Russia of "wheeler-dealers" as opposed to the old Soviet Union of bureaucrats and officials.

Building on past U.N. activities, additional steps could be taken by the United States to make use of U.N. bodies to help institutionalize and routinize attention and concern about nonproliferation in U.N. member states. Creation of a U.N. rapporteur on proliferation, as suggested by France, could be a useful step. It would help ensure that matters of proliferation concern came to the attention of the Security Council. A rapporteur also would provide a potential source of information on proliferation that could be more acceptable or neutral in the eyes of developing countries. If that rapporteur were required to prepare an annual report on the "state of proliferation," this would provide another vehicle to direct both the General Assembly and Security Council members' attention to proliferation issues. In turn, possibly establishing a quarterly debate within the Council on the "state of proliferation" would be another means to routinize attention to this issue. Not least, one consequence of greater attention to proliferation on the U.N. agenda would be to provide a partial forcing event for officials and bureaucrats in capitals to take it up.

Security Building

At least three types of security-building roles related directly to lessening proliferation pressures stand out. These concern respectively: strengthening security assurances to countries threatened with NBC blackmail or attack; regional conflict avoidance and prevention; and, more narrowly, the maintenance by UNSCOM and the IAEA of a robust long-term monitoring regime in Iraq.

In connection with the NPT Review and Extension Conference, held from April 17–May 12, 1995, the five acknowledged nuclear weapon states made parallel statements in the Security Council expressing their readiness consistent with their obligations under the Charter to come to the assistance of NPT countries that are victims of an act of, or an object of a threat of, aggression in which nuclear weapons are used. Reflected in Security Council Resolution 984 (April 1, 1995), this reaffirmed the earlier *security assurances* provided by the United States, the United Kingdom, and the Soviet Union and acknowledged by Security Council Resolution 225 (1968). Equally important, it extended the earlier 1968 security assurance to include commitments by France and China, which have since joined the NPT. (This updated resolution also takes note of the commitments, expressed with differing conditions, of the five nuclear powers not to use nuclear weapons against nonnuclear weapon states parties to the NPT.)

Reaffirmation and extension of this assurance are a welcome step. Nonetheless, a number of additional Security Council actions might be considered to help ensure that this new Perm-5 Security Assurance—unlike its 1968 predecessor—does not become simply a soon-forgotten formality of NPT extension. Passage of a Security

Council resolution stating that "proliferation is a threat to the peace" would be one such step, thereby giving legal status to the statement of the 1992 Security Council Summit. Should a rapporteur for nonproliferation be established, a report might be prepared for the Council on what types of responses could be made, and any needed contingency planning to do so identified. As part of any annual debate on proliferation matters, the Council could reaffirm this earlier pledge. Further, consideration might be given to extending this nuclear pledge to a broader Security Council assurance of support in the event of threats of biological weapon (BW) or chemical weapon (CW) blackmail or attack.

Initiatives first to *lessen regional tensions* and then to deal with the underlying sources of political-military conflict are one essential element of a longer-term U.S. strategy to contain and roll back proliferation in the Middle East, South Asia, and on the Korean Peninsula. The primary responsibility for such efforts continues to fall on the countries within those regions, encouraged and supported by the United States and other outsiders. For its part, however, the United Nations may be able to contribute in modest ways to this process. U.N. forces may be part, for example, of monitoring mutual troop disengagements under future Israel-Syria and Israel-Lebanon peace agreements. Within South Asia, U.N. conferences and studies could contribute to both sides' readiness to discuss enhanced confidence-building measures and the identification of possible next steps.

Finally, under the conditions of Security Council Resolution 715, Iraq agreed to *long-term monitoring* to ensure that it did not seek to resume its NBC weapon programs. In achieving U.S. nonproliferation objectives in the Middle East, it is difficult to exaggerate the importance of enduring Security Council support for such monitoring by UNSCOM and the IAEA. Should monitoring cease, there is every reason to believe that Saddam Hussein, or any likely successor, would move rapidly to reconstitute Iraq's now-banned programs and covertly deploy NBC weaponry. The renewed prospect of Iraqi possession of nuclear, chemical, and biological weaponry would spill over throughout the region. It would further reinforce Iran's motivations to acquire nuclear weapons (and not to give up its probable BW and CW capabilities), generate pressures in Saudi Arabia to gain access to nuclear weaponry, lessen prospects for capping Israel's nuclear capability, and undermine efforts to bring the Chemical Weapons Convention into force for countries in the Middle East. The United States needs, therefore, to continue to use its diplomatic and political influence to maintain Security Council backing for UNSCOM's activities.

Nuclear Crisis Management

Twice within the past decade, in 1986 and 1990, India and Pakistan have moved toward a military confrontation. Longstanding suspicions about each other's motivations were reinforced by poor intelligence about the other side's military dispositions and activities. Nuclear threats apparently also were conveyed. In both instances, outside diplomacy, including, in 1990, U.S. provision of information to both sides concerning the disposition of military forces on the other side, contributed to resolving each crisis short of war.

The primary responsibility for resolving any future crisis involving new nuclear powers is likely to rest on the parties themselves. Depending on the situation, bilateral U.S. involvement, as occurred in the 1990 India-Pakistan crisis, could be valuable. Here, too, use of the United Nations could sometimes reinforce U.S. crisis management efforts. Under some conditions, for example in a future South Asia nuclear crisis, the secretary-general, at the request of the Security Council, could offer to mediate in an attempt to break the momentum of events. Or emergency deployment of U.N. observers might provide a means of reassurance about each side's military dispositions. More broadly, the Security Council may have a role to play in legitimizing political and diplomatic intervention by the United States and others in an attempt to defuse a future NBC related crisis.

Buttressing Nonproliferation Compliance

In recent years several developments—first UNSCOM's activities in Iraq, then the 1992 Security Council Summit, and more recently Council debate on North Korea's noncompliance with its safeguards obligations—have focused increased attention on the Security Council's potential role in backstopping compliance with nonproliferation treaties. U.S. nonproliferation objectives would be served by seeking to buttress such a Security Council role. Depending on the specific situation, the prospect of action by the Security Council in the event of treaty noncompliance might help to deter such violations or reinforce other efforts to restore compliance. Security Council political, economic, diplomatic, or military sanctions in response to a violation also could influence third parties' calculations of the risks of noncompliance. Security Council action also would lessen the corrosive impact of isolated instances of noncompliance on the overall credibility of the treaty regimes.

Experience reminds us, of course, that constraints exist. The Council's members, especially the Perm-5, may have different views of whether, when, or how to respond. Some developing countries already are concerned about too great a Council role, lest it become a new form of outside domination. Nonetheless, a number of possible steps might be taken with U.S. support in an attempt to buttress the prospect of Security Council action in response to nonproliferation noncompliance. These include both actions involving the Council and actions to strengthen the Council's linkages with other bodies.

Assuming readiness to turn the January 1992 Security Council Summit Declaration into a formal resolution, this would make that declaration's commitment to "tak[ing] appropriate measures in the case of any violations notified to them by the IAEA" into a Council commitment. The Secretariat could be authorized, as well, to assess past U.N. experience in imposing sanctions in order to identify what measures proved most useful, under what conditions, and why. Such an assessment is likely to demonstrate that the particular mix of political, economic, financial, and military sanctions needs to be tailored to the country in question; but the very fact of undertaking such an assessment could serve to increase the presumption of action—both in the minds of potential treaty violators and Council members. Annual debates on the "state of proliferation," proposed elsewhere, would also help to create a presumption of Council action.

In turn, more routine, perhaps quarterly, reporting by the

IAEA director general to the Security Council on the status of safeguards implementation might be explored. This would build on recent establishment of a secure communications link between the IAEA and the U.N. secretary-general and discussion of technical enhancements of communications between the IAEA director general and the Security Council. As preparations continue for creation of the Organization for the Prevention of Chemical Weapons to implement the Chemical Weapons Convention, comparable mechanisms and procedures for access to the Security Council could be put in place. Again, part of the reason for doing so would be to shape perceptions of the likelihood of a Security Council response to noncompliance.

Toward an Enforceable Global Taboo on NBC Use

Despite intensified nonproliferation efforts, the risk of use of NBC weapons is likely to grow in the years ahead. Faced with that risk, today's U.S. response emphasizes prudent defense planning initiatives both to deter aggressors from using nuclear, chemical, or biological weaponry or, should deterrence fail, to prevail militarily without responding in kind. These measures are necessary. At the same time, it is not too soon for U.S. policy makers to begin thinking about what steps might be taken over the longer term to create an enforceable global taboo against any use of nuclear, chemical, or biological weapons.

An enforceable global taboo against use of nuclear, chemical, or biological weaponry would enhance the legitimacy of U.S. responses to future threats or use of NBC weaponry against U.S. forces, friends, or even the American homeland. Equally important, over the longer term policies of national self-help and deterrence may not be sufficiently credible or compelling to avoid increasing use of NBC weapons in regional clashes. Instead, for the leaders of some potential aggressors armed with such weapons, only the prospect of international outlawry and the collapse of their regimes might suffice to convince them not to use these weapons. Further, without an enforceable international taboo, a slow spread of NBC weaponry—and ad hoc national self-help in response—could result in eventual conventionalization of these weapons. As a result, threats to U.S. security would grow.

The U.N. Security Council comprises the best—if not, indeed, the only—body through which to seek over the decade ahead to create and maintain such an enforceable nonuse taboo. It has responsibility for dealing with threats to the peace. It would give needed legitimacy to efforts by the United States and others to establish and enforce such a rule. It would provide a venue for working out in practice what types of action might be entailed, up to and including use of military force by the Perm-5 on behalf of the Security Council.

From the U.S. perspective (or, for that matter, the perspectives of the other Perm-5 countries), pursuit of an enforceable taboo against NBC use would pose few problems with regard to either chemical or biological weapons. The United States, like the other Perm-5, has renounced the right to possess, produce, or use such weapons. However, establishment of an enforceable taboo against nuclear use would require a major shift in U.S. policy (and that of all of the other Perm-5 except China).

Specifically, for the past decades, the United States has been unwilling to renounce the option to use nuclear weapons first in response to major aggression in Europe. Even now, U.S. NATO allies resist any change in U.S. declaratory policy as potentially signaling a lessening of the U.S. tie to Europe, despite the fact that the collapse of the Soviet Union has eliminated that military rationale for retaining a nuclear first-use option. More important, how to deter use of biological weapons as terror weapons against U.S. friends, forces, or the American homeland has emerged as a significant new concern. In particular, there is a new reluctance to give up the possibility of responding to use of biological weaponry with nuclear weapons lest deterrence be undermined.

Many considerations would need to be weighed by U.S. policy makers in deciding whether to renounce nuclear first use. In some situations, uncertainty about how the United States might respond to biological weapons attack—including the possibility of a nuclear reprisal—could well influence an aggressor's calculations. Conversely, the threat of a nuclear response might be less credible than other actions, up to and including concerted U.S. supported international action to treat as an international outlaw and bring down any regime that had used biological weapons in violation of a global taboo. This is so partly because any U.S. president would be extremely reluctant to use nuclear weapons short of a situation of retaliation for nuclear use by an aggressor. Actual use of nuclear weapons in response to biological weaponry, moreover, could have the undesired effect of encouraging more countries to seek nuclear weapons, while also undermining restraints on still additional nuclear use. Perhaps most important, the costs of giving up the option of uncertainty about the U.S. response to use of biological weaponry would need to be balanced against the longer-term payoffs of an enforceable taboo against any use of nuclear, chemical, or biological weaponry.

Faced with these complexities, a possible alternative to a "no first use of nuclear weapons" pledge has sometimes been suggested. The United States could declare that it would never be the first country to use weapons of mass destruction. From one perspective, this declaratory policy would narrow the conditions under which the United States might contemplate recourse to nuclear weaponry. In effect, it also would put the United States on record in support of the view that nuclear weapons should not be regarded as instruments to assert power, but only as last resort deterrents of other weapons of mass destruction. Nonetheless, from another perspective, this type of pledge would be viewed by many developing countries as significant backsliding from the current U.S. assurance not to use nuclear weapons against NPT parties, resulting in an erosion of the NPT regime. More important, highly visible U.S. assertion of the option to respond to use of chemical or biological weapons with nuclear weapons would likely enhance incentives to acquire nuclear weapons in other countries. They, too, could view the threat of nuclear retaliation as an essential response to CW or BW proliferation. As a result, over the coming decades, the role of nuclear weapons—and the risk of their further use—would likely be increased, not decreased.

Assuming a U.S. decision to seek to build an enforceable global taboo against use of nuclear, biological, or chemical weapons, a first step would be to affirm a U.S. belief that use of biological or chemical weapons cannot be tolerated by the international community. In addition, the United States could declare that pending their ultimate elimination, in its view, the only purpose of nuclear weapons should be to deter the use of other nuclear weapons. The United States could seek to build a consensus among the five nuclear weapon states first on the principle of movement toward an enforceable nonuse taboo, then on how to implement that principle.

In pursuit of this goal, the United States could take advantage of the fora provided both by the General Assembly and the Security Council. Eventually, agreement among the Perm-5 on the principle of a global taboo against use of nuclear, chemical, or biological weapons could be reflected in a Security Council resolution. This could express the Council's belief that pending the ultimate elimination of all nuclear weapons, the only purpose of such weapons should be to deter use of other nuclear weapons. Such a resolution could reaffirm, as well, the total bans on use included within the Biological and Toxin Weapons Convention and the Chemical Weapons Convention. It also could commit the Council to treat any country that used such weaponry in effect as an international outlaw, responding appropriately.

The character of any such response would depend very much on the specific situation at the time, whether nuclear, chemical, or biological weapons had been used, how, and with what consequences. However, should the notion of an enforceable nonuse taboo be accepted in principle, consultations among the Perm-5 could be undertaken to define the range of potential responses and how to implement them under the auspices of the Security Council.

For now, even the idea of moving toward an enforceable global nonuse taboo may appear at best illusory, and at worst dangerous. This may be so. But following a next use of chemical, biological, or nuclear weaponry—particularly if such use entailed major death and devastation—attitudes could well change dramatically. Throughout the postwar period, it has been just such proliferation shocks that have repeatedly triggered new ways of thinking about how to confront the proliferation challenge. Consequently, thinking now about the whether, what, and how of an enforceable nonuse taboo is essential to take advantage of the opportunity likely to be provided by the shock of use, especially nuclear use.

Conclusion

Both the United Nations and the threat of nuclear destruction emerged from the devastation of World War II. Five decades later, new thinking is being given to how to realize the promise of the United Nations as a means of enhancing international order and security. In so doing, it is important to reflect on how the United Nations—from the General Assembly to the Secretariat, the Security Council to associated organizations—can play a greater role in helping the United States to meet a changing and more dangerous proliferation challenge in the decades ahead. Incremental steps, building on past roles, are a place to start, and progress can be made. But it also is none too soon for U.S. policy makers to think about a more far-reaching, indeed radical goal: working with the other Perm-5 through the Security Council to create an enforceable taboo against the further use of nuclear, chemical, or biological weapons. Success could well be essential to containing the longer-term threat proliferation poses to the security of the United States, our friends, and our allies.

Notes

[1] My thinking on these issues has been stimulated by my colleague Burrus Carnahan as well as by my fellow members of a United Nations Association of the United States of America study group on the role of the Security Council in nonproliferation. The views in this chapter are those of the author, not necessarily those of SAIC or any of its sponsoring agencies.

4

The U.N. System and Sustainable Development

CATHERINE GWIN AND MAURICE WILLIAMS

Multilateral Aid as a Component of U.S. Policy

Since the end of World War II, the United States has been the lead architect and a major contributor to the development efforts of the United Nations and a host of other international organizations and programs. Today, both that support and leadership role are in decline. This chapter argues that it remains in the interest of the United States to support a U.N. role in development, but that a streamlining and reform of that role should be pressed by the United States acting in conjunction with other countries.

CATHERINE GWIN, vice president of the Overseas Development Council, directs ODC's international policy research program. Prior to joining ODC, she was a special program adviser to the Rockefeller Foundation, senior associate at the Carnegie Endowment for International Peace, on the staff of the United States International Development Cooperation Agency, and executive director of the Council on Foreign Relations' 1980s Project. Her publications include *Pulling Together: The Interna-*

U.S. Leadership in Building the U.N. System

The United Nations, International Monetary Fund (IMF), World Bank, and General Agreement on Tariffs and Trade (GATT)—the four pillars of the U.S. led postwar system—were ambitious in projecting broad political, social, and economic objectives. There was the promise of collective security from aggression and of economic cooperation designed to promote growth, full employment, and stability through increased international trade and investment. Since most Americans were determined to avoid another devastating war and the isolationist foreign policy that had led the country to stand aside from the League of Nations, support in the United States for these endeavors was widespread.

The outbreak of the cold war, together with the coming of independence to countries throughout what came to be called the Third World, provided additional rationale for U.S. leadership and support of the build-up of the U.N. system. As U.S. government officials emphasized in the early cold war days, U.S. support for the United Nations, the Bretton Woods institutions, and other international agencies contributed to the peace and solidarity of the free world, and it demonstrated the rich countries' commitment to helping the newly independent countries advance their economic life under free institutions. As its war-torn allies recov-

---

tional Monetary Fund in a Multipolar World, edited with Richard Feinberg; *U.S. Relations with the World Bank 1945–92;* and "A Comparative Assessment of the Bretton Woods and U.N. Development Institutions."

MAURICE WILLIAMS is president emeritus of the Society for International Development (SID), editor of the SID journal *Development,* and ODC senior associate. He was executive director of the U.N. World Food Council (1978–85), chair of the OECD Development Assistance Committee (1974–78), deputy administrator of USAID (1970–74), and assistant administrator of USAID for South Asia and the Near East (1967–70). He was adviser to the U.N. secretary-general for UNCED and a founder of the Earth Council. His publications include *U.S. Development Cooperation Policies, Aid Coordination and Effectiveness* and *U.N. Programs for Technical Assistance in Africa.*

ered, the United States also pressed them to share the burden of development aid by contributing funds through both bilateral and multilateral channels. This was the purpose of the U.S. initiated Development Assistance Committee (DAC)—a bilateral donors' club set up "to design and monitor compliance with equitable standards of burden sharing in the provision of aid." Aid burden sharing was also a motivating factor in U.S. support for the proliferation of multilateral agencies and programs.

As part of the initial construction of the United Nations, the Food and Agriculture Organization (FAO), the U.N. International Children's Emergency Fund (UNICEF), and the U.N. Educational, Scientific, and Cultural Organization (UNESCO) were established in 1945 and 1946. Also, the specialized agencies of the League of Nations—including the World Health Organization (WHO), the International Telecommunications Union (ITU), and the International Labor Organization (ILO)—were incorporated into the U.N. system.

In designing the U.N. economic structure, the United States and other member governments were influenced by the idealist theory of international relations that functional specialists were more effective in facilitating practical regimes that bridged political and national differences than were diplomats and politicians. According to this view, functional cooperation would gradually erode the tenacious hold nationalism exerts on international politics, and would form the fabric of an international society. The approach shaped the formation of the network of U.N. specialized agencies, each independently governed by councils of country specialists with only nominal association with the United Nations.[1]

The original mandates of the specialized agencies were cast almost entirely in terms of research, compilation of data, and standard setting for activities with international implications in their respective fields. With the independence of former colonies and the related explosive growth of U.N. membership, the promotion of economic and social development and execution of technical cooperation projects in the newly independent states became an increasingly central role of all U.N. agencies with support from the United States.

In 1950 a U.S. initiative launched the United Nations on an

Expanded Program of centrally funded technical assistance by the specialized agencies to developing countries. The United States also proposed the Special Fund for U.N. preinvestment feasibility studies. Both the Expanded Program and Special Fund were later consolidated into the United Nations Development Programme (UNDP). At about the same time, UNICEF—initially a temporary relief fund—was given an expanded role; and, after much developing-country pressure to add a capital assistance function to the United Nations, the United States proposed creation of the International Development Association (IDA), as a soft loan window under the auspices of the World Bank.

Other results of U.S. endorsed institutional growth include the World Food Program (WFP), the Fund for Population Activity (UNFPA), and the Inter-American Development Bank. Moreover, international conferences often generated mechanisms to implement their conclusions, including the United Nations Environment Programme (UNEP), the World Food Council (WFC), and the International Fund for Agricultural Development (IFAD), all of which the United States supported.

The build-up of multilateral development institutions stabilized during the 1970s at thirty-five agencies—including U.N. funds, programs, and specialized agencies, and international financial institutions. They were chosen instruments of aid for many donor and recipient governments throughout the 1970s; collectively, multilateral aid achieved an impressive funding growth, rising to 31.7 percent of total DAC aid in 1978—its highest proportion before or since. In addition to burden sharing, the comparative advantages of multilateral aid were seen by the United States to include coordination of donor efforts in response to emergencies and capital investment needs, and the encouragement of policy reforms in recipient countries.

Growing Dissatisfaction

By the mid-1970s, however, American policy makers began to have serious reservations about multilateral development aid. There was concern about the explosive growth of Robert McNamara's World Bank, whose level of lending quadrupled during his ten-year reign. The United States expressed even greater concern about both the mushrooming budgets of the U.N. specialized agencies imposed by the Third World "automatic majority," and the tendency toward personal empire building by the heads of U.N. agencies, which often meant they took positions at variance with U.S. interests. Also, competition among the agencies intensified, and there were increasing examples of duplication, mismanagement, and wasted resources. In response, in 1977 the United States adopted a policy of zero growth in U.N. budgets.

At the beginning of the 1980s, the Reagan administration took office with the stated intention of significantly reducing U.S. bilateral and multilateral development assistance. Yet the administration wound up increasing bilateral aid levels as a result of large increases in foreign military assistance. Moreover, the debt crisis in the early 1980s, followed by the fall of the Berlin Wall a half-decade later, reversed the early multilateral policy. Resources were needed to meet threats to the international banking system and to support transformation in post-Communist countries, and since the United States was not going to shoulder the burden alone, these had to be found within the multilateral agencies. These events led to important innovations in the roles of the international financial institutions supported by the United States— including extended terms for IMF credit and a new form of World Bank structural adjustment loan. Moreover, in the late 1980s the United States supported the creation of yet another regional development bank, the European Bank for Reconstruction and Development (EBRD), and currently the United States is pressing for a new Middle East bank.

Yet a chorus of criticism of foreign aid in general and multilateral aid in particular has escalated over the past ten to fifteen years. In retrospect, many in the United States have concluded that the system of multilateral agencies has expanded too far without sufficient consideration of overlapping functions and the difficulties of coordinating so many diverse agencies. Maintenance of such a large system calls for a degree of collective agreement and discipline among governments and among the international bureaucracies that has yet to be achieved. As a result, it now seems to many policy makers and analysts alike that the system of multilateral development assistance, which the United States so actively helped to create, has spun out of control.

Temporary withdrawal from the ILO for the two years 1977–78 and the departure from UNESCO since 1984 have been the most dramatic expressions of growing U.S. dissatisfaction. In addition, the UNDP and other U.N. programs now face sizable cuts, and the United States is in arrears in its payments to several of the concessional windows of the multilateral development banks (MDBs).

It must be recognized, however, that the current critiques of the decentralized, sprawling, international development system are calling into question a central feature of the postwar institutional architecture for which the United States was a principal proponent. The United States insisted upon autonomy for the specialized agencies. It was also U.S. policy to retain a distinction between the technical assistance activities of the U.N. agencies and the capital investment programs of the World Bank.

The United States has a major responsibility, therefore, as well as an important interest, in revising and reviving the U.N. system. As the initial architects, fifty years ago, and with so much change occurring in the world, it is time that the United States, along with others, examine how well the existing international structure fits the needs of the twenty-first century. A revised and more effective U.N. role can serve U.S. interests by:

- increasing countries' capacity and willingness to work cooperatively on shared problems such as the spread of communicable diseases, drug trafficking and related crimes, and environmental degradation;
- building more cost-effective mechanisms to prevent, where possible, or to respond forcefully, where necessary, to humanitarian crises and post-crises reconstruction; and
- mobilizing resources to meet agreed goals of poverty reduction, democratization, and global problem solving.

What follows are a review of the United Nations' proven capabilities, a consideration of new challenges, a history of shortcomings, and recommendations for reform.

U.N. Capacity for Sustainable Development

The organization of the United Nations, as envisioned in its Charter, has several characteristics that shape its role in the economic and social fields:

- the definition of economic betterment as a core objective, which has directed U.N. assistance efforts to human well-being;
- a universality of membership, which has made the United Nations a key forum for dialogue and consensus building on the norms and agenda for collective action;
- a broad mandate, which has engaged U.N. funds and programs in social and political, as well as economic, dimensions of development; and
- a decentralized operating structure and extensive field presence at the regional and country level.

These features have provided the United Nations with unique potentials that have translated into major accomplishments over the years. Among the main achievements in the social and economic fields are the following.

Decolonization. A basic tenet of the United Nations from its origin has been the right of people to self-government. Active pursuit of this objective, with strong U.S. support, accelerated the process of decolonization and determined the universal character of the organization, encompassing nations of diverse cultures at varied stages of economic development.

Human Rights and Democratization. The United Nations effected a conceptual and moral revolution for human rights that—although not always even-handed—has helped to establish international norms for the conduct of governments toward their citizens. At the 1993 U.N. World Conference on Human Rights in Vienna there was acceptance that alleviation of extreme poverty—as a fundamental human right of development—is central to meaningful exercise of political and civil rights.

Freedom from economic deprivation has been a persistent theme of U.N. concerns and programs on behalf of seriously disadvantaged and vulnerable people, including refugees, victims of wars and natural disasters, and women and children. Because there is growing recognition that the suffering of people is a matter of concern for the whole international community, the United Nations' universal character confers a moral authority across political boundaries shared by no other political entity.

Moreover, in recent years, the United Nations has contributed to the building of new democracies through support for election monitoring; reform of military, judicial, and parliamentary institutions; and the strengthening of nongovernmental organizations. While much of this democracy-building work is new and in need of strengthening, it forms an important part of the U.N.'s role in sustainable development, which other international institutions—including the World Bank and IMF—are not well equipped to provide.

Humanitarian Emergency Relief. The United Nations provides important instruments for collectively mobilizing and coordinating international relief for humanitarian interventions in emergency situations. The United Nations High Commissioner for Refugees (UNHCR), the WFP, and UNICEF sustain successful humanitarian relief programs. Additionally, the United Nations has set up special entities in response to such complex emergencies as the Congo and Biafra in the 1960s, the African famines of the mid-1970s and 1980s, Cambodia from the early 1980s, and relief of victims of civil strife in Somalia and Bosnia. The new Department of Humanitarian Affairs provides a U.N. focal point for coordination of emergency responses.

Technical Cooperation for Development. The United Nations contributed substantially to earlier priorities of nation building for countries emerging from colonial rule and currently sustains grant technical assistance—largely separate from capital aid—of about $2 billion annually for their continued development. UNDP is at the center of U.N. technical cooperation, funding—both directly and through cooperating agencies—about half of such U.N. activities from voluntary contributions. The other half is provided by donors directly to the budgets and trust funds of twenty-seven U.N. programs and specialized agencies. While U.N. technical cooperation accounts for only 6 percent of official economic aid to developing regions, it provides 25 percent of total technical assistance, with the largest proportion directed to the poorest countries.

Mobilizing Action to Address Global Problems. Through a series of world conferences and specialized programs, the United Nations has mobilized world concern and established the basis of collective action on a number of problems that reflect global interdependence and require concerted actions among nations. Global problems of this nature include population growth, migration, status of women, protection of children, control of infectious diseases, drug trafficking, poverty, food security, the special needs of least developed countries, and global commons including regimes governing use and protection of the seas and environmentally sustainable natural resources.

In addressing such global problems, the United Nations provides nations with means for gaining consensus on the precise nature of problems of common concern and on actions for dealing with them. This involves negotiation to narrow policy differences and to establish cooperative regimes and programs for implementation. An example is the consensus reached on the injury to people resulting from the depletion of the ozone layer and the accord to scale down chlorofluorocarbon emissions. Another example is the understanding gained on the threat to social and ecological stability of uncontrolled population growth and the agreement on a broad program of action reached at the 1994 U.N. Conference on Population and Development in Cairo.

Contributions of the U.N. Specialized Agencies. Important contributions have been made by the U.N. specialized agencies in establishing norms, providing services, and advancing solutions to sectoral problems of global significance.

The four major specialized agencies—FAO, ILO, UNESCO, and WHO—have each been activators of global efforts to address important needs. These have included problems of world food supply and nutrition, unemployment and international labor standards, primary education and literacy, and global targets for clean water, sanitation, and preventive health services, along with programs for the eradication of infectious diseases. An outstanding success is the eradication of smallpox. Important contributions have also been made in agricultural development through efforts to transfer research findings and technology in such areas as pest control, soil conservation, and water management.

Future Challenges and the Need for Reform Despite this record of past accomplishments, the United Nations has failed in many respects to live up to the mandate of its Charter. North-South as well as East-West divisions have in the past distorted and often paralyzed the United Nations' work. Institutional shortcomings, which were left unattended in these politically acrimonious decades, now appear in stark relief as serious obstacles to the increased international cooperation required to meet the many challenges facing the United Nations and its member countries in today's post-cold war era.

New Challenges for the United Nations

Although substantial progress in global economic growth and social development has been made over the past half-century—including increases in per capita income in most regions of the world, reduction in population growth rates, and a rise in literacy worldwide—much remains to be accomplished. Currently, over a billion people live on the margin of survival, and in the poorer regions population growth of almost 100 million people annually over the next three decades threatens to cause great suffering and social and political disorder. Unemployment and stagnant economies in failing states—particularly in sub-Saharan Africa—along with civil and ethnic strife fuel massive refugee migrations and spreading areas of lawlessness and chaos. The United Nations is increasingly called on to manage such complex emergencies and to lay the basis for transitions from conflict to peaceful reconstruction. These challenges must be addressed, however, within a context vastly different from the one in which the organization was founded.

- The end of the cold war removes a preoccupation with super-power nuclear rivalry and erases an East-West divide that dominated and distorted international development cooperation efforts. But it also eliminates the principal rationale for the vast build-up of development aid. A new rationale—based on a recognition of shared problems and common goals—has not yet taken hold.

• Even before the fall of the Berlin Wall, belief in a centrally planned approach to development had eroded throughout most of the developing world; with the collapse of communism, market based economic policies and democracy have been embraced as the only viable development paradigm. This shift has presented international development institutions with new clients and major new tasks ranging from the promotion of private sector development to the fostering of democratic political reforms and the strengthening of organizations of civil society.

• Simultaneously, the world has become increasingly aware of the dangers and the costs of environmental degradation and of other global problems such as drug trafficking, state supported terrorism, and the spread of new communicable diseases. Few of these global problems, intensified by increased interdependence and revolutionary technological change, have adequate international institutional arrangements to facilitate the degree of international cooperation that is required to cope with them.

• State-to-state relations remain at the center of world affairs, but another feature of the changing world is the emergence of a vast array of non-state actors. The first generation of post–World War II international institution building had little to do with these forces; the second generation will need to forge new connections between public and private actors.

Sustainable development is the term that has come to encapsulate the economic, social, political, and environmental agenda needed to meet these new challenges. Its basic insights are that: 1) growth, poverty reduction, and environmental preservation are intricately interrelated—you cannot have one on a sustainable basis without the other two; 2) democratic participation improves the quality, effectiveness, and durability of development efforts; and 3) the well-being of future generations should not be sacrificed to the interests of present generations.

In the fall of 1994 the U.N. secretary-general issued an "Agenda for Development" that embraces the goal of sustainable development and identifies as its five central dimensions peace, the economy, environmental protection, social justice, and democracy. The "agenda" provides a compelling vision of development grounded in the universal values of the U.N. Charter, correctly casts development as a complex process, and highlights the comparative advantages and roles of the United Nations in promoting development. But given its generality, failure to identify the U.N.'s particular areas of comparative advantage, and failure to specify adequate ways to rationalize and restructure U.N. programs, the "agenda" risks contributing further to a widely held view that the United Nations suffers from lack of focus, excessive overlap of efforts, and bureaucratic paralysis.[2]

In his response to the secretary-general's report, the president of the U.N. General Assembly, S.R. Insanally of Guyana, observed during the 1994 World Hearings on Development that "no agenda for development would be of interest unless it included proposals for serious change, not just tinkering with the existing structures and routines." The nearly universal consensus of the General Assembly hearings was that the U.N. system needs to set sharper priorities and address its institutional shortcomings.

Institutional Weaknesses

Both U.N. member governments and independent analysts point to the following problems as among the most serious institutional weaknesses now crippling the U.N. system.[3]

Policy Incoherence. International development cooperation is hindered by the lack of international policy coherence both across fields of money, trade, and development finance, and, within the development field, across major institutions and programs. Absent is an organizational locus for 1) maintaining an ongoing watch on international economic trends and conditions and their impact on development; 2) regular review and monitoring by donors and recipients of international development assistance policies—both bilateral and multilateral; and 3) effective oversight of the diverse U.N. development funds and programs and their interactions with other international development agencies.

Cross-sectoral policy coherence cannot be achieved effectively by any single entity. It does not work well in the Group of Seven (G-7) summit process. It does not even work well within national governments. Rather, international policy cooperation has been most effective on a sector-specific basis, and there is need to strengthen the policy roles of each of the major institutions in the monetary, trade, and development assistance fields. But there is also need for ongoing oversight, review, and dialogue among developed countries, transition economies, emerging markets, and the poor countries whose economies are lagging.

Program Sprawl. Not only has the number of development agencies increased markedly but also, within the different agencies and funds, the agenda has broadened, operational activities expanded, earmarked funding (as distinct from agency or program support) increased, and the demands and expectations of both donor and recipient governments escalated, usually without regard to institutional capability or the structure of the system overall. Repeated partial efforts to improve coordination often conflict with individual agencies' efforts to gain or maintain resources and turf, with individual recipient governments' determination to capture as large a share of the funding as possible, and with individual donor governments' determination to control the use of its resources and gain credit for its development contributions. The one-country/one-vote rule of U.N. agencies and funds exacerbates this problem by reinforcing each member government's tendency to look at its own piece, rather than the whole of the pie. As a result, most programs fail to establish priorities, set concrete goals, and organize resources to meet them.

Agency Competition. When aid resources were increasing, there was less of a tendency for agencies to see themselves in competition with one another (although this has always been something of a problem). In recent years, however, competition—both between the central U.N. programs and the Bretton Woods institutions, and among the U.N. programs and funds themselves—has impeded operational cooperation and coordination. At one time the United Nations was the principal provider of multilateral technical assistance. With the greatly increased role of the MDBs, especially the World Bank, in the provision of technical assistance, along with capital investment loans, one might ask: why maintain the historical separation? Why not, say, let the World Bank and the other MDBs—which have the bulk of the resources, the analytic rigor, and the dominant policy leverage—do it all?

The simple answer is that the Bretton Woods institutions and the U.N. programs have different mandates and different institutional capabilities. The U.N. programs have a broader mandate, as noted, which their assistance programs reflect; their assistance is generally provided on a smaller scale; and, in contrast to the largely headquarters based structure of the World Bank, programs such as UNICEF and UNDP have the bulk of their staffs in the field. These features make the U.N. programs, in principle, well suited to a range of social, political, and institutional development and national capacity-building tasks. They also suggest the potential for fruitful cooperation between the World Bank and U.N. programs that is essential for addressing today's much broadened development and global issues agenda. But this potential for complementary cooperation is too infrequently realized.

Administrative Laxness. As virtually all recent assessments of the United Nations have emphasized, the role of the organization is seriously undermined by weak personnel, poor accountability, and lack of transparency procedures. Member governments are as much at fault for these shortcomings as the agencies themselves: a virtual "national patronage" mentality has a "profoundly negative" effect on the appointment process.[4]

Governance by Member States. The United Nations is often blamed for poor coordination that is actually due to inconsistent policy guidance from member states. Governments must recognize that improving many current weaknesses depends on improving the quality of personnel appointed and that uniform policy instructions from governments to relevant governing bodies are essential to reform. Much of the responsibility for improving the U.N. system therefore falls on governments themselves.

A Reform Agenda

Numerous proposals for U.N. reform have been made over the years. In response, the secretary-general has taken some steps— e.g., to strengthen the Secretariat in areas of peacekeeping and humanitarian assistance and to clarify responsibilities for social and economic affairs. However, neither senior management nor the collectivity of member governments has yet fully committed themselves to major institutional change.

It would be an oversimplification to say that the longstanding division between "North" and "South" prevents such change. Differing views and perceptions of interest are more diverse than that. A coalition of reform-minded developed and developing countries will be needed, therefore, if weaknesses in the system are to be overcome.

The United States has manifested its own dissatisfaction by withdrawing from certain agencies and by cutting back on funds, but it has not taken the lead in encouraging major reforms. Within a system based on one-country/one-vote, U.N. reform is not something that the United States can engineer alone. It can unilaterally and selectively continue to withdraw or pull back from the programs it views as ineffective or irrelevant, but that will not produce the international institutional capacity that is in U.S. interest. It is time, therefore, for the United States to join with others to foster significant reform and revitalization to improve the United Nations' contribution to the promotion of sustainable development.

The U.N. does not have the wherewithal to play a lead role in support of economic and social policy reform; nor does it have the resources to finance major infrastructure or institutional developments. Where it does have a valuable role to play is in helping countries build their capacities to meet essential human needs, in advancing democracy and human rights, in assisting conflict resolution and reconstruction, and in responding to complex emergencies.

This chapter recommends that the United States urge a streamlining of the U.N. development role around these areas of comparative advantage and in so doing give priority attention to the following.

1) *Consolidate the central U.N. development funds and programs.* A U.N. General Assembly "capacity study" and follow-up "consensus resolution" in 1970 sought to establish coherence in the delivery of technical cooperation to developing countries by a tripartite partnership among governments, the UNDP, and U.N. agencies. Governments would program their development with the technical help of the agencies, and the UNDP would centrally fund and coordinate projects, which would then be executed by the agencies. However, despite the UNDP's initial role in core funding, the U.N. system proved resistant to the coherence intended by the "consensus resolution" and the resolution broke down. As a result:

- The U.N. specialized agencies generally have overextended themselves in administration of technical cooperation projects from extra-budgetary resources, which has lessened the influence of their governing bodies and adversely affected the quality of their performance. There has been a weakening of the relevance of the specialized agencies, relative to private and other technical entities, both in their mandated functions and in their technical cooperation operations.
- The UNDP has increasingly become one of the many implementing agencies of technical cooperation projects, either directly or by actors outside the U.N. system. While the UNDP continues to assist developing countries in building capacity for management of development and encourages national execution of technical cooperation projects, its role as a central coordinator of the system is largely lost.
- It is the poorest countries with their high dependence on external aid that are victimized by the lack of coherence among the many U.N. and other donor entities that largely overwhelm weak governments with separate agency program criteria, administrative procedures, and competitively guarded institutional identities.

Middle income countries with better developed management are able to impose some coherence on external resources, but the poor countries are not helped to gain that capacity by the way external aid is administered. Many of the African and other less developed countries lacking means to assure coherence of U.N. and other donor assistance are in danger of becoming failed states. A new consensus resolution is needed to achieve:

1) a more focused set of priority objectives;

2) consistent policies and procedures at the country level;

3) high performance assistance programs.

The current plan within the United Nations is to follow up the recent and still-to-come major U.N. conferences with a synthesis of the multiple goals and objectives that have been or will be approved, and to establish the interagency task forces to pursue their implementation. This approach simply will not go far enough in streamlining and strengthening the provision of increasingly scarce U.N. development assistance. Instead, we recommend a merger of the central U.N. funds and programs (specifically, UNDP, UNFPA, and UNICEF), together with IFAD and many of the separate technical trust funds of the specialized agencies, into a single U.N. development fund.

The basic purpose of this unified development fund would derive not from a notion of country entitlements to aid, but from the U.N. Charter's commitment to human security and individual well-being. With a single governing board, executive, staff, and country offices, the fund would build on the best features of the existing programs. That is, it would combine 1) the focus on basic human well-being, the high-profile advocacy, and the goal oriented approach of UNICEF; 2) the national capacity-building orientation and permanent field presence of the UNDP; and 3) UNDP's newly expanding role in democratization, conflict prevention, and peacebuilding.

The latter area, which is an important and growing feature of U.N. activity, needs much conceptual clarity and program development. There is broad agreement today that the United Nations system as presently constituted, mandated, and funded is not adequately prepared to deal with the multiple complex emergencies and conflicts laid at its door. The three most frequently cited weaknesses are 1) inadequate coordination within the United Nations and between it and other agencies (both official and nongovernmental); 2) the absence of processes that link emergency relief to more sustained development; and 3) the difficulty of designing and implementing comprehensive post-conflict programs that combine peace negotiations with reconciliation and reconstruction efforts. The agencies—especially UNDP, UNHCR, and the Secretariat's new Department of Humanitarian Affairs—along with outside critics, have expressed continuing concern that existing agency mandates result in both gaps and disjointed programs.

A unified U.N. development fund could play a crucial role in improving this situation, but not by playing the role of an emergency relief organization. Rather, short-term emergency relief should be left to separate actors as discussed below. The strength of the fund would lie in its permanent field presence, and it is at the field level that it could play a key role in 1) serving as broker or neutral intermediary among internal and external actors and between the two; 2) defining a strategic approach to emergency prevention, contingency planning, and post-emergency rehabilitation and reconstruction; 3) fostering or serving as a clearinghouse or information exchange at the time of an emergency; and 4) facilitating field-level coordination of official and NGO emergency relief efforts.

The U.N. development funds and programs with their field staffs, small grant operations, and extensive NGO working relations have a potential comparative advantage in helping to promote basic human needs, democratic reforms, conflict prevention, and emergency and peacebuilding assistance. Unifying the existing programs under a common set of priority guidelines, management structure, and governing board would result in a more effective U.N. development assistance effort—one that could avoid currently wasteful duplication and cross-purposes and draw renewed worldwide support.

Some will argue against such a merger because: 1) donor governments have shown no inclination to coordinate their efforts; 2) recipient governments believe that more spigots mean more aid and more independence; and 3) the agencies, especially UNICEF, fear that their special missions and related fundraising capabilities would be undermined. It is time, however, to put the imperative for a truly effective U.N. development assistance system above partisan and sectoral interests. Otherwise, support for the U.N. development system will continue to erode, and the system will pass into the class of noble but failing enterprises.

The effort to restructure and focus the U.N. development programs should aim also to improve working relations between the United Nations and the Bretton Woods institutions. As already noted, these two sets of organizations have markedly different mandates, characteristics, and resultant strengths and weaknesses. When and where their institutional comparative advantages have been mutually recognized, they have often established effective working relations. But by all accounts, the cooperation is less systematic than is in the interests of their intended beneficiaries. No one step will cure this problem. The important consideration for governments is that each of the separate components of the international development system carries out its mandate and purpose effectively and is held accountable for doing so.

2) *Streamline and revive the quality roles of the U.N. specialized agencies.* As much as when the United Nations was first established, the world needs a set of strong sectoral agencies to monitor global trends and spotlight emerging problems; to set standards, promote norms, and advocate for priority uses of limited resources; to advise on technical matters; and to provide neutral fora for policy debates. To this end there is need to a) rebuild the analytic capacity of the specialized agencies so that they can serve as "centers of excellence" in their respective fields, and b) terminate certain of their activities that have become obsolete or irrelevant. In particular, as indicated above, their roles in the provision of technical assistance need to be redefined.

Recent reviews of the work of the specialized agencies have concluded that their programs have become too heavily oriented toward technical cooperation operations to the detriment of their basic roles of building substantive expertise. This has adversely affected their capacity to set standards and manage growing areas of global interdependence in their respective fields. Worse, there has been a deterioration in the quality of their technical assistance operations, which are increasingly below the standards achieved by personnel in the developing countries. There are differences among the agencies, and diverse factors contribute to their diminished effectiveness, including budget constraints, personnel policies, and in some cases poor management.

Redressing the balance will not be easy. It will mean: 1) purposeful direction by the governing bodies of the agencies aimed at improving substantive capacity, and 2) reallocation of staffs and budgets, forgoing extra-budgetary resources that are not in line with agency core priorities. This may involve some increases in regular budgets to facilitate the transition and upgrade professional standards. Most important is a clear perspective on the roles of the respective agencies and on the relevance of current programs and structures to changing needs. FAO is currently engaged in such a review; the same is needed at WHO.

Redefinition of the role of the specialized agencies in provision of technical cooperation will mean scaling back their execution of projects, particularly at the national level, and increasing their role in sectoral analysis and policy advice. The agencies' criteria for technical cooperation operations should be their clear relevance to the agency core priorities and quality expertise, so that analytic work and technical operations are mutually reinforcing.

Coordination of the overall direction of the United Nations in the economic and social sphere must rest in the first instance with governments, specifically with a reformed role of the Economic and Social Council (ECOSOC), as discussed below. To assist in this process, there should be an annual meeting of the elected presidents of the governing bodies of the specialized agencies with the executive bureau of ECOSOC to review broad policy and coherence of the U.N. system.

The current meetings of the Advisory Committee on Coordination (ACC) of U.N. agencies and entities, chaired by the secretary-general, bring together some sixty U.N. officials and serve as "town meetings" for information exchange but are a totally ineffective means of program coordination.

3) *Create a single emergency relief organization.* As already noted, emergencies—both natural and human-made—are swamping the international assistance system. Experience with the range of emergencies from simple to complex suggests that much reform of the roles and procedures of international agencies is required. This chapter has argued above that certain responsibilities for setting the development framework within which emergency assistance is provided best fall within the mandate of a unified U.N. development fund. However, the rapid delivery of short-term emergency assistance requires a separate, highly flexible organizational arrangement. Establishment in 1991 of the U.N. undersecretary and Department of Humanitarian Affairs (DHA) and the creation of a central emergency revolving fund were half measures toward better equipping the United Nations to respond to emergencies. However, current U.N. coordinating mechanisms—always fragile at best—are without explicit authority to effectively direct the multiplicity of U.N. agencies and other governmental, international, and NGOs involved in relief efforts. Key U.N. agency roles in times of crisis remain open to negotiations, resulting in confusion, overlapping operations, and the risk of costly delays. This current

organizational structure hinders effective responses.

Given the continuing number and scale of complex emergencies requiring timely and well-directed international interventions, there is need to complete the task of strengthening the humanitarian relief capabilities of the United Nations. This can be achieved by establishing explicit authority for central direction of core U.N. relief operations, both among the agencies and at the country level, as a basis for coordinating the overall relief efforts of the international community.

The approach recommended is to consolidate U.N. emergency efforts into a single U.N. emergency relief organization that would incorporate the operational functions of the Department of Humanitarian Affairs, the UNHCR, and the World Food Program. Central direction of the relief efforts of these programs by the under secretary for humanitarian affairs, with the full support of the U.N. secretary-general, would provide a solid basis for effective coordination. The under secretary should be able to designate U.N. humanitarian coordinators for specific country operations on the basis of the official best equipped to deal with them. It would be a mistake, however, for this integrated relief organization to seek to expand its mandate into conflict prevention and post-conflict activities as the DHA is showing a tendency toward. Instead, it is essential for the relief organization to be bureaucratically lean and procedurally flexible and to rely on good working relations with NGOs and relief aid donors. It is also essential that in peacekeeping operations, the relief coordinator work closely with, indeed, under the authority of the secretary-general's special representative in cases where one is assigned. (The early actions of the U.N. Office of Humanitarian Assistance Coordination (UNO-HAC) in Mozambique, which functioned independently of the special representative, designed activities in isolation from donors, and downgraded coordination from donors, are an example of much that is wrong.)

Overall, the U.N. emergency relief organization would provide essential data, act as something of an international clearinghouse on what relief is needed and who is doing what, and respond quickly and flexibly to unmet needs. If it is going to be able to do so, however, major bureaucratic and administrative reforms will be required—and governments should, as a matter of priority, review everything from personnel to procurement procedures that now impede the United Nations' emergency relief role.

Admittedly, the work of the UNHCR involves human rights and protection issues for refugees. Under the UNHCR statute, the "work of the High Commissioner shall be of an entirely nonpolitical character; it shall be humanitarian and social and shall relate, as a rule, to groups and categories of refugees." This special character of the high commissioner's role must be preserved. However, as the high commissioner has repeatedly stressed, with the massive increase of the numbers of displaced persons, distinctions as to the causes of their displacement have tended to blur. In any case, protection of refugee rights does not mean that the UNHCR must run its own supply operations. Provisioning could and should be the operational responsibility of a consolidated U.N. emergency relief organization with the UNHCR responsible for establishing terms and conditions of the treatment of refugees, negotiation of safe havens, etc.

Moreover, there is little rationale for maintaining an independent emergency food relief operation. At the heart of every emergency is the disruption of basic food supplies for the afflicted people. Delay in delivering food supplies exacts a terrible toll. The food needs of people in current emergencies are enormous at several millions of tons annually, and appear likely to continue. The World Food Program is now entirely directed to emergency relief and providing food to the most vulnerable people. Its logistic capacities are well developed, but its program procedures need to be streamlined and brought more fully under the central direction of the U.N. Department of Humanitarian Affairs, which should have a wing for operations and a separate one for prevention, early warning, needs assessment, and fundraising.

This consolidated U.N. emergency relief organization would still need to build working relations with the International Committee of the Red Cross and with other important NGOs whose operations on the ground have been an important aspect of flexible humanitarian assistance efforts and will continue to play a major role in the years ahead to help to ensure rapid responses and political neutrality. It would also need to forge close working relations with the proposed U.N. human development fund (combined UNDP and UNICEF discussed above) for the handling of the emergency-to-development "continuum."

4) *Activate the United Nations' institutional structure for implementation of the Earth Summit conclusions.* A critical question during the United Nations Conference on Environment and Development (Earth Summit) process was what international institutions should be created or improved to assure follow-up of the summit conclusions. To facilitate integration of economic and environmental approaches, the summit purposefully avoided recommending a specialized agency for the environment.

The conference consensus centered instead on the new high-level Commission for Sustainable Development (CSD) to set program priorities and monitor progress. The U.N. secretary-general was to assure support and coordination of the U.N. system and seek periodic advice of eminent persons. The Global Environment Facility (GEF) was to be democratically restructured and its scope expanded. New ground was to be broken by associating NGOs and the business community with the work of the commission. These pieces are mostly in place, but they have yet to be fully and meaningfully activated.

The CSD—reporting to ECOSOC—after two sessions appears to be settling into a routine of statements by government officials based on mundane Secretariat preparations. This has not been effective, but it is too early to write off the commission. What are needed are independently prepared reports on key agenda topics to focus commission deliberations. Specifically, the relations of the commission with the NGO community and the business sector should be institutionalized by establishing two advisory groups, each of which would meet before the commission and issue independent reports.

After an initial pilot phase, the GEF has been strengthened and restructured in innovative ways that engage developing and developed country representatives in program priority setting, with the World Bank, the UNDP, and the UNEP providing project development and execution. The GEF has been extended for three years at a somewhat restricted level of over $2 billion focused sharply on the global priorities of the ozone layer and climate change, biological diversity, and international waters. While the precise GEF agenda and priorities are still being determined, a great deal of the sustainable development agenda and financing remains outside the writ of the GEF, including all the local environmental problems of developing countries in water, health, agriculture, industry, chemicals, waste management, and most energy concerns.

Part of the success of the Earth Summit is that public and governmental focus on the environment has gained dramatically increased attention, and that U.N. agencies seek to adjust their programs accordingly. Both the World Bank and the UNDP have greatly strengthened their environmental staffs and work, and the U.N. specialized agencies and programs have established environmental units that competitively seek funding for operational projects.

Aside from the GEF, there is no effective U.N. coordination over environmental assessment and operational activities. The U.N. subcommittee of the ACC set up for this purpose plays the usual game of agency turf defense. Nor is the UNDP as one of the competing agencies able to exercise a coordination role.

The UNEP has sought faithfully to follow the Earth Summit recommendation by "ceding operational authority and strengthening relations and coordination with other agencies" both in and outside the U.N. system. However, it has not gained the strength in overall monitoring and assessment of environmental problems envisioned for it by the Earth Summit. On the contrary, the UNEP appears to be losing ground as other agencies set up competing services. The UNEP's mandate as the central coordinating agency for monitoring and assessment of environmental trends and conditions needs to be clarified, and its monitoring role and financing strengthened.

While it is reasonable that the UNEP should not itself engage in operational project activity, it should be ceded a central role of technical review and coordination for environmentally sustainable projects within the U.N. system. This would parallel the UNEP's role for technical vetting of all projects funded by the GEF. To establish a clear division between such project coordination and its role in assessments, the UNEP should establish a separate technical project office outside Nairobi—perhaps in cooperation with the U.N. Economic Commission for Europe, which has a well-developed network of technically competent environmental specialists.

It would be for donors to insist that their funding of environmental projects by the U.N. system—whether funded through the GEF or independently—be technically coordinated by the UNEP's proposed Office of Technical Project Coordination. In this way it may be possible to gain some coherence on the environmental activities of the U.N. agencies.

5) *Reinvent ECOSOC.* Concern about the lack of policy and program coherence have led to recent calls for the creation of a new "Economic Security Council." The idea seems neither feasible nor necessary. It is premised on a false analogy with the U.N. Security Council, which has functions not assigned to subordinate organizations with their own governing boards, as is the case in the economic field. Instead, ECOSOC (which is empowered by the U.N. Charter to monitor and to make recommendations regarding the U.N. specialized agencies and programs) should be reinvented so as to:

1) serve, through its high-level convening process, as a forum for regular global scanning that can spotlight gaps, inconsistencies, or emerging problems likely to fall between the purviews of the sector-specific institutions in the fields of money, trade, and development;

2) perform the functions of an international development assistance review committee that provides a regular joint donor and recipient assessment of the aid policies, programs, and practices of both bilateral and the many varied multilateral assistance agencies and funds;[5] and

3) improve its oversight of the U.N. development funds and programs with a particular eye to management efficiency, program effectiveness, and interagency coordination.

The responsibility for seeing that ECOSOC is reformed sufficiently to perform these tasks rests largely with the member governments. It will require that developed countries cease to dismiss the council, and that developing countries cease to abuse it. One proposal that is being discussed informally and seems worth serious consideration would create a constituency based executive committee of ECOSOC, comprised of some twenty or so members, that would meet regularly; and then, convert ECO-SOC into a committee of the whole that would meet only once a year.

6) *Improve overall performance, forge relations with nongovernmental actors, and eliminate what is no longer necessary.* In addition to the above reforms, several kinds of across-the-board improvements are needed. First, member governments and senior U.N. management must, by whatever means necessary, improve the personnel, oversight, and evaluation procedures throughout the central U.N. organization and the specialized agencies, and must make the operations of each of the funds and programs more efficient, transparent, and accountable. This change is the real sine qua non to any future U.N. development role. It is essential for both the reestablishment of support for the activities of the United Nations and for the achievement of results needed in emergency and long-term development efforts. The recent establishment of an independent inspector-general was an important step that will have to be watched for a time to see if it accomplishes its purposes.

Much of the responsibility for effecting these administrative reforms lies with the Secretariat and the management of the U.N. departments, agencies, and funds. But member governments must also commit themselves to these changes and to quality appointments in the Secretariat, the programs, and their own U.N. missions.

Second, with democracy expanding worldwide and globalization of economic affairs, the need for involvement of citizen and nonstate actors at the international level to strengthen the support base of the United Nations has become increasingly important. Nonstate actors need to build advisory processes into the U.N. system's deliberative bodies along the line indicated above for the U.N. Commission on Sustainable Development.

Lastly, as part of an effort to reinvigorate essential programs and agencies, it is time to eliminate those parts of the system that either have completed their tasks and are no longer needed, or have never performed well and do not warrant continued support in a time of resource tightening and rising new demands. The unified development fund, proposed above, would consolidate a number of currently separate funds and programs. That is a start. In addition, as others have also suggested, at least two other agencies should be eliminated: U.N. Conference on Trade and Development (UNCTAD), whose important functions in helping the poorer countries benefit from an open trading system should now be absorbed into the new World Trade Organization (WTO), and the U.N. Industrial Development Organization (UNIDO), which has failed to justify its separate existence.

This proposed combination of streamlining as well as revitalizing and restructuring is necessary to tone up the U.N. system to meet the challenges that lie ahead and to sustain member government support in an era of policy redefinition and resource constraints.

Financing the United Nations' Development Role

Finally, it is necessary to turn attention to the issue of financing. Two recent assessments have been made that are striking in their conclusions and recommendations, and with which we are in broad agreement.[6] Indeed, we can do no better than to synthesize their findings and reiterate their recommendations. Four key points underlie the recent studies' concluding recommendations.

The first is that there is an urgent need to find ways to match multilateral funding with recognized international needs and agreed objectives. The increasing discrepancy between the tasks imposed on the United Nations and its available resources should not continue. The current situation suffers from problems of both quantity and quality (e.g., predictability and stability).

Second, to secure an increased and stable funding base for the different U.N. emergency and long-term development efforts, it is imperative to achieve more equitable burden sharing in future. Initially, the main support for multilateral institutions came from a small group of donors led by the United States. Later, a group of small, like-minded countries became important donors for the U.N. system. Although certain countries, notably Japan, have significantly increased their overall aid levels, the "like-minded" (e.g., the Nordics) still contribute a disproportionately large share. This situation is becoming less and less acceptable to them, as the following comment from the 1991 Nordic U.N. project indicates:

A stronger and more effective UN in the economic and social fields must be built on the basis of the joint responsibility of its members. To a greater extent than is presently the case the sharing of funding among member states must reflect their ability to pay.[7]

Third, the present funding arrangements, which are based on assessed and voluntary contributions, have some strengths; however, they also have weaknesses. On the one hand, they provide flexibility for member states to support programs that are of particular relevance to their foreign policy interests or are judged to be particularly effective. On the other hand, the combination of assessed and voluntary contributions provides an inadequate means of mobilizing the resources required to match agreed objectives.

Some agencies, including the central U.N. organization and the specialized agencies, depend on assessed budgetary support supplemented by voluntary contributions; others, including the UNDP and UNICEF, depend almost entirely on voluntary contributions (with limited subventions from the U.N. budget). Overall, roughly 70 percent of the total budget for U.N. technical assistance is based on voluntary contributions.

These funding arrangements differ markedly from the negotiated replenishment processes for the "soft loan windows" of each of the MDBs. The MDB replenishment process occurs in two stages: first, donors agree on a proposed funding target for total contributions to meet agreed objectives over a specified period of time (normally three years); second, donors negotiate the burden sharing among themselves.

Fourth, it is unlikely that the U.N. funding situation will improve (i.e., funding will be increased and provided on a more predictable basis) without some change in governance procedures and better accountability and transparency in U.N. management and operational procedures. Having already touched on the accountability issue, we turn here to the governance issue.

There is nothing surprising about the fact that donor contributions to the MDBs, in which donors exercise dominant influence through a system of weighted voting based on contributions, have increased over the past decades far more than contributions to U.N. programs, which are governed on a one-country/one-vote basis. The introduction of weighted voting into the U.N. system would, however, have implications for the character and concept of the United Nations. Efforts need to be made, therefore, to find an acceptable middle ground; delay in doing so only risks permanent erosion of the United Nations' development assistance role. As the Nordic U.N. study concluded, corrective measures need to focus on solutions "which give donors greater say in determining agency budgets, management, and programs without necessarily diminishing rights of recipients or quality of assistance. The alternative is for all technical assistance to gravitate to the MDBs where recipients have little say at all."[8]

In sum, a revised funding system is needed to underwrite the United Nations' development and emergency roles. The two recent studies proposed a revised funding system that combines contributions from three sources: assessments, negotiated pledges, and additional voluntary contributions. Administrative costs, the study argues, should be shared by all member governments who participate in the U.N. programs: funding the machinery should be a matter of agreement and commitment by all participating countries on the basis of ability to pay.

Consistent with the organizational reform suggested above, negotiated pledges (or replenishments) rather than voluntary contributions should provide the resources for the technical assistance programs of the proposed new U.N. development fund. Along with this change, we would propose that the governance of the new fund resemble the innovative arrangement reached in the restructuring of the GEF—an arrangement relying on a process of double majorities. The intended outcome is both greater predictability and greater likelihood of continuing support for the United Nations' development role.

Future Direction of U.S.
Multilateral Aid Policy and Funding

The reforms proposed aim to:

* reduce costly U.N. bureaucratic overhead;
* focus scarce grant resources on key areas where the U.N. has a strong comparative advantage—including immediate needs, emergency relief, human rights, and conflict resolution and reconstruction;
* put emphasis on building capacity within countries to handle these problems on their own; and
* diminish problems of lack of coherence among the many U.N. and other donor agencies.

These changes should, we believe, provide the bases for building greater confidence in and support for U.N. assistance operations.

Clearly the potential for the United Nations to play an influential role in the world supportive of American interests is greater today than in the past. U.N. aid facilitates cost-effective burden sharing. Properly directed, it can help build national capabilities and an international culture of cooperation vital for building peace, safeguarding human rights, protecting the environment, and solving other shared problems. Moreover, with the progressive dismantling of the U.S. overseas Agency for International Development missions, the U.N. development field staffs assume importance as a common facility for all donor agencies.

But if the benefits of a shared address to global common problems is to be realized, the United States must take a more active role in reforming the economic and social components of the United Nations to assure that it sets an example for others by the quality of its appointments to a merit based U.N. personnel system, and by a clearly indicated willingness to contribute its fair share of resources needed by the United Nations to perform the reformed economic and social role recommended by this report.

At the same time, if the United States is to do its part in the reform and revitalization of the United Nations to meet the needs of the twenty-first century, then it is reasonable to expect firm assurances of transparency and efficiency in U.N. activities. No longer can we accept bureaucratic bloat. There are too many important jobs to perform in such key areas as peacekeeping and humanitarian relief and too few resources. The U.N. administration must do what governments and private firms and institutions are expected to do, namely, improve services while controlling costs.

If the partnership between the United Nations and the United States begun in San Francisco fifty years ago can be renewed with these mutual assurances on both sides, then a global system of cooperation in the economic and social areas will emerge that will prove more effective than any alternative either the United States or the United Nations could achieve alone. The costs are manageable. The entire U.N. system, including peacekeeping, got 0.7 percent of the $285 billion the United States spent annually in the two years 1993–94 on international security. That translates to a price per capita for the United States—for everything from blue helmets for peacekeeping to vaccines for children—of less than $7 a year or the price of a film show.

Although current reviews of the United Nations are mixed and its prospects unclear, the United States would fail in its responsibility if we take too narrow a view of the opportunities that are now at hand. For decades we have espoused the merits of free markets, free elections, human rights, and the opportunity for economic progress. In this new era we have the opportunity to see real movement toward higher standards of international behavior and cooperation. International organizations, and especially the United Nations, are central to this effort.

Notes

[1] Mitrany (1966) provided the seminal work on functionalism that influenced post–World War II planners. Hans Morganthau, a political realist, asserted that: "The future of the civilized world is intimately tied to the functional approach to international organization." Cited in Thompson (1980). The most successful application of the functional approach internationally has been among European states where the Coal and Steel Community and the Common Agricultural Policy have contributed to progress toward political union.

[2] United Nations Secretary-General (1994).

[3] Among studies on the need for U.N. reform: Bertrand (1985); United Nations Association of the United States of America (1987); North South Roundtable

(1989); South Commission (1990); Nordic U.N. Development Project (1991); Danida Study (1991); Netherlands Ministry of Foreign Affairs (1991); Dadzie (1993); Childers and Urquhart (1994).

4 Franck (1985).

5 Existing mechanisms all fall short of this role. The DAC is a donors club. The Development Committee is a joint body of the IMF and World Bank and focused largely on their activities.

6 Nordic U.N. Development Project (1991); Independent Advisory Group (1993).

7 Nordic U.N. Development Project (1991), p. 82.

8 Nordic U.N. Development Project (1991), p. 82.

5

Protecting Human Rights

FELICE D. GAER

In August 1992 international media showed horrifying pictures of emaciated prisoners behind barbed wire, accompanied by reports of depraved torture and prisoners beaten to death as part

FELICE D. GAER is director of The Jacob Blaustein Institute for the Advancement of Human Rights of the American Jewish Committee. Ms. Gaer was appointed a public member of the United States delegations to the World Conference on Human Rights in 1993 and to the United Nations Commission on Human Rights in 1994 and in 1995. She is a member of the Council on Foreign Relations, a member of the Board of Directors of the Andrei Sakharov Foundation, a member of the core group of the Human Rights Council at The Carter Center of Emory University, and vice president of the International League for Human Rights. Ms. Gaer is the author of recent articles on human rights at the United Nations, the relationship of the U.N. and CSCE, and the U.N.'s role in former Yugoslavia. She has led human rights fact-finding missions to former Yugoslavia, Nagorno-Karabakh, Chile, and elsewhere. She has provided expert testimony at hearings of the U.S. Congress on a wide range of countries. She previously served as executive director of the International League for Human Rights, as executive director for European programs at the United Nations Association of the USA, and as a program officer at the Ford Foundation.

of a policy of "ethnic cleansing" in the conflict in Bosnia-Herzegovina. The United Nations Commission on Human Rights and the U.N. Security Council urgently convened meetings to condemn the abuses and to gather authoritative information on the actual state of affairs in the Serb-run northern Bosnian camps and nearby. The first ever emergency session called by the fifty-three-member United Nations Commission on Human Rights met in Geneva and appointed former Polish Prime Minister Tadeusz Mazowiecki as special rapporteur on former Yugoslavia, dispatching him immediately to the region. The U.N. Security Council condemned "any" violations of humanitarian law (human rights being too controversial for it to consider), and called for "substantiated" data on such violations to be sent to the secretary-general. Later, these actions helped the Security Council to establish the first post–World War II War Crimes Commission and the first international war crimes tribunal.

Underlying these efforts was the expectation that once an accurate account of human rights violations was obtained and reported upon, the United Nations could, at a minimum, publicize the truth about atrocities in the region and mobilize pressure against the offending parties to stop them. Those had been the traditional tools of human rights advocacy, outside as well as inside the U.N., but U.N. efforts to "mobilize shame" may have diminished some abuses, but did not end the vicious war. Indeed, some prisons were emptied (after a time), many individuals were permitted to leave, and, according to the War Crimes Commission, certain abuses, such as rape employed as part of "ethnic cleansing," diminished substantially after international publicity reached unprecedented levels.

In appointing a special rapporteur at an emergency session, the Commission on Human Rights dramatically advanced the scope and means of U.N. human rights monitoring employed by the U.N. Centre for Human Rights, the U.N. Secretariat agency primarily responsible for human rights. From the outset, the special rapporteur was authorized to take measures, utilize personnel, and act in ways that would cut across the often restrictive, limited human rights investigatory mandates established until then, with great difficulty, by the U.N. Commission. Mazowiecki was authorized to utilize the *combined expertise* of the U.N.'s other independent human rights experts (on torture, executions, the internally displaced), who, for the first time in Human Rights Commission history, accompanied a country "special rapporteur" to carry out urgent fact finding. Mazowiecki's continuing reports (fifteen issued from August 1992 through February 1995) are even sent to the Security Council, which has long rejected addressing human rights findings. Mazowiecki soon recommended—and the General Assembly eventually agreed—to dispatch the first-ever deployment of commission human rights field monitors to reside in the country under scrutiny in order to examine human rights on a continuing basis.

Yet in 1994, after vigorous reporting, abundant recommendations, and a level of staffing (eight persons) and support (including $500,000 in voluntary contributions from the U.S.) unprecedented in the U.N. Centre for Human Rights, the rapporteur bitterly assessed the slow pace or inaction of other U.N. agencies, including the Security Council, in taking measures to stop or prevent further rights abuses. Their lack of responsiveness, he argued, highlights the very weakness of U.N. human rights rapporteurs. In this conclusion, he is painfully correct. Over the years, many governments have worked prodigiously to ensure that the human rights programs of the U.N. remain modest, ineffective, and unable to connect to operational policies of the world body. Their aim has been to delegitimize concern for human rights as an acceptable consideration in the policies and programs of the U.N. Years of neglect and intimidation could not be overcome in one dramatic stroke. The Mazowiecki mandate reflects these system-wide problems.

No one could expect that a single prominent human rights investigator with a handful of staff could *resolve* a conflict as complex as that in Yugoslavia, particularly when he was appointed a full year after the fighting erupted in Croatia, and four months after ethnic cleansing's worst atrocities ravaged Bosnia. But his authoritative findings, active intervention, and targeted recommendations should have clarified the responsibilities of the respective parties to the conflict, and ensured that other U.N. bodies and personnel would employ at least some protection strategies he recommended to prevent further atrocities and "ethnic cleansing."

The lack of coordination and receptivity to human rights issues by other U.N. agencies engaged on the ground in former Yugoslavia, particularly the 40,000-person peacekeeping force "UN-PROFOR," which still has not assigned any of its staff to address human rights issues, has meant that the world body has not taken advantage of its own expert advice on how to utilize human rights reporting and information to help protect victims of abuses in Bosnia and neighboring states, prevent further atrocities, or maintain the U.N.'s own credibility as an impartial international force committed to upholding U.N. principles.

There is much more the rapporteur could do—but not alone. The U.N.'s human rights programs will need to be developed substantially to take early measures to prevent human abuses and the outbreak of violent conflicts, to identify and report upon human rights violations objectively and independently, and to provide more effective response mechanisms for stopping gross rights abuses. Such a multilateral capacity to combat abuses will need the strong support of engaged member states, committed to building a more effective human rights program that is able impartially, but intelligently, to identify, report on, and respond to severe violations of human rights and to engage in this effort operational agencies of the U.N. other than the Centre for Human Rights. The establishment in December 1994 of the office of U.N. High Commissioner for Human Rights, at the initiative of nongovernmental organizations (NGOs) and because of extremely strong political leadership of the Clinton administration, offers hope that the U.N.'s capacity to address violations of human rights in the post–cold war period might gain greater focus and effectiveness.

However, the high commissioner, Jose Ayala Lasso of Ecuador, in trying to stop the genocidal atrocities in Rwanda was also hampered by the weakness of the U.N.'s human rights machinery. He took up his post on April 5, 1994. The Rwandan president's plane crashed the very next day, and this was followed by incitement and the start of mass killings. The high commissioner personally undertook a mission to Rwanda, issuing statements from its capital in May 1994. He suggested, and Canada formally initiated action leading to another emergency session of the Commission on

Human Rights, convened in late May, which set up very much the same kind of machinery as established for former Yugoslavia: a special rapporteur with wide authority to investigate and monitor human rights. The high commissioner has tried to work with other U.N. agencies on the ground in Rwanda, including a War Crimes Commission and tribunal set up again by the Security Council, and has begun establishing field monitors in Rwanda and technical assistance programs in neighboring and volatile Burundi. His efforts have been plagued by bureaucratic inaction, inefficiency, financing problems, a lack of trained staff, and the absence of an emergency operational response capacity for establishing human rights monitors both within the U.N. system as a whole and the Centre for Human Rights in particular.

For all the problems encountered, the substantial U.N. human rights responses on former Yugoslavia and Rwanda, unique in U.N. history, were possible only in the post–cold war era. Over the years, the United Nations' human rights programs have been kept weak, initially concentrating exclusively on obtaining consensus about norms. Establishment of effective, impartial, and independent mechanisms to implement those human rights standards and to report on violations, long a U.S. goal, has been the subject of intense controversy and widespread opposition. Whereas the Soviet Union and its allies provided an umbrella for numerous dictatorships and abusive regimes until the late 1980s, the shift toward democracy in East and Central Europe left regimes elsewhere temporarily leaderless—and having to speak for themselves.

The United States and other countries have helped build mechanisms to enforce the human rights guarantees of U.N. instruments, but American support has lacked the priority, and sometimes the consistency, needed to create and support a truly independent and objective international system to protect human rights. The U.S. expression of "dissatisfaction" with U.N. Human Rights Centre Director Theo van Boven's outspoken criticism of "disappearances" and similar abuses in Argentina, Guatemala, and other Latin American countries that led U.N. Secretary-General Perez de Cuellar to fire van Boven as his first public act is particularly well known. Less familiar is the continuing reluctance to this day of the U.S., under all administrations, to ensure adequate funding of the Human Rights Centre, whether through regular or voluntary contributions, and to make certain that it can report and act effectively to protect against human rights violations. America's elaborate "Draft Action Plan" for human rights protection through the U.N., drawn up just before the 1993 World Conference on Human Rights, has yet to be pursued with the vigor, or the necessary financial resources, to make the serious vision presented there a reality.

This chapter will explore ways that the United States government can and should be more involved in the development of more effective U.N. activity to combat human rights abuses.

Human Rights as a U.S. Foreign Policy Priority

The fact that the U.N. addresses human rights issues at all is nothing short of revolutionary, and was in strong measure due to American leadership half a century ago. Indeed, the initiative to turn the United Nations Charter into an instrument concerned with promoting respect for the human rights of individuals came from many of the forty-two American organizations present as "consultants" to the United States delegation at the founding conference in San Francisco in 1945. Their conviction that respect for human rights and the dignity of the individual was essential to peace and conflict prevention stemmed not merely from deep-seated American values, but reflected their realistic assessment of contemporary events: the failure of interwar treaties aimed at protecting only a few minorities in a few countries, and a world war stoked by the fires of hatred and dehumanization of Jews and other minorities and nationalities. Convinced that only if the rights of all people were protected would the rights of particular minority, ethnic, and religious groups be ensured, and future conflicts avoided, they persuaded the American delegation and other drafters of the Charter to make the new world body different from its predecessor.

The Charter's opening words, "We the peoples . . ."—rather than the more familiar treaty language of "The High Contracting Parties"—signify these differences. For the first time, the rights of individuals—and not solely the rights of states—had become a matter of principal concern for an international organization. Encouraging respect for human rights is one of the four purposes of the United Nations set forth specifically in its Charter, which also calls for studies, recommendations, and joint and separate action by member states to achieve human rights goals, and permits consultation with nongovernmental organizations in this effort.

Whether garnering public support for human rights as a main purpose of the U.N. or in setting goals for engagement abroad, a focus on human rights helps forge a better U.S. foreign policy that can muster public support: a foreign policy "that thinks like Americans," to paraphrase President Clinton's description of his cabinet.

Promoting human rights does more than express American aspirations and beliefs or make people "feel good." It "does good" and is a policy rooted in realism. Famed Soviet dissident and Nobel Peace Prize laureate Andrei Sakharov argued effectively that countries that do not respect the freedoms and dignity of individuals living within their borders, and that are not accountable to their citizens, are also more likely to start aggressive wars abroad, both because of a lack of domestic restraints and a callous disregard as to how armed conflict affects combatants and civilians. The Clinton administration has argued the corollary to this, namely, that countries that respect human rights are less likely to upset regional and global stability. A free press, democratic political process, and independent court system require governments to be accountable to their people about actions abroad as well as at home. Such institutions encourage states to resolve internal disputes through peaceful measures of dialogue and domestic democratic institution building rather than through "disappearances" and forced displacement of populations. This reinforces both domestic and international stability. Moreover, as Secretary of State Warren Christopher told the Senate Foreign Relations Committee on February 15, 1995, there is a long-term American interest in "a world where information flows freely and the rule of law protects not only political rights but the essential elements of free market economics."

Studies have shown that most of the ethnic conflicts in the world today identify systematic discriminatory treatment, usually political or economic, as a root cause. In their efforts to prevent violent clashes, it is important for policy makers and negotiators alike to focus early on longstanding grievances, on the way people are treated and the rights they lack or possess, before cynical politicians use these grievances to foment hatred and even violence. Accurate human rights reporting can provide early warning of conflicts and, through democratic and participatory institutions, may help shape policies aimed at early prevention of armed uprisings.

The salience of the human rights factor in national and international policy formulation is thus perhaps greater than ever. And paradoxically, because of the increasing priority of economics in interstate relations, and the numbing effect of a plethora of televised information on abuses, human rights grievances may seem less urgent because of an abundance of data and the multiplicity of factors involved in policy formulation. In such situations, there is a growing need for effective multilateral institutions able to sound the warning bell authoritatively and independently, and to respond effectively to emergency situations thereby relieving the burden on any one state to adopt unilateral economic sanctions or other enforcement measures when they are necessary. Furthermore, there is a palpable need for preventive action that must be based in part upon the reaffirmation and strengthening of the universal applicability of rights and the legitimacy of international concern about human rights violations.

Unilateral and Multilateral Human Rights Policies

U.S. Human Rights Policy

U.S. policy to promote and protect human rights has focused primarily on stopping egregious violations, particularly assaults on physical integrity such as torture, political killings and arbitrary arrest, and other civil and political rights. American policy thus emphasizes protection over promotion, action over words, a country-specific focus over global generalities, and the building of institutions rather than drafting additional human rights norms.

The U.S. unilateral approach has generally been to expose (or confirm) gross human rights abuses, to demand their end, to establish sanctions (such as the cutoff of military aid or trade), and to build institutions of accountability, including official bodies authorized to investigate abuses. These range from national human rights commissions to U.N. established ad hoc international criminal tribunals created for former Yugoslavia and Rwanda.

Within the federal government, the U.S. Congress has been the major force mandating that assistance to countries—whether unilateral or multilateral—be linked to observance of human rights. Legislation in 1976 mandated the creation of a human rights bureau in the Department of State headed by an assistant secretary. Congress later required an annual report on observance of international human rights standards for all proposed U.S. aid recipients, expanded thereafter to include all countries. Subsequent legislation has called on the U.S. government to oppose torture, to deny economic and military assistance, and to oppose multilateral loans to any government that engages in a consistent pattern of gross violations of internationally recognized human rights or that practices imprisonment for political purposes. The Jackson-Vanik amendment denied most-favored-nation tariff status and credit or investment guarantees to nonmarket economy countries that deny their citizens the right to emigrate, and was responsible for hundreds of thousands of Soviet emigres leaving for Israel and the U.S. Finally, American law requires that countries trading with the U.S. take measures to ensure workers' rights. A country is eligible for the General System of Preferences under the Trade Act only if it provides workers with the basic rights of freedom of association, freedom to organize and bargain collectively, and acceptable conditions of work, and prohibits forced labor. Similar provisions apply to the Overseas Private Investment Corporation and the Caribbean Basin Initiative. Often, human rights conditions are built into aid bills for specific countries.

Other U.S. programs supplement traditional human rights fact finding and reporting providing hands-on engagement that has a preventive and long-term efficacy. On the institution-building front, "rule of law" programs established in 1990 in the State Department aim to strengthen legal structures. They have focused on legal reform and training judges and law enforcement officials. The Clinton administration has expanded this approach, encouraging the building of institutions to promote democracy (a policy of the Reagan and Bush administrations), to contain racial, ethnic, and religious conflict, and to ensure accountability.

To the extent that the U.S. has become associated with telling the truth about conditions in countries, and with efforts to end abuses, it has won respect from those struggling to end repression. The Statue of Liberty model forged by Tiananmen Square demonstrators vividly expressed this attitude. There is another obvious benefit to U.S. human rights policies: tens and hundreds of thousands of victims of repression have been freed or have had their suffering reduced because of U.S. attention to their cases. Sadly, the opposite is also true: when American officials have been indifferent to repression abroad, or actively engaged in efforts to excuse or justify political killings, disappearances, or torture, resentment, alienation, and diminished respect and credibility for the United States have followed, abroad and at home. The result has often been more people killed, imprisoned, or tortured.

Multilateral Human Rights Policy

Building Human Rights Standards, Commitments, and Machinery. While U.S. human rights policy focuses on combating violations, United Nations human rights programs have emphasized standard setting and voluntary commitments by states to adopt and implement the norms. Only in the last fifteen years, and with great difficulty, has the world body developed machinery able to address violations; it remains very weak and under attack.

Eighteen years after the U.N. proclaimed the Universal Declaration of Human Rights in 1948, it agreed to give the declaration's rights binding legal status in two treaties, the International Covenant on Civil and Political Rights and the International Covenant on Economic, Social, and Cultural Rights. Other treaties have been adopted since then, but the member states have failed to establish effective means to implement or enforce these rights. In an early resolution member nations—including the Soviet Union and the United States alike—proclaimed the U.N. had no power to look into individual cases or situations of human rights abuse. For years, this rendered the United Nations Commission on Human Rights largely a talk shop for talented lawyers.[1]

At present, the U.N.'s human rights strategy focuses primarily on building a web of commitment: first, committing states to observe the norms in the many treaties by voluntarily signing them and thereafter committing the states to cooperate with the various treaty bodies, to adopt policies to implement the norms, and start educational projects to spread knowledge about them. In some cases, the U.N. aims to strengthen a state's capacity for commitment by offering "advisory services," a form of technical assistance advice including training by U.N. human rights staff or outside consultants on how to write human rights reports or how to construct institutions ranging from a law school, to a court system, or an emergency unit to combat "disappearances."

As this web of commitment is expanded, the acceptance of the universality of human rights standards could similarly expand, but only if such hands-on advisory services programs of the U.N. are effective, rather than cosmetic.

As nongovernmental human rights organizations have shown, people are protected from abuses as a result of heightened embarrassment over specific violations, directed against specific individuals, and not from vague expressions of concern over generic rights problems. Publicly issued reports on specific atrocities—torture, disappearances, political killings and massacres, among others— have enabled a number of governments, including the U.S., to forge consensus within the U.N. Commission on Human Rights itself to establish a confidential procedure (Resolution "1503") to look into documented complaints of violations (begun in the late 1960s), and later, to scrutinize gross violators in public.

The countries identified for public criticism by the Commission on Human Rights have commonly reflected the politics of the U.N. and its member states rather than independent judgments about the intensity of the abuses themselves on any absolute scale. Not surprisingly, the first special human rights investigative teams looking into violations were set up to examine South Africa (1967), Israel (1968), and Chile (1975). In the years that followed, the Commission on Human Rights, composed of government representa-

tives, would cite specific countries for their human rights abuses—
but only when the votes could be gathered. Early subjects of scrutiny were comparatively small countries, often reflecting the cold
war ideological divide, with each side sponsoring criticism of some
countries and shielding "their own." Thus after Chile came under
scrutiny and Argentina technically avoided it, three more rightist
authoritarian Latin American states were cited publicly: Guatemala (1980), El Salvador (1981), and Bolivia (1981). In response,
with great difficulty, the U.S. pressed the commission to add Po-
land (1982), Afghanistan (1984), and Iran (1984). In each case, a
single individual (alternatively called an "expert," "special representative," or "special rapporteur") was appointed to investigate
the facts and report back. A major U.S. led effort later focused on
obtaining criticism of Cuba, whose skill in the pyrotechnics of
U.N. procedures at first blunted specific criticism; eventually, U.S.
persistence resulted in the 1991 appointment of an investigator,
which has been renewed annually.

Abusive governments have continued to be the subject of special resolutions and machinery set up by the Commission on
Human Rights—but only when appropriate political support
could be mustered. Thus despite years of NGO reporting on
atrocities in Iraq, it was first cited for human rights abuses only *after*
the Gulf War, in 1991. Myanmar (Burma), Sudan, and Zaire came
up for public scrutiny in the 1990s after years of "consideration" in
confidential sessions under the "1503" procedure. Global televi-
sion news reports led the commission to hold the emergency sessions on former Yugoslavia (1992) and Rwanda (1994).

In the main, powerful countries have escaped scrutiny and criticism. None of the permanent five Security Council members has
been the subject of resolutions of the commission—with the exception of the mildest of chairperson's statements (based on consensus) regarding the Soviet Union's use of excessive force in the
Baltic republics (1991), and another statement on Chechnya (1995).
Efforts to censure China since the suppression of the 1989 democracy movement have not, to date, succeeded, although in 1995 the
United States achieved the first defeat of China's procedural
shield, a "no-action" motion, at the commission, and came within
one vote of winning censure. In 1995 Amnesty International iden-

tified five countries as priorities for commission consideration: Turkey, Indonesia, Colombia, Algeria, and India. Four of the five were commission members (Turkey having rotated off), and all have been beyond the reach of a public resolution, although Indonesia has been the subject of a consensus chairperson's statement on East Timor.

Precisely because of the difficulty of obtaining the votes necessary to criticize countries engaged in gross violations of human rights, major efforts have been made to establish effective U.N. human rights machinery able to examine and respond to violations independently, impartially, and wherever they occur. In the late 1970s the Commission on Human Rights established a regionally balanced, five-person Working Group on Forced or Involuntary Disappearances. Horrific reports of "disappearances" in Argentina prompted concern, but the inability to gather enough political support to name Argentina in a resolution led to the tactical decision to create a body capable of examining "disappearances" *everywhere*. This global approach turned out to be a strategically brilliant breakthrough that has already led to the creation of about ten similarly conceived "thematic mechanisms" consisting of one additional working group (on arbitrary detentions) and many single expert investigators or "special rapporteurs" (on summary executions, torture, religious intolerance, freedom of expression, violence against women, sale of children, independence of the judiciary, internally displaced, and contemporary forms of racism). Each of these is able to act urgently to inquire into individual cases of threatened or existing abuses, and to examine implementation of the right under scrutiny in countries throughout the world. Persons appointed to these bodies serve as independent experts, not as government representatives.

The Disappearances Working Group and other "thematic mechanisms" capitalize on the U.N.'s strength, which lies in its legitimacy as the premier global international institution, its ability to reach out or into virtually every society, and to establish norms applicable universally. They are able to look into human rights violations affecting individuals, to contact governments on an emergency basis, and to report their findings and recommendations publicly. Together, the complex web of thematic rapporteurs and working groups and country-specific rapporteurs represents the building blocks of a universal, impartial human rights program able to take action against abuses. Alongside them, helping to implement the norms, six separate committees of experts review and comment upon *every* state party's compliance with each of the U.N.'s principal human rights treaties.

Discrediting and Diminishing the Human Rights Machinery. Opposition to the U.N. being operationally active in combating violations through these instrumentalities has been intense: it has been directed both against the specific allegations of abuse and against the world body developing the capacity to investigate or respond to them. Commonly, the very countries that have been—or are likely to be—objects of scrutiny have made prodigious efforts to keep the human rights mechanisms and programs of the United Nations weak, distracted, and marginalized.

It is routine for a country accused of human rights violations to deny the charges. It will often challenge the U.N.'s competence to look into these matters—claiming protection from the U.N. Charter's article II, para. 7, which calls for noninterference in internal affairs. The next step is usually to deny that the specific violations have occurred at all or that, if they occurred, they were in fact violations. For example, Argentina and El Salvador used to argue that there were no "disappearances"—claiming individuals may have gone abroad seeking employment or to get away from their families. Other states, such as China and Iran, have denied that political killings or summary executions of demonstrators, political prisoners, or members of religious minorities are violations at all, citing national law or custom as justification for these acts. Like courtroom lawyers, those countries accused are quick to challenge the veracity of information and the intentions and bona fides of the witnesses—ranging from victims and their families, to local human rights defenders (who risk harassment, imprisonment, and death to collect the information in the first place), to international human rights organizations (who bring reports of abuses to the United Nations itself). The U.N.'s special rapporteur is called "biased" and the nations voting for a resolution are accused of "selectivity" and a lack of impartiality—i.e., refusal to treat everyone, violators and those who observe human rights, as equal. If a

special rapporteur is eventually appointed to examine alleged violations, accused governments often refuse to cooperate, denying
permission for the rapporteur's official visit to their country. In this
way, the investigator is denied both information and credibility.

The human rights secretariat of the U.N. is also kept weak so
that even if the commission or General Assembly censures a country for its human rights practices, U.N. personnel will be unable to
carry out investigations and report effectively. Despite a burgeon-
ing of U.N. treaty bodies, special procedures, and new mechanisms to address violations, the total U.N. staff assigned to all
human rights issues is considerably smaller than that of Amnesty
International in London alone. Following the 1993 World Conference on Human Rights, many of the temporary staff posts assigned in the past to "special procedures" and mechanisms dealing
with alleged violations were regularized in the U.N. budget. With
these included, a total of $18 million was allocated for 1995 for all
programs and activities and staffing of the Centre for Human
Rights for all countries in the world. (This includes additional
staffing to carry out the extensive program of action affirmed in
Vienna [$1.3 million], and the office of newly created High Com-
missioner for Human Rights [$1.2 million in total for his salary,
travel, two senior professional staff, and two assistants].) In all, just
over 1 percent of the total regular U.N. budget is assigned to
human rights activities. By comparison, the U.N. agreed to allocate $28 million in 1995 alone for the war crimes tribunal on
former Yugoslavia. The United States spent over $40 million on its
Iran-Contra investigation. Most country or thematic rapporteurs
have less than one full-time staff assistant assigned to help investigate, prepare and submit inquiries, and assist with their reports.

Governments seeking to dismantle, or at least diminish, the
U.N.'s capacity to address violations have been zealous in diver-
sionary agenda cluttering at the Commission on Human Rights,
which absorbs Human Rights Centre staff and resources year
round. Thus, for example, the human rights aspects of such issues
as development, housing, economic debt, scientific and technological innovations, sometimes addressed by entire other U.N. agencies, are routinely added to the agenda of the Commission on
Human Rights with requests for new reports, seminars, and other

activity. Without wishing to diminish the importance of these subjects, it is noteworthy that governments advancing their consideration tend to be the same as those that oppose mechanisms to respond to human rights violations.

Furthermore, marginalization and delegitimation of human rights within the U.N. system have been both physical and substantive. In 1973 the Secretariat staff and meeting site of the commission were moved permanently to Geneva, designed to get them away from the press, activist nongovernmental organizations, and the center of U.N. activity. Programmatically, human rights concerns have been pronounced out-of-bounds for U.N. development programs and for the Security Council (although both carry on some human rights related activities). Information on alleged violations is kept relatively inaccessible to the public and media.

Since governments make the decisions to create—or eliminate—human rights rapporteurs and other procedures at the Commission on Human Rights, the decisive issue when that body meets is to mobilize political support for one position or another. Violator countries compete for seats on the commission and to pack it with others like themselves. It is no accident that recent members included Iraq, Libya, Sudan, Syria, Indonesia, China, and Cuba. The U.S. has argued, so far to no avail, that states that run for election to the commission should meet certain rights related qualifications.

When the number of countries and mechanisms focused on violations began to grow, Cuba launched a successful initiative in 1990 to increase the membership of the Commission on Human Rights from forty-three to fifty-three, with the ten added members all from developing countries. Since resolutions for country rapporteurs continue to receive decisive majorities, Cuba, India, and others have begun to press vocally for a new rule requiring either a two-thirds majority or consensus on any country resolution.

There has also been a continuing, but increasingly concerted effort to restrict NGO representation, speeches, and access to proceedings. In addition, it is common for the states cited by the U.N. to threaten to remove U.N. accreditation from the international human rights organizations that have been most effective in bringing cases of abuse to the attention of the world body.

Despite the General Assembly's decision that formulating concrete recommendations to improve the effectiveness of U.N.
mechanisms and activities in human rights was one of the objectives of the June 1993 World Conference, the subject got short
shrift there: one brief and grudging call to strengthen the "thematic mechanisms" and special rapporteurs and to hold periodic
meetings to "harmonize and rationalize their work." And like so
many words used in U.N. documents, even this has two meanings:
a) genuine rationalization, which everyone favors; b) official sanc-
tion for cutting back the thematic mechanisms.

Many of the "rejectionist" violator states have been among the
most vocal in advancing the argument that human rights are not
universal, and that regional and national "particularities" should
predominate. Although this view was rejected in Vienna, the argument continues to be advanced vigorously as a further challenge to
the findings and decisions of the special mechanisms set up by the
Commission on Human Rights.

As a universal, multilateral body the United Nations has the
unique capacity to be global in its examination and reporting on
compliance with all human rights. Its assessments can be authoritative. But its credibility will rest upon the accuracy, independence, and objectivity of its analysis. Because the principal human
rights bodies are made up of governments, whose delegates are
instructed when it comes to votes on the practices of specific countries, it must be a principal strategic aim to develop human rights
fact-finding and implementation instrumentalities and mechanisms in the U.N. that are independent of governments. In view
of the weakness and political susceptibility of U.N. Secretariat personnel, it has become regular practice to appoint (or nominate for
election) independent outside experts to carry out the U.N.'s fact
finding into violations, and to serve on specialized implementation
bodies for assessing compliance with treaties and other norms.

Confronted with so many obstacles, it is no wonder that U.N.
staff have found it easier to emphasize human rights programs that
focus on expanding voluntary commitments by states rather than
programs aimed at exposing violations or establishing sanctions.
But a "voluntary compliance" approach alone is morally indefen-

sible for the U.N., ineffective unless linked to independent assess-ments of human rights performance, and out of step with the urgent needs of preventive diplomacy in the post–cold war era. Moreover, a cooperation-only approach would be politically un-tenable vis-à-vis most donor states, and particularly so for the U.S., which has been the world's leader in showing that public exposure of human rights violations and the threat of sanctions are an effective foreign policy tool that can diminish human rights violations.

Priority Objectives for U.S. Human Rights Policy through the U.N.

A significant burden will fall to the U.S., as a leading power and leader in linking human rights to international relations, to mar-shall substantial, sustained support for the development of a more effective, independent capacity at the U.N. to report on human rights violations as the core of a human rights program aimed at combating such abuses.

Three elements–1) strengthening universality; 2) preventing gross abuses of human rights; and 3) establishing an effective emer-gency response system to combat gross violations—emerge as the priority objectives for the U.S. to strengthen the human rights bodies and instrumentalities of the United Nations in the coming years. Intensified U.S. engagement in U.N. human rights bodies, demonstrating strategic and intellectual leadership accompanied by sustained financial support, will prove decisive in achieving these goals. Strengthening the special rapporteurs, and more im-portantly, the High Commissioner for Human Rights, must be the American tactical focus.

Strengthening the Universality of Human Rights

One of the strongest attacks on the U.N.'s human rights mech-anisms focused on violations has revolved around the question whether human rights norms are universal in scope and applica-bility or whether regional differences or "particularities" such as culture, tradition, religion, or history render some of the concepts invalid for non-Western regions. This argument intensified just prior to the 1993 World Conference on Human Rights. It is vital for the United States to remain actively engaged in defending universality, first, because it is central to efforts to hold governments to account for their actions, and secondly, because the U.N.'s comparative advantage as an institution engaged in human rights matters lies precisely in its authority and global reach, and in its capacity to speak as the sole universal intergovernmental body.

In fact, those who argued in favor of "particularities" at the Vienna World Conference also gave lip service to the universality of human rights in their speeches, noting that the rights are accepted by the international community. Iran, for example, stated human rights are "inherent in human beings . . . [and] cannot be subject to cultural relativism."[2] Indonesia, speaking as chair of the nonaligned movement, cited "our shared view on the universal validity of basic human rights." The essence of the quarrel lies elsewhere:

1) with the idea that any body—whether an international organization, a country or a group of countries, or a private monitoring association—can decide about these matters in place of a national government, or insist on "compliance" rather than voluntary "cooperation";

2) with the identification of any one set of rights, or any specific right, as preeminent over any others, and with an emphasis on the rights of individuals rather than the interests of the community or state;

3) with the objectivity, impartiality, and bona fides of those who demand international compliance with human rights norms.

This advocacy of "particularity" contains a distinct overlay of the postcolonial drive toward cultural independence and autonomy; an anti-Western and anti-American fury is palpable. Yet these positions echo old, familiar arguments concerning:

1) the principle of national sovereignty, and noninterference in internal affairs of states;

2) the preeminence of economic and social rights over civil and political rights, and of the interests of the state over those of the individual; and

3) the selective, political misuse of human rights and of the international machinery of human rights to subjugate other states.

Iran has charged, for example, that those Western states that advocate human rights—whose political predominance is "temporary"—possess neither "admirable pasts" nor "consistency" in their own behavior regarding human rights worldwide. Indonesia's foreign minister, using an ironic metaphor, proclaimed to the world conference that "no country or group of countries" can be "judge, jury and executioner over other countries" by demanding compliance (rather than cooperation) with particular human rights norms.

Such vocal Third World challenges to the universality of human rights have emerged since the collapse of the Soviet Union, which had long propounded them. During the cold war, Western countries commonly confronted those positions by affirming the preeminence of civil and political rights on the grounds that they could be immediately implemented and were a basis for economic development. Economic and social rights, they noted, could only be implemented gradually, as financing and other tangible resources permitted. The Reagan and Bush administrations further polarized the arguments by insisting that the economic and social rights affirmed in the Universal Declaration of Human Rights and later in the Covenants are not rights at all but merely goals or social policies. They explained that rights may only *limit* state action, and cannot *establish* international *entitlements*.

During the 1980s an understanding was reached in U.N. human rights forums wherein governments declared that all human rights are indivisible and interrelated (and occasionally, "interdependent") and that "the promotion and protection of one category of rights should never exempt or excuse states from the promotion or protection of the other." Yet despite this verbal consensus that the two categories of rights were related, intense United States opposition to economic and social rights—often displayed in lone "negative" votes on resolutions affirming the indivisibility and interdependence of the two sets of rights—sent a clear message that the U.S. (and the industrialized North) was indifferent, if not openly hostile, to economic development needs of impoverished Third World countries. This created a further polarization between North and South that human rights violator countries were able to exploit successfully in U.N. human rights forums.

At the World Conference on Human Rights, universality was defended by the U.N. secretary-general, and affirmed by representatives of 171 countries, spurred on by thousands of NGO representatives from all world regions, and by an active presence of international media. Boutros Boutros-Ghali and others who supported universality pointed out that the human rights instruments were adopted by consensus, and the norms widely accepted, many as customary international law. Others affirming universality sounded many of the points in Secretary of State Warren Christopher's speech, recalling that none of the world's faiths or cultures tolerates torture, rape, racism, antisemitism, or arbitrary detention, and that none of these abuses can be justified by the demands of development or political expediency. The real chasm, Christopher stated, "lies between the cynical excuses of oppressive regimes and the sincere aspirations of their people."

Vocal, visible support for this view came from nongovernmental organizations from the same countries that defend "particularity." These NGO representatives firmly insisted that human rights were universal and rooted in the cultural, historical, religious, and legal traditions of their societies. They called upon all assembled governments to take strong action to stop violations of human rights. They expressed impatience with arguments about "particularities" from the very governments committing atrocious abuses of human rights.

Ultimately the World Conference affirmed universality by stating:

All human rights are universal, indivisible and interdependent and inter-related. The international community must treat human rights globally in a fair and equal manner, on the same footing and with the same emphasis. While the significance of national and regional particularities and various historical, cultural and religious backgrounds must be borne in mind, it is the duty of states, regardless of their political, economic and cultural systems, to promote and protect all human rights and fundamental freedoms.

With this reaffirmation of the universal applicability of *all* human rights standards, the U.S. once again stated that it recognized economic and social rights *as rights*. In this way, the Clinton administration indicated its commitment to work together with all nations of the world to strengthen respect for all human rights and to develop democratic institutions essential to sustainable economic development. It also stressed that the U.S. remains committed to the fundamental principle of the unmistakable importance of individual rights, and the centrality of civil and political rights in establishing a democratic participatory political setting in which other rights can be pursued.

The United States can best respond to challenges to universality not only by reaffirming it, as Secretary Christopher did in Vienna, but also by taking the offensive in exposing the cynicism of the arguments of the proponents of particularity. For example, in response to the three underlying complaints of the proparticularity countries, the U.S. should take firm and constructive stands.

1) To claims that "noninterference in internal affairs" shields countries from scrutiny, the United States should recall and continue to seek explicit confirmation, as it accomplished in Vienna, that human rights monitoring is a legitimate concern of the international community. It should also take political and financial measures to ensure such monitoring occurs, is professional, and widespread.

2) To those questioning the alleged "imposition" of one set of rights, the U.S. should take an active role in helping define how the rights are in fact interrelated, and stressing the importance of the case, or individual approach to these matters.

3) To those challenging U.S. bona fides, more active U.S. engagement on the points raised above and vigorous followthrough to identify gross violators will speak for itself. Ratification of international human rights treaties would not only send a positive

signal about U.S. intentions but would also provide an avenue for authoritative involvement in the definition and interpretation of the treaty norms.

The United States must avoid establishing itself as hostile to bona fide economic and social rights issues by becoming the sole opponent of them. The World Conference demonstrated that U.S. participation in the definition of these issues is productive: U.S. verbal acceptance of economic and social rights and the right to development created an atmosphere that enabled affirmation of universality; it also brought about universal acceptance that a country's level of development can never be used as an excuse for failing to protect human rights, and that "priority be given to action to promote democracy, development, and human rights" as well as to building human rights institutions and strengthening pluralistic civil society.

Using the opposite tactics—opposing economic and social rights altogether—the U.S. actually helps promote the solidarity of all Third World states against the U.S. on these issues, and, in turn, in favor of those arguing for "particularity."

In the future, the U.S. needs to distinguish two distinct aspects of the issue: 1) the applicability and acceptance of the norms in the Universal Declaration of Human Rights and the Covenants and 2) the means by which norms are implemented and the laws and institutions are established to give them effect. It is widely acknowledged, even in the Vienna Declaration, that the norms are indeed universally applicable and must be upheld. On the other hand, the international community has no single prescription for the means by which countries are to implement these standards: neither the laws adopted nor the institutions created need to conform to a single internationally mandated model. On the contrary, the various treaty committees and other U.N. bodies charged with monitoring implementation have demonstrated a very broad approach to these questions and a genuine openness to national decisions as to the specific means by which the norms will be implemented. Indeed, those monitoring compliance readily recognize that for issues other than physical integrity of the person (right to be free from torture, arbitrary executions, etc.), history, culture, and religious tradition may shape the precise laws and institutions set up to implement the rights nationally. But as the Vienna Declaration affirmed, none of the details of institutional tinkering excuses the duty of a state to uphold the norms and standards of international human rights instruments.

Treaty Ratification

Universality will be strengthened by U.S. support—and that of other nations—for the Vienna Declaration's call for universal ratification of the principal human rights treaties by the year 2000. While some 120 to 150 nations subscribe to the principal treaties, several major countries and an unusually large number of the same Asian states who most vocally challenge universality (including China, Indonesia, Malaysia, and Pakistan) are not parties to the principal human rights treaties. In the last decade, the U.S. has itself finally ratified four of the major treaties, Genocide, Torture, the Civil and Political Covenant, and the Racial Discrimination Convention, and has signed the Rights of the Child Convention. A 1994 effort to ratify the Convention on the Elimination of Discrimination Against Women failed to reach the floor of the U.S. Senate.

America's formal ratification of these treaties not only strengthens initiatives aimed at universal ratification, but also adds greatly to the credibility—the bona fides—of the U.S. as an actor in U.N. human rights bodies where universality is under attack. U.S. leadership in demanding that the U.N. censure gross violator states such as Iraq, Iran, China, or Cuba was often (unsuccessfully) parried by the argument that the U.S. itself was using a double standard, as it had not ratified the treaties it used to criticize others. U.S. ratification also opens the door to participation of American experts on the committees that monitor compliance with the human rights treaties and further define the obligations entailed by the standards themselves. Only parties to the treaties can nominate experts to serve on these supervisory committees. By its non-ratification, the U.S. has closed itself out of this important process, eliminating any U.S. perspective on how to uphold and implement the universal norms and the requirements for fulfilling them.

Additionally, universality will be strengthened to the extent that reservations attached to the treaty norms are kept to an absolute minimum and/or withdrawn. The U.S. attached extensive reservations, understandings, and declarations to the treaties it signed largely to overcome political objections to ratification by the U.S. Senate. To a considerable degree these limitations undercut U.S. interests in affirming universality precisely because they restrict the applicability of the treaties and their relationship to domestic law and appear to question the universal application of the norms themselves. The U.S. should express concern about broad reservations attached by other treaty signatories, and will need to look closely at its own reservations to explore means of narrowing or even withdrawing some of them.

In ratifying the covenant, the U.S. did not commit itself to do anything that would require any change in current American law or practice, at either the state or federal level. Additionally, the U.S. has declared the substantive provisions of the covenant are "not self-executing," and would require implementation by separate laws adopted by the Congress and state legislatures to give them effect—whether or not existing constitutional or other legislative provisions already render them effective and whether or not it is constitutionally necessary to require special laws. By insisting on such exceptions, the U.S. appears to affirm that national law (and even state law) may predominate over universal international law. Yet in most matters affecting human rights practices by other countries, the U.S. rejects similar arguments about the relevance of national law or practice over international. The U.S. must establish a means of involving state officials in a systematic review of state laws to ensure they too conform to international standards.

In its General Comment on reservations to the International Covenant on Civil and Political Rights, the Human Rights Committee, the most highly regarded of the bodies that monitor compliance with U.N. human rights treaties, indicates that sweeping reservations are harmful to the treaty regime:

Of particular concern are widely formulated reservations, which essentially render ineffective all Covenant rights which would require any change in national law to ensure compliance with Covenant obligation.

No real international rights or obligations have thus been accepted. . . . So that reservations do not lead to a perpetual non-attainment of international human rights standards, reservations should not systematically reduce the obligation undertaken only to those presently existing in less demanding standards of domestic law.

Definition and Analysis of Rights. The U.S. should try to play a leading role in further interpretation and analysis of those rights in the International Covenant on Civil and Political Rights. Additionally, the United States could help shape international understanding of universality by becoming engaged in the now quite active intellectual analysis and development of guidelines for implementation of economic and social rights, and the controversial right to development, and their interrelationship with civil and political rights that define the playing field on which to seek access to these rights. The Vienna Declaration and Programme of Action reiterated that the right to development (first proclaimed by the General Assembly in 1986 by a vote of 146-1-8, with the U.S. casting the sole negative vote) is "inalienable," "universal," and "an integral part" of human rights. It emphasized, in particular, the close relationship among democracy, development, and human rights and recalled that the human person is the central subject of development. The Vienna Declaration cautioned—for the first time—that the level of development may never be used as an excuse for the abridgement of human rights.

A fifteen-member expert working group was created by the Commission on Human Rights after the World Conference to identify obstacles to implementing the declaration on the right to development. There is no American member, and one can hardly expect the three Western group members (Australia, France, and Finland) to take the initiative in clarifying the intellectual content to the right to development or to succeed in keeping attention focused on human rights and the human person as the central subject of development, rather than on "global economic policy."

The right to development, accused correctly of being "intellectually amorphous," needs sustained intellectual attention, to assess ways that the centrality of the individual in development can be advanced, and explore how effective development policies at the national level can be formulated that underscore the importance of individual participation in democratic governance regarding all decisions, including those about development. The U.S. and like-minded states will want to rally intellectual analysis and leadership to ensure that the right to development is analyzed in terms of its components—the specific rights of the two covenants—and not in terms of political criteria such as the desire for debt relief, international financial transfers or entitlements, or reform of structural adjustment programs required by international financial institutions. To do this effectively may require the U.S. to become more directly engaged in this issue, serving on the working group alongside Cuba and Malaysia, among others.

The eighteen-member Committee on Economic, Social, and Cultural Rights reviews country reports regarding observance of the treaty and issues General Comments on the meaning of the covenant, modeled on those by the Human Rights Committee (which supervises the Civil and Political Covenant). General Comment No. 2 (1990)—hereafter "GC-2"—offers an excellent example of how creative engagement in defining both substantive issues and working methods of the committee can lead the U.N. human rights program to enter other areas of U.N. activity from which human rights considerations had been barred. GC-2 draws attention to the obscure article 22 of the covenant, and argues that this authorizes the committee to recommend country-specific policy suggestions arising from the country reports that the committee reviews to "virtually all UN organs and agencies involved in any aspect of international development cooperation," mentioning by name UNDP, UNICEF, the World Bank, ILO, WHO, as well as the Commission on the Status of Women. The committee argues that since the two sets of rights are interdependent, development agencies should "scrupulously avoid involvement in projects which, for example, involve the use of forced labour in contravention of international standards, or promote or reinforce discrimination against individuals or groups . . . or involve large-scale displacement of persons. . . ." It calls for integration of human rights concerns into development and for human rights impact statements as part of development projects. Following these suggestions would offer the U.S. an opportunity to advance U.S. interests in sustainable development, good governance, democracy, and human rights. Core human rights issues such as promoting women's rights and/or combating discrimination against ethnic minorities have a substantial base in both sets of rights. Rather than deny their validity, the U.S. can help shape understanding of their interrelationship.

Preventing Gross Abuses of Human Rights

Preventing gross abuses requires the capacity to know what is happening and to analyze it properly to identify probable behavior, and the ability of leaders and institutions to respond to channel the grievances in ways that are more likely to reduce violent conflict.

To achieve this, the U.N. must be able to collect key information in a timely manner, analyze and review it regularly, and draw it to the attention of those bodies and officials able to take early action. Earlier, I described how the U.N. has established factfinding and reporting mechanisms through "special rapporteurs" and thematic mechanisms—and the opposition that has kept these instrumentalities weak. The U.S. must also focus attention on building better technical assistance programing in human rights by strengthening the analytic, organizational, and operational planning component of the U.N. Centre for Human Rights that engages in technical assistance in human rights, so that it can be the intellectual (rather than operational) center for U.N. activities encouraging the integration of human rights perspectives into U.N. development programs, as well as peacemaking (conflict resolution) and peacekeeping.

Technical Assistance in Human Rights

Establishing voluntary nationally based programs of technical assistance would seem, in theory, to be the area in which the United Nations, because of its global reach and legitimacy, would have a comparative advantage over any United States bilateral program for ensuring the *universal* implementation of human rights, a major aim of U.S. human rights policy. The U.N. is broadly engaged in technical assistance programs in fields ranging from economic development to health care to election assistance and monitoring. Such programs are particularly important because they can bring the words and principles adopted in meeting halls in New York and Geneva to life in specific national contexts, and may actually assist individuals at risk.

U.S. human rights policy emphasizes the building of democratic institutions such as human rights commissions, human rights verification and monitoring projects (for example, as part of peacekeeping or "postconflict peacebuilding" programs authorized by the Security Council), which may include independent court systems and, where appropriate, "truth commissions" or international criminal tribunals. The U.S. Draft Action Plan prepared prior to the June 1993 World Conference on Human Rights identified the strengthening of U.N. advisory services in human rights as second in priority only to creation of the high commissioner's post. In particular, it called for development of expertise on the administration of justice and rule of law, national institutions supporting democracy, human rights education, including the training of law enforcement and judicial officials. To accomplish this, the Draft Action Plan proposed that human rights be integrated with all U.N. development, humanitarian, conflict resolution, peacekeeping, election monitoring, and related programs.[3] To make this plan a reality throughout the U.N. will require substantial U.S. engagement, financial support, and political persistence. It is worth the effort involved.

The U.N. clearly has great potential to expand its technical assistance into the field of human rights institution building and a special legitimacy in so doing that derives from its universal membership. The need for better system-wide coordination of human rights with development, peacekeeping, and humanitarian programs is urgent.

The integration of a human rights perspective and programing into the work of other U.N. agencies, and particularly those engaged in operational activities, is not a task that can be accomplished overnight. At present, the Centre for Human Rights, the lead Secretariat agency responsible for human rights programs, is neither well structured, professionally staffed, nor even remotely well enough financed to carry out large operational "advisory services" programs in human rights. The Centre for Human Rights has no field orientation and little operational field experience. However, the centre is the lead U.N. agency engaged in defining human rights standards, reviewing country implementation (particularly through the reporting to treaty bodies), and identifying gross abuses and violations (through the rapporteurs). Without having to conduct operations itself, the centre could play a leadership role within the United Nations in identifying and elaborating upon the standards that need to be implemented and strengthened through technical assistance programs, and providing guidance and training to other U.N. agencies about what constitutes appropriate human rights technical assistance. Because they know what the norms are and can assess human rights implementation on the national level in each relevant country, the centre can provide key assistance in identifying appropriate targets of opportunity and means to provide human rights technical assistance, and to develop standard operating procedures for political troubleshooters, peacekeepers, and humanitarian aid workers. Both military and civilian peacekeepers need to learn how to monitor and report on human rights violations that occur before their eyes, how to provide a protective presence against added violations, and how to press local officials for corrective action.

Unfortunately, the other U.N. agencies that have experimented with addressing human rights issues—in peacekeeping, humanitarian assistance, UNDP projects, and political analysis and early warning, as well as the lawyers and politicians constructing the U.N.'s two new ad hoc criminal courts—have carried out their activities with only the most pro forma acknowledgement to the centre or contact with its staff. This stems from institutional and financial jealousies, one-upmanship, concern over operational field competence, and a deep-seated sense that the centre is politically stigmatized, and thus not a desirable public partner in such assistance projects.

It is still politically premature to establish an ongoing formal interrelationship between U.N. development programs and those advancing human rights. Indeed, the resistance of Third World governments to human rights concerns as a factor in the organization's development work remains very strong. Only a few years

ago, the U.N.'s own system-wide in-depth evaluation of the
human rights program suggested that the Centre for Human
Rights advise on UNDP country projects involving human rights
(e.g., human rights education, university law school development
and training, drafting texts, etc.) by communicating through
UNDP resident representatives. This recommendation provoked
such controversy that the evaluation was not formally endorsed by
the Economic and Social Council. And, in 1991, when the
UNDP's *Human Development Report* included a Human Freedom
Index, the Third World reaction was so intense as to launch formal instructions to forbid mention or inclusion of the subject ever
again. Despite refinement in the index's methodology (including a
name change to the "Political Freedom Index") and promises to
consult before evaluating countries, the Group of 77 made it clear
to a February 1992 special session of UNDP's Governing Council
that Third World governments rejected inclusion of such an index
or ranking in any future studies. Among the Group of 77's principal concerns was the likelihood that the index—and a country's
human rights performance—would be used to condition aid. Indeed, the issue of aid conditionality (and even "unilateral coercive
measures," the term Cuba uses to describe U.S. sanctions) has
been denounced by U.N. human rights bodies. At the World Conference, the Vienna Declaration stated specifically that ". . . the
promotion and protection of human rights and fundamental freedoms at the national and international levels should be universal
and conducted without conditions attached."

Despite some positive developments such as the cooperation of
many newly democratic states in UNDP programing addressing
core human rights and electoral issues, opposition to integration
remains a political priority for most Third World states. This view,
in turn, reinforces further efforts to marginalize the Human Rights
Centre and delegitimize its programs and personnel.

In considering how the U.S. can effectively promote a linkage of
human rights and technical assistance, it is essential to reiterate
that conditionality remains a particularly powerful tool in promoting human rights compliance. Faced with such intense Third
World political opposition to it, several polar approaches immediately suggest themselves: the U.S. could resign itself to the aban-

donment of conditionality within the U.N. altogether.

Alternatively, and particularly in the case of gross violators, the U.S. could insist that conditionality and sanctions be triggered automatically after receipt of certain information on repeated action by the U.N. Commission on Human Rights or reports from its special rapporteurs. The U.S. could even try to organize a donors' boycott in order to persuade receiving countries to accept human rights conditionality. Doing so would no doubt be effective in the short term, but runs the risk of further exacerbating the anti-Western resentments that have triggered so many of the problems for U.N. human rights programs. Another approach, more effective in the short run, would be to work quietly, but firmly, to achieve the same thing through a select number of U.N. organizations and international banks—such as the UNDP and the World Bank—that have already shown a growing receptivity to the need to promote good governance and to explore linkages of human rights to their own lending programs and projects. Already there is a great deal of human rights activity, for example, in UNDP programs in Central America and some in the newly independent states. Such an "actions speak louder than words" (or resolutions) approach would strive to break down the U.N.'s political barriers to integrating human rights into development for those states that agree to it, for whatever reason. The U.S. should actively support projects through voluntary funds, specialized agencies, and multilateral banks that can be targeted specifically to stopping or preventing violations in particular countries. These programs also offer an opportunity to engage U.N. agencies in building democratic institutions of accountability in countries where the U.S. cannot go on a bilateral basis, or cannot go alone for political reasons.

Until now, U.N. advisory services in human rights have been channeled exclusively to and through government agencies—and not to and through nongovernmental groups that can help build and strengthen civil society and rule of law. The U.S. should support involvement of NGOs in receiving and conducting human rights voluntary assistance programs that are preventive.

For the U.S. to encourage the U.N. to develop its capacity to provide human rights technical assistance, it must also begin to

provide substantial "in-kind" contributions of expert personnel to
design and evaluate programs and possibilities, and must make
sizable voluntary contributions. The capacity to design and engage in these programs cannot be attained without substantial
funding allocated for it, and considerable concentration of talent
and attention. The U.N. Centre for Human Rights lacks such
skills at present, and it will take considerable time and substantial
resources to build its capacity. The nonearmarked U.S. contribution of over $1 million in 1995 to the U.N. voluntary fund for
technical services was an excellent first step, but the U.S. will need
to undertake far more targeted support, and efforts to encourage
joint support from other donor countries, if it is to establish the
operational technical capacity to organize and carry out technical
assistance in human rights.

Human Rights, Conflict Resolution, Peacekeeping, and the International Criminal Courts

The focus of most international emissaries and teams sent by the
U.N. to "do something" about conflicts is to find ways to contain
the conflict (by ceasefires, troop withdrawals, sending in traditional peacekeeping forces) rather than to resolve the issues at the
heart of the conflict. To have more effective conflict prevention
and resolution, there must be a much more serious and sustained
effort to address the core issues of the conflicts, in particular the
sense of injustice that fuels them. "Human rights" and means for
protecting these rights must be factored into conflict resolution
design, procedures, outcomes, and follow-up. As the Organization
for Security and Cooperation in Europe (OSCE) High Commissioner for National Minorities Max van der Stoel has pointed out,
"Even if violence has come to an end, very often the underlying
causes which led to the conflict have not been removed. . . . renewed armed clashes are not unlikely."[4]

United States experience in institutionalizing attentiveness to
human rights in the State Department and embassies worldwide
gives America both special expertise and operational perspective
in how to integrate human rights concerns more broadly into
United Nations policy. And as a permanent member of the Secu-

rity Council, the U.S. has the access and power to exercise leadership that will shape the integration of human rights into the work of the U.N.'s political operations.

The U.N. Department of Political Affairs needs to ensure that human rights is a central element in its efforts to provide early warning of conflicts, and strategies for resolution of disputes. The U.N.'s Peacekeeping Department will need more than the capacity to integrate human rights factors into its analysis; it must integrate human rights behavior into the operational presence of military and civilian personnel. At present, the capacity to do either of these is very limited and is commonly created without—or despite—the findings and expertise of the Centre for Human Rights.

Approaches to conflict prevention and resolution devised in the U.N. Department of Political Affairs are rarely based on any overarching human rights concept or realization of specific human rights standards. Instead, analysts and negotiators commonly claim either that the issues are not relevant to the disputes fomenting violence and instability, or that they have "intuitively" factored in human rights. Too often in post–cold war negotiations and preventive actions addressing conflicts, the fact finders, negotiators, and conflict resolvers simply lack awareness of what the relevant human rights standards actually are and what means of human rights implementation have been employed in similar circumstances. Those engaged in early warning conflict prevention missions too often conduct their fact finding in the field without the benefit of expertise as to the political, historical, or cultural background to the conflict, and, what is more, without expertise about how to investigate or document discrimination or the violation of other human rights. Rarely do members of official teams of the U.N. or other international agencies have any specialized legal or medical-forensic skills that nongovernmental organizations often bring when they examine an ethnic conflict situation that has already erupted in violence.

Sometimes, negotiators claim that they cannot address human rights concerns because these are the "grievances" of one party against another, and that they cannot conduct fact finding or make the results public—because this would transform the negotiator's role into one that is "judgmental," forestalling any prospect of reaching a solution to the dispute. They declare that they must be impartial. Yet impartiality should not mean indifference or even neutrality—not toward such fundamental U.N. principles as those of nondiscrimination and respect for universally accepted human rights. Yet too often, that is precisely what they mean.

Clearly, a capacity to consider such human rights grievances must underpin and imbue diplomatic negotiations that the U.N. engages in—so that the outcome comports with human rights principles. Otherwise, U.N. special envoys and negotiators run the risk of fashioning agreements devoid of basic human rights principles (i.e., based on whatever agreement one can reach), or that do not address the underlying causes of the dispute. The resultant agreement may result in a temporary "peace" and may bring some toleration of a minority group involved in a conflict. However, its implementation remains essentially subject to the whims of the current leaders of the state concerned. Unless an outcome of such negotiations establishes or explicitly reaffirms fundamental rights, an aggrieved minority will live with the anxiety that its negotiated solution might be easily bartered away again. While such solutions may curtail violent conflict for the moment, they lack staying power.

Investigating and reporting the facts accurately, independently, and in a timely fashion are critical to the process of conflict prevention: aggrieved groups seek the confidence to know that their grievances are heard, their problems examined, and, whenever possible, that those responsible acknowledge it.

Remedy, compensation, and accountability are crucial parts of conflict resolution and reconciliation. By burying, ignoring, or diminishing them, negotiators undermine the very processes they seek to succeed in. The international criminal tribunals established by the Security Council for former Yugoslavia and Rwanda will play an important role after conflicts, when human rights abuses have not been combated or prevented. The ability of the international community to prosecute those responsible for heinous war crimes and human rights abuses can have both a preventive role and a role in the reconciliation of societies, identifying clearly that individuals—not ethnic groups or "states"—are responsible for their own actions when they constitute atrocious violations of humanitarian and human rights law. Continuing to support such tribunals will offer a major opportunity in future conflict resolution efforts of the U.N.

Peacekeeping has become more complex than the mere interposition of lightly armed peacekeepers between two opposing armies along a "green line." For example, the Yugoslav conflicts have brought a whole new array of skills to U.N. peacekeepers: the ability to move from observation/interposition (traditional peacekeeping), to escorting humanitarian aid during conflict, to implementation of no-fly zones, safe areas, and cooperation with the European Union, NATO, and others. The pace of change has been stunning for the U.N. (which has not welcomed it) but the performance of these tasks has shown severe problems as well, and has been seriously limited in almost every instance by the preference of U.N. civil and military officials to utilize traditional Chapter VI approaches to the implementation, regardless of the Security Council's instructions.

Key operational lessons from U.N. engagement in the former Yugoslavia are to act earlier rather than later; to establish U.N. physical and moral authority—on the ground—early and firmly; and to follow up on threats when U.N. ultimata are openly flaunted. The U.N. performance in former Yugoslavia—exemplified, on the one hand, by the image of the lone Serb with a clipboard holding up U.N. convoys one by one or, on the other, by U.N. commanders explaining yet again that the organization's mandate won't permit the use of force to protect people from atrocities occurring in front of the peacekeepers—suggests strongly that without major reform of procedures and policies, inside and out, the collective security organization created in 1945 with great hopes cannot address the complex internal conflicts of the post–cold war era.

The U.S. can play a leadership role by pressing, and helping the organization to build up an internal capacity to address such conflicts fully and effectively: for example, developing standard operating procedures that require U.N. forces to be more than silent or indifferent witnesses to atrocities that occur around them and that call for a truly impartial and properly trained force that upholds the principles of international law and humanitarian norms that the Security Council repeatedly affirms. Some U.N. peacekeeping programs have included separate human rights components, primarily for the postconflict phase, as in El Salvador. Such components have had the capacity to monitor, actively investigate, seek corrective action, and report upon allegations of human rights abuses.

Other U.N. peacekeeping operations have concentrated, with mixed results, on beginning the process of rebuilding institutions in the postconflict stage. Whether this should be a part of a peacekeeping project or an auxiliary U.N. agency project remains controversial. But it is clear that in both preconflict and postconflict stages of ethnic and other severe disputes, the United Nations can and must encourage the establishment of human rights protection institutions as part of this process: ombudsmen, national human rights commissions, international courts or tribunals. The United States can and must provide the leadership, and often the technical assistance and financing, to see that such human rights institutions and issues are part of the U.N.'s reforms and new approaches to early warning and early action. The U.N. clearly needs a much more rich and complete policy formulation and analysis capacity than it presently has, an internal command and control system with depth and rapid response capabilities including a capacity to provide protective presence, when needed, and greater accountability for its actions.

The extraordinary leadership role played by the United States in the establishment of the war crimes tribunal for former Yugoslavia demonstrates that it is possible, in some circumstances, for the United Nations to do the impossible. It takes effort and determination by the leading states, and particularly by the U.S.

Combating Serious Violations of Human Rights

The U.N. has codified and reaffirmed the universality of the human rights standards it has adopted and aims to commit states to affirm, enact, ensure, educate, and engage experts to advance human rights. The overriding U.S. priority for the U.N., which also reinforces American human rights policy, remains to enhance the capacity of U.N. human rights bodies and mechanisms to examine, report, and take action to stop egregious human rights violations. And, despite the fact that the U.N.'s human rights mechanisms are still weak in this area, U.S. policy should remain focused on enhancing U.N. capacity to report on and combat human rights violations as a top, long-term priority.

To the extent that U.N. mechanisms for responding to serious violations are strengthened, these human rights entities would provide a means for advancing U.S. interests, with the added benefit of demonstrating global approval and offering cost and responsibility sharing. As described earlier, the U.N.'s special thematic and country-specific rapporteur and working groups have been the main agents of the U.N.'s activities aimed at responding to violations. They are also the primary building blocks of a reporting system that is the first element of early warning.

The Thematic Mechanisms and Special Rapporteurs

The credibility of any international protection mechanism depends, of course, on its independence of governments, professional competence, and universality of focus. But its effectiveness also depends upon its ability to find and evaluate facts quickly as well as fairly, make its findings known (to the victims, members of the U.N. body or other institution, the public, and/or offending governments), and recommend measures to alleviate the abuse, and, indeed, to follow up. As to whether such instrumentalities should also be able to bring relief in individual cases or conduct general human rights investigations, only a few mechanisms have the flexibility to undertake whichever they feel is most warranted in the circumstances. Ultimately, human rights victims look to the international protection mechanisms for *prompt* and effective protection, not years of procedural and political wrangling. Thus the ability to initiate a prompt investigation, perhaps on-site, and not merely react to incoming data, is another means of enhancing a mechanism's capacity to stop violations. Similarly, the ability to intercede speedily with relevant authorities and without excessive formality can save lives and prevent abuses.

While the U.N.'s early years of sloth and indecision about establishing and using protection mechanisms are now behind us, there remain a significant number of governments that prefer to im-mobilize any greater activism, as described earlier.

The special rapporteurs and members of thematic working groups at the U.N. have now held two meetings to assess their methods of work and future needs. Where there were only four such mechanisms dealing with countries or thematic issues in 1980, there were thirteen in 1990, and the post–cold war, post–World Conference atmosphere has brought about their expansion in many directions, to a total of twenty-six in 1995. At these meetings, the individuals who carry out this work, without honorarium or adequate staff, have identified a number of problems hampering their effectiveness. The United States should focus, as its top operational priority for U.N. human rights programs, on strengthening these fact-finding and reporting mechanisms. An effective operational structure for integrating human rights factors in development, peacemaking, and peacekeeping is dependent, first and foremost, on the enhanced capacity of these procedures. Priority concerns to strengthen the rapporteurs and thematic mechanisms must include:

- better U.N. receipt and handling of the information upon which all their inquiries and interventions with governments are based, including greater speed and assuring that an ongoing dialogue occurs with the sources of the information, to better ascertain if the responses (usually denials) from governments comport with the facts of the individual cases;
- stronger fact-finding capacities, including conducting more in-country investigations, with improved staff preparation for the missions, and with the addition of better emergency reaction capacities; rapporteurs should be better coordinated with one another, undertake joint missions, and in certain cases dispatch or take with them experts on forensics, gender related abuses (as in the investigation of rape), and medical and other technical matters.
- greater personal security guarantees for the special rapporteurs, U.N. staff, witnesses, and local human rights defenders with whom they consult on their missions;
- serious discussion and consideration of findings and recommen-

dations by the Commission on Human Rights and the General Assembly, where the results are often reported, but not debated or probed, and more dialogue between the special rapporteurs and interested government and NGO representatives;
- fuller analysis of official governmental responses to these special procedures;
- regular follow-up with those contacted about specific cases, when these are not satisfactorily resolved; and
- better presentation, circulation, and publicity for the reports.

In reflecting upon the suggestions cited above, one overriding factor emerges: the gross inadequacy of the staffing and funding of these specialized procedures. The expert rapporteurs and working group members receive no salary or honorarium for their activities, and very little staff support from the Centre for Human Rights (normally less than one full-time person per mandate, whether it is to address torture in every country or to examine the situation only in Iran).

Establishing more on-site human rights monitoring is of particular importance. The quality, credibility, and utility of such information and the protective or corrective presence of the U.N. monitors are infinitely more useful than reports written and issued in Geneva alone.

Yet the funding and political support for such monitors has been tenuous: the small field staff of the U.N. rapporteur on former Yugoslavia has been supported by voluntary financing, governmental and private; at the end of 1994 it was extended only through a major effort. A request to set up monitors within or on the borders of Iraq has not yet been funded. Delays in finding start-up funding for monitors in Rwanda were a major embarrassment to the new high commissioner and the whole human rights program. At the Vienna World Conference, the assembled nations agreed that human rights officers could be "assigned to regional offices" of the U.N. and only "to disseminate"—not to collect— human rights information and training, at the request of states. With such precarious financing and support, it is no wonder that the capacity of the thematic mechanisms and special rapporteurs is less than it should be to enable the U.N. to stop gross violations.

To integrate human rights concerns into the mainstream of U.N. activity focused on conflict prevention, and early warning, U.S. activity must focus intently on strengthening the core reporting capacity of the United Nations human rights programs of the future, with the high commissioner as the central focal point.

Despite the substantial efforts by the rapporteurs and thematic mechanisms to investigate and report on allegations of violations in all parts of the world, the U.N. issues no global report on human rights. Each of the country and thematic mechanisms produces one or two reports annually, but there is no means by which these are compiled, analyzed, or sent forward as an authoritative U.N. "world report" to its parent bodies or to the public. Even if the U.N. never develops an effective operational capacity to stop human rights violations, it must be able to report fully and impartially if it is to provide "early warning" and engage in preventive diplomacy. The establishment of a global report should be high on the U.S. agenda.

The High Commissioner for Human Rights

The long-awaited creation in December 1993 of the post of U.N. High Commissioner for Human Rights has raised hopes that the U.N.'s capacity to respond to and stop serious violations of human rights will dramatically improve. This post, sought almost since the creation of the U.N., was revived by the approach of the World Conference and ardently supported by the Clinton administration. In advocating its establishment, the U.S. stated that it sought to energize U.N. programs on human rights and ensure that human rights takes its proper place as one of the key pillars of the U.N. system, as set out in the Charter. It wanted to create a high commissioner who would be a "champion and spokesperson" for human rights worldwide—and a focal point for implementation of human rights and its integration into peacekeeping, peacemaking, and humanitarian assistance programs of the U.N., the coordinator of all U.N. programs in human rights, including regular interaction with UNDP, UNICEF, WHO, ILO, and others. But beyond this, the Clinton administration called for a high commissioner who would have independent authority to dispatch envoys on fact-finding missions and undertake other initiatives, as well as to request the secretary-general to bring to the attention of the U.N. Security Council serious violations of human rights when they threaten international peace and security.

The mandate assigned to the high commissioner is less specific and less activist than the U.S. proposal. However, its vagueness provides adequate flexibility for a committed human rights leader to shape the post in the direction suggested by its most avid proponents inside and outside the U.S. government. However, the U.S. must undertake substantial efforts to help develop an effective strategy for action by the high commissioner.

In creating the post the General Assembly reaffirmed the need for a "continued adaptation" of U.N. human rights machinery to meet the needs of the future, and to improve its coordination, efficiency, and effectiveness. The high commissioner's specific responsibilities encompass making recommendations to U.N. bodies for the promotion and protection of all rights, including the right to development; playing "an active role" in the elimination and prevention of violations of human rights around the world; providing overall coordination of human rights activities throughout the United Nations system; enhancing international cooperation in human rights, including the provision of technical assistance; coordinating education and public information programs in human rights; and rationalizing, adapting, and strengthening U.N. human rights machinery. Organizationally, he is based in Geneva, but has an office in New York.

For the high commissioner to be effective, protection of human rights must assume the central role in strategic planning and actions. Human rights protection means the high commissioner should have the ability to respond effectively to human rights violations wherever they occur, and includes, at a minimum, monitoring and ensuring respect for human rights obligations and responding to violations through, *inter alia,* effective fact finding, public reporting, and securing relief and redress for victims of violations, including efforts to establish accountability for those responsible for gross abuses. In short, it is widely expected that the high commissioner must make a palpable difference in actually preventing and stopping human rights violations.

At the tactical level, there has long been considerable agreement that the most effective activity to stop violations is to bring maximum publicity to bear on governments. This, as the nongovernmental human rights sector has demonstrated much better than the intergovernmental, often brings an end to abuses. Publicity may also, in turn, trigger unilateral or regional economic sanctions. It is thus of considerable concern that the first high commissioner, Jose Ayala Lasso of Ecuador, has begun his tenure so quietly: in his first year in office he visited twenty countries (beginning with Austria and Switzerland, but including hot spots such as Rwanda and Cuba), largely to engage in diplomatic discussions, not to assess violations, but to explore cooperation with other U.N. machinery.

The U.N.'s special rapporteurs and thematic mechanisms are at primitive stages of effectiveness. The high commissioner will need to coordinate and facilitate their activities, strengthen their working conditions, and enhance their financial and political support.

The U.S. must encourage the high commissioner to take the initiative to enhance the capacity of the UN to protect human rights and stop gross violations. He should begin to submit regular monthly reports to the Security Council advising it of urgent situations warranting attention because of their threat to international peace and security; he could energize and convene the Commission on Human Rights in emergency sessions, such as those convened for former Yugoslavia and Rwanda; he could submit reports to and appear before other U.N. bodies such as UNDP, the international financial institutions, World Conferences, or others—as well as relevant regional organizations.

In 1994, shortly after his tenure began, the high commissioner tried to examine and establish ameliorative human rights instrumentalities in Rwanda (as an emergency situation) and Burundi (as a preventive measure, under advisory services). He found that there were severe difficulties in establishing an on-the-ground presence, and has publicly called for assistance to provide him with a rapid response capacity for such atrocious violations. In his first report to the Commission on Human Rights Ayala identified the following three long-term needs for securing support to carry out activities rapidly and effectively in situations of serious human rights violations and where preventive action is necessary:

1) logistical assistance capacity on a standby basis to provide material, communications, and other support for emergency or preventive field missions;

2) establishment and maintenance of an international roster of specialized staff to be available at short notice for human rights field missions (investigation teams, field officers, legal experts, etc.); and

3) increased contributions to the Voluntary Fund for Technical Cooperation.

The fact that the Centre for Human Rights has none of these capacities at present is indicative of the point made earlier: the centre lacks a field orientation, and has been starved of resources—both human and financial. If the U.N.'s human rights programs, and the high commissioner in particular, are to be able to play a major role in combating gross violations of human rights, they will need resources and political support. The U.S. can provide no more important support to the U.N. than to enhance the high commissioner's capacity to combat violations.

The high commissioner has reported that he is reviewing "how best to adapt the structure of the Secretariat to the new priorities of the Vienna Declaration and Programme of Action and to respond to the gaps and weaknesses" in the Secretariat identified by a June 1994 review conducted by the Office for Inspections and Investigations, the predecessor of the Office of Internal Oversight Services. In so doing, he is examining strategic priorities, restructuring of the Secretariat's program of work, the strengthening of administrative services, and training of personnel. One of the important criticisms of the centre's programs raised in this review is its lack of a country-specific orientation. In years past, such an orientation would have been politically unacceptable; today, it would dramatically assist the high commissioner and his staff in developing strategic, country-specific plans for action that could combat human rights violations.

This is a time of considerable institutional reformulation and fluidity in the U.N.'s human rights programs. Supporting the high commissioner to undertake a more activist role in setting the agenda of other agencies to address human rights, and in making the Centre for Human Rights more responsive to violations and more effective in stopping them, must be the highest priority objective of United States' human rights programs at the U.N.

The high commissioner's broad mandate includes responsibilities for proper coordination of human rights throughout the U.N. The high commissioner can bring the talents and human resources of the Human Rights Centre into this picture, energizing actions together with other agencies with the resources and field experience to do this work promptly and well.

To carry out such activities, the high commissioner will need greater system-wide authority to ensure strategic direction to the U.N.'s hands-on human rights technical assistance activities. The high commissioner must have the power to integrate human rights concerns into all aspects of the U.N.'s work—from development, to conflict resolution, to peacekeeping—and not merely hold cosmetic "coordination" meetings on integrating human rights concerns that then have no follow-up, and over whose implementation he has no authority. As the Vienna Declaration suggests, such system-wide authority should extend *inter alia* to programs affecting human rights of women, children, indigenous populations, as well as humanitarian aid and criminal justice programs, election monitoring, and such key operational activities as peacekeeping and postconflict peacebuilding.

Such responsibilities mean that the high commissioner cannot be tied exclusively to the Centre for Human Rights in Geneva. He must be freed from day-to-day line management responsibilities there. Access to the secretary-general and the principal U.N. development and conflict resolution bodies—including the Security Council—will be essential to effective functioning of the high commissioner in these areas. Therefore it is important that he be able to interact regularly with top officials in New York, and be included in the secretary-general's regular "cabinet" meetings with the heads of political affairs, peacekeeping, and other departments. The high commissioner will need to take the initiative and report and make recommendations not only to the Commission on Human Rights, but to the General Assembly (in plenary), its various committees, as well as to governing councils of specialized agencies.

These activities should not, however, distract the high commissioner from his principal role: to protect people from human rights violations and to respond effectively when such abuses occur. The U.S. must press him to do so with vigor and speed, and must assist him strategically, operationally, and financially.

The needs are substantial. They will not be developed by happenstance, or as a result of American passivity or disinterest. Past and recent experience has shown that when the U.S. does lead politically, and sometimes even financially, in the U.N., its engagement can be decisive. But for U.S. leadership, the post of U.N. High Commissioner for Human Rights would not have been created. Earlier, the U.S. played a key role in establishing the Working Group on Disappearances, and initiated efforts to have a Special Rapporteur on Religious Intolerance. The emergency session on former Yugoslavia resulted from U.S. leadership in calling the special meeting, carving the mandate, and later, financing the handful of added monitors assigned to work on-site in the region. The war crimes tribunal would not have happened and would not be under serious development today without abundant energetic American leadership—and loans of personnel, equipment, and the like. The U.N.'s human rights emergency initiative on Rwanda was started by Canada, and taken up by the U.S., albeit after an embarrassing delay, but was then given substantial U.S. political and financial support.

These success stories signal the importance of more energetic involvement, leadership, and sustained financial support by the U.S., working together with like-minded states when possible, if the U.N. is to develop an effective emergency human rights response capacity. The opportunities are abundant. The challenges are formidable. As the U.N. enters its second half-century, the United States can once again lead in making this world organization different and better than its predecessors.

Notes

[1] The Commission on Human Rights is a political decision-making body composed of fifty-three government representatives, which reports to the Economic and Social Council. It has appointed ad hoc investigators (special rapporteurs, working groups, etc.). The Human Rights Committee is one of six technically independent bodies, composed of experts elected by state parties to human rights

treaties, for the purpose of monitoring compliance with the treaties. Despite the similarities in names they are very different bodies.

[2] See Jan Bauer, *Report on United Nations World Conference on Human Rights,* October 31, 1993, pp. 131–132.

[3] U.S. Department of State Bulletin, June 21, 1993, pp. 444–446.

[4] Keynote speech, CSCE Seminar on Early Warning, Warsaw, January 1994.

6

Refugees, Displaced Persons, and the United Nations System

FREDERICK C. CUNY

Introduction

Nowhere is the United Nations system under more stress than in the field of refugees and internally displaced persons. Bosnia, Somalia, southern Sudan, Rwanda, the former Soviet Union—more countries and more conflicts keep being added to

---

FREDERICK C. CUNY is founder and president of INTERTECT, a Dallas based emergency management consulting firm. Starting with Biafra in 1969, he has worked in scores of emergency relief operations. In 1991 he was senior advisor to the U.S. military's civil affairs units during Operation Desert Storm and was the principal advisor to the U.S. government on humanitarian operations in northern Iraq during Operation Provide Comfort, the international effort to rescue the Kurds. He worked for two years on humanitarian operations in Sarajevo during the siege there and led efforts to provide aid to the victims of the conflict in Chechnya, Russia. Mr. Cuny is author of numerous books and articles on humanitarian and peacekeeping operations. He is also a part-time, nonresident associate of the Carnegie Endowment for International Peace and a member of the Council on Foreign Relations. The editors regret to state that Fred Cuny was reported missing in Chechnya in April 1995. Search efforts to locate him continue as this volume goes to press.

the list. Few of these crises are quickly resolved, and the costs, both in human terms and in international resources, continue to expand. In the principal United Nations agency mandated to protect and care for refugees, the U.N. High Commissioner for Refugees (UNHCR), expenditures increased from slightly over $8 million in 1970 to over $1 billion in the early 1990s. The global number of refugees climbed from 2.5 million in 1970 to over 20 million in 1990. The number of internally displaced persons, those within their own countries, is estimated to be even higher—at least 25 million in 1994. No fewer than seventy-one countries were generating or hosting significant numbers of refugees in 1995.

Though the resources devoted to international crisis operations are substantial, they are inadequate to address the number, severity, and scope of the problem. Increasingly, development aid is being diverted to meet emergency needs, and emergency aid and disaster relief account for a substantial portion of the aid budgets of the major donor countries and the U.N. system.

At the same time, many of these missions have become entangled in the very crises that they were sent to help ameliorate. In Bosnia and other parts of the former Yugoslavia, humanitarian operations became a substitute for political and military action to solve the crises. When peacekeeping forces sent to Somalia subsequently became embroiled in the conflict themselves, humanitarian activities came to be identified with the military objectives of the intervening force, and relief operations were subsequently constrained. In many conflicts, the U.N. organizations entrusted with the lead role were reluctant participants, often being the last on the scene or the first to leave when the situation became unstable. U.N. leadership was questioned, comprehensive planning and strategic thinking were absent, and despite millions of dollars and hundreds of thousands of tons of relief aid, change for the better was often slow in coming and sometimes nonexistent. Under these circumstances, many questioned whether these efforts had only served to produce "well-fed dead" and prolonged the conflicts.

Humanitarian assistance from 1970 onward has been largely media-driven. The United Nations, without a mechanism for spreading resources according to needs, has been forced to respond to the newer crises by diverting aid and resources away from the old ones, leaving many of the older, sorely afflicted populations with vastly reduced international assistance. Higher than normal death and disease rates have become accepted as the norm. Places such as Afghanistan, Angola, and Cambodia, once at the center stage of cold war politics, now suffer in relative obscurity with few controls on the incessant violence.

But this does not tell the entire story. There are many other groups affected by crisis that fall outside the scope of the U.N.'s concern. They include guest workers suddenly expelled by their host country for political or economic reasons, such as the Ghanians and other West Africans expelled from Nigeria in February 1983, the Asians who fled the Middle East prior to the Gulf War of 1991, or the millions of people each year who flee from extreme economic hardship, famine, and political repression, but who are unable to obtain refugee status. Of special concern are nationalities or ethnic groups subjected to persecution or ethnic cleansing; they usually cannot be protected by the U.N. system until they become refugees.

All these groups need protection, assistance, and an advocate to plead their case to the international community. Yet when resources are scarce, costs are rising, and the numbers of people who qualify according to the already strict definition of refugees is increasing, there is great reluctance on the part of the U.N. to take on any more categories of distressed populations. Increasingly, the staff of the high commissioner resorts to rigid interpretations of its mandate to keep from being drawn into newer emergencies.

Trends

Not only are the numbers of refugees and the costs associated with their care and maintenance doubling at an alarming rate (a 100 percent increase in the caseload from 1985–1995), the gap between humanitarian assistance needs and the international donor response is widening. In 1990 appeals outpaced donor response by about 25 percent. By 1995 only 50 percent of the needs identified by appeals were met. Clearly, needs are beginning to outrun resources.

This problem is being exacerbated by a major shift in the locus of the caseload. Prior to 1988 there were few emergencies in the northern, colder latitudes. Virtually all the major disasters that the international system responded to were located in warm, tropical climates, principally in Africa and the southern parts of Asia. With the break-up of the Soviet Union and the end of the strict Socialist regimes in Eastern Europe, countries such as Bosnia, Armenia, Georgia, and Russia have been added to the list of countries in crisis. Before 1991 emergencies in the Soviet Union were the exclusive domain of the Russians. Now these newly independent states turn to the Western industrialized countries for humanitarian assistance. The operational implications are immense.

However, the international relief system is still largely oriented toward providing assistance in tropical zones. Relief operations in colder regions will have higher attendant costs per capita than in tropical areas. Furthermore, the people in these areas are used to a much higher standard of living and will be less able to sustain themselves than refugees or displaced persons in the Third World. In the higher latitudes, the winters are fierce. Refugees will require sleeping bags—not blankets—and heavy foods with substantially more calories. Fuel—not just for cooking but for heating—will be a critical issue. In just one case, Bosnia, the United Nations High Commissioner for Refugees spends upwards of 40 percent of its entire budget on taking care of refugees and displaced persons. As other northern countries become embroiled in crises, the costs are likely to be even greater, because the distances will be farther from the donor countries and the countries will be poorer than those in the Balkans.

Another trend is the increasingly Islamic makeup of the caseload. In 1950 Muslim refugees and displaced persons represented only a small percentage of the world's refugee population. By 1970 they made up 50 percent. In 1990 almost 75 percent of the world's refugees were Muslim. Furthermore, most of the potential new crisis areas in the northern latitudes of Middle Asia and the Caucasus involve substantial Muslim populations. In the Russian Federation, where over 10 percent of the population is Muslim, many of its internal nationalities problems are likely to have an Islamic dimension.

At the end of the cold war there was hope that a new world

order would emerge that could deal with ongoing, low-intensity conflicts and bring them to an end. But just the opposite has happened. The Western countries have been reluctant to engage while the forces that held the Socialist countries together in the post–World War II era and the controls on ethnonationalism were removed. As the end of the century neared, many countries faced partial or total disintegration. In the two-year period 1991–92, five new countries emerged from the former Yugoslavia; four immediately became involved in conflict. At the same time, the Soviet Union dissolved and six, or almost half, of the republics that emerged (Azerbaijan, Armenia, Moldova, Russia, Tajikistan, and Georgia) were involved in active warfare within three years. Four of these new conflicts involved Muslim populations.

The Aid System

By the early 1990s the United Nations' humanitarian systems were being challenged as never before. The donor countries, especially the United States, were increasingly disturbed by the seeming inability of the U.N. to effectively manage existing and newly emerging crises. In the last year of the Bush administration, the United States joined with the Nordic countries in pressuring the United Nations to revise its mechanism for coordinating international emergency response. The U.N. Department of Humanitarian Affairs (DHA) was established to provide more effective coordination among the U.N. agencies and to assist nongovernmental organizations (NGOs) in managing their humanitarian emergency services. By 1995 the international aid system was loosely structured as follows:

1. DHA was at the pinnacle of the U.N.'s humanitarian system. It was headed by an under secretary-general tasked with coordinating the international response to complex emergencies.

2. The United Nations High Commissioner for Refugees remained the designated focal point for protection and coordinating humanitarian assistance for refugees.

3. United Nations International Children's Emergency Fund (UNICEF), the United Nations Development Programme

(UNDP), the World Health Organization (WHO), and other specialized agencies of the U.N. were charged with implementing specific projects or programs for refugees and displaced persons.

4. Private, nongovernmental organizations served as implementing partners of the U.N. or worked as independent aid providers under the U.N.'s umbrella (sometimes funded by or through various United Nations agencies).

Another important actor is the International Committee of the Red Cross (ICRC). ICRC is completely independent and operates under its own international conventions; it plays a major part in providing assistance and protection to people living in zones of conflict. Yet the organization operates under major constraints, especially in civil conflicts, and often many needs of people in conflict zones go unmet despite ICRC's presence.

The major deficiency in the international aid system is that there is no U.N. agency specifically tasked with providing assistance to the internal refugees, or displaced persons, or others under attack by their own government. This is largely due to a structural problem of the U.N. The organization represents *nations* and works under the authority, and only with permission, of the host government. The U.N. must be invited to assist—it cannot go independently. Even when the Security Council authorized member states to intervene in northern Iraq to protect the Kurds and provided a legal framework under Resolution 688, the United Nations operational agencies—UNHCR and UNDP—were reluctant to enter the country without permission from Baghdad. At the time, there was no precedent for such an action.

The protection of and assistance to refugees is guided by international law, principally the 1951 U.N. Convention on the Status of Refugees and the 1967 Protocol. The mandate of the U.N. High Commissioner for Refugees derives from these conventions, and, until the 1980s, the bulk of UNHCR's efforts were aimed at providing legal protection—in other words, trying to bring refugees under the rule of law in the countries in which they seek asylum. Provision of relief, or assistance in U.N. terms, was viewed as a minor part of its work, even though there were provisions for it, until the late 1970s.

A major change in attitudes occurred in 1979 with the influx of Khmer refugees from Cambodia into Thailand. UNHCR had been involved in refugee emergencies before, but never to such an extent and with so much publicity. For six months, the attention of the world was focused on the Thai-Cambodian border. In that situation, UNHCR, with strong support from the American government, generally rose to the occasion, and efforts were immediately made to try to codify the lessons learned there and to develop a better emergency response capability. In 1980 work began on establishing an emergency unit. In 1984 a specialist support unit aimed at improving UNHCR's technical capabilities was also added. Yet emergency response was still inadequate. In 1985 major failures by UNHCR in Sudan led the United States to spearhead an effort to select a high commissioner who was more operationally minded. In late 1985 an emergency management training program was instituted by UNHCR for all midlevel and senior staff members. The specialist support unit was expanded, and UNHCR further improved its field capabilities. These efforts led to a significant improvement in the way UNHCR responded to emergencies, and, indeed, the organization became the principal repository for knowledge and skills about emergency management of refugee crises. While there were still many problems, they were less from a lack of knowledge about how to respond than from the inability of the organization to expand sufficiently to handle all the needs, especially in the ever-expanding number of crises that it was called upon to manage.

To a large measure, the donors failed to understand the nature of the problem. Even within the upper levels of the Bush administration, the failures of the UNHCR were interpreted as mismanagement or poor use of resources. American diplomats have never fully understood the role of UNHCR in emergencies and the inherent structural difficulties the organization faces in responding to crises. In 1991, when the Kurdish refugee crisis exploded on the borders of Turkey, the United States urged UNHCR to take the lead U.N. role. Senior administration personnel believed that the U.N. could be fully operational in a matter of a few days. A week after Resolution 688 was passed, UNHCR had still not deployed to the Turkish-Iraqi border, and senior administration officials were furious. One official called UNHCR to demand why it had not deployed dozens of camp planners and scores of medical personnel to the area; he was told that in the entire UNHCR staff, there was only one refugee camp planner and two full-time medical officers. Administration officials had failed to grasp that UNHCR is not an operational agency. UNHCR views its role as coordinator and catalyst for operational activities. Field staff are likely to be generalists and protection officers, not technicians. When the Bush administration chose to back the plan to create the DHA, the United States had interpreted the problem as one of a lack of coordination rather than a host of structural problems or one of limited mandates and mission capabilities.

Strengths and Weaknesses of the U.N.

The great strength of the United Nations in the refugee field lies in the prestige of the organization. This, in turn, is based on the U.N.'s Charter and international refugee law. The Charter defines the principles under which all United Nations agencies must act, and establishes the U.N. as a neutral, nonpartisan body to regulate disputes among nations. Because the United Nations has adhered to its strict definition of neutrality, nonpartisanship, and, in relief operations, transparency, it is usually regarded as nonthreatening to the host countries, and its organizations, such as UNHCR, are routinely given access to refugees and permitted to provide a wide range of protection and services.

The operations of UNHCR are guided by international law. These laws confer legitimacy on its actions and provide the basis for policy, doctrine, and operational responsibilities. More important, they structure the behavior of nations and demand that they conform to certain norms relating to civilians who have been displaced and sought asylum in nearby countries. UNHCR is not only the principal beneficiary of international refugee law, it is also the trustee. The high commissioner must ensure that all nations that are signatories to the conventions comply with the provisions and, if they do not, must bring pressure to bear on the country to accede to the norms set out in the various covenants.

Were it left up to the staff, UNHCR would probably focus on protection. The organization has always been uncomfortable with its assistance role. But, as noted, since 1980 the organization has expanded its operational role far more than any other part of its activities, and it is now the central player, operationally, in virtually all refugee emergencies. The U.S. government has been foremost in urging the development and expansion of the UNHCR's operational capabilities.

As UNHCR's emergency operations capabilities expanded, the organization developed several approaches to widening its capabilities. The first was standby arrangements with some of the stronger NGOs. Organizations such as the Norwegian Refugee Council, the International Rescue Committee, and CARE entered into agreements to provide specialist support to UNHCR to enable it to deploy more quickly and to manage field operations. These standby arrangements have greatly extended the capabilities of the organization.

The recognition that UNHCR needed to be more fully aware of problems in the refugees' countries of origin, as well as the fact that it was getting harder to distinguish between refugees and groups of people affected by conflict, drought, or famine in the same area, prompted UNHCR to enter into a series of experiments known as cross border/cross mandate arrangements with sister U.N. agencies, especially UNICEF. This strategy came from a realization that their traditional approaches to refugee assistance had not led to solutions or tackled root causes, but had worsened dependencies.

Normally, UNHCR approaches relief on an individual basis, that is, it makes a determination as to whether a person qualifies as a refugee, registers those who do, and then provides aid accordingly—but only to those people who meet the definition. Other U.N. agencies provide assistance to *groups* of people under the assumption that wider programs will reach down to and benefit individuals. Under the cross mandate approach, UNHCR would operate on a community-wide basis, providing assistance to all people in need regardless of whether they are refugees or not. Refugee camps would be avoided unless necessary for protection concerns. Nor would UNHCR take the lead in providing assistance in communities where mixed needs occurred if other U.N. agencies had a presence and the capacity to deliver aid. A U.N.

liaison office would be established under the auspices of the agency
with the most substantial presence in that area, and the other
agencies would participate in integrated programing and provide
in-kind assistance and financial support to the lead agency. The
approach was tried in Ethiopia and later in Kenya along the
Somali border. The principal problem is that UNHCR is the only
agency with a responsibility for refugees; internally displaced persons, conflict victims, and migrating drought victims fall outside
the concern of any U.N. agency. Therefore, UNHCR does not
have a sister agency to cross mandates with in many communities
and situations. Nonetheless, despite mixed results, the approach
did point to further opportunities for collaboration among the
agencies.

As a result of these changes, the U.N. system is getting stronger
operationally, especially the UNHCR. But there are still ongoing
problems. They include:

1. insufficient numbers of high caliber managerial personnel and
   technicians;

2. bureaucratic procedures that delay operations;

3. a generally narrow focus on defining refugees strictly according
   to UNHCR's mandate (that is, persons who have crossed an
   international border, not those who are still inside their own
   country);

4. an overly legalistic approach to protecting refugees; and

5. an overly rigid adherence to the principle of neutrality.

Unquestionably, the most outstanding set of problems is related
to the issue of how the U.N. system can assist and protect civilians
caught in conflicts inside their own borders. Because the U.N. has
no mandate to work in a country with the internally displaced, the
body of international law protecting civilians is weak. No U.N.
agency has developed doctrines, procedures, or the special skills
necessary to help these groups. From an operational point of view,
this means that aid falls largely to nongovernmental organizations.
While they struggle valiantly to provide a range of services in these
circumstances, overall coordination is often lacking, critical needs
go unmet, and emergency operations are characterized by a high

degree of ad hocism. But while many NGOs are willing to provide assistance, no one provides protection. This means that minorities who are threatened—such as the Muslims of Bosnia, the Tutsis of Rwanda, the Chechens of Russia—have no advocates and no on-site agency to represent them or to intercede on their behalf to stop gross human rights abuses, ethnic cleansing, and genocide.

Recognition of this structural weakness within the U.N. came to the fore with the war induced famine in southern Sudan. Three years later, the UNHCR's failure to seize the initiative in northern Iraq early in the operation because it was reluctant to cross the border further highlighted the problem. Yet the major donors fixated on the effort to improve interagency coordination and pressed ahead with the establishment of DHA, while the fundamental question of which agency should be responsible for the displaced remained outstanding.

When the Bosnian war broke, the UNHCR had offices in Bosnia to assist refugees fleeing from the conflict in Croatia. The high commissioner, Sadako Ogata, lobbied for the role of assisting the victims of the war of Bosnia, not just refugees fleeing to Croatia but also civilians remaining in the war zone. UNHCR representatives negotiated agreements between the warring factions to grant UNHCR virtual supernumerary authority over all relief operations. NGOs worked under UNHCR's umbrella and received implementing partner status, badges, and documents—without which it was extremely difficult to work in the conflict zone.

To UNHCR's credit, the Bosnia operations have gone fairly smoothly in the areas under Bosnian government control, especially in central Bosnia and even in besieged Sarajevo. Despite incredible obstacles, international relief agencies, working under UNHCR's umbrella, were able to deliver hundreds of thousands of tons of relief supplies, and mass starvation and hunger were largely averted except in the most remote enclaves. But in Bosnia, thousands of people continued to die—not from lack of food, but from bullets—and over 2 million people were displaced or became refugees in neighboring countries. The U.N. system failed to develop effective strategies to prevent forced population transfers, gross human rights abuses, and campaigns of murder and terrorism aimed at ethnic minorities throughout the country.

Early in the operation, UNHCR announced that one of its primary goals in Bosnia was preventive protection. It would attempt to take measures to protect the Muslim and Croat populations in the Bosnian Serb-held areas. In practice, UNHCR was never able to develop an effective approach to the problem. The number of UNHCR personnel deployed in the Serb-held areas was minimal. There was disagreement among the senior staff about how proactive protection officers should be. The U.N. was fearful of challenging the Serb leadership for fear that the limited supply operations in the Serb-controlled zones would be curtailed, and that relief convoys traveling through Serb-held zones to the Bosnian government areas would be halted. Furthermore, there was a feeling within UNHCR that advocacy for human rights on behalf of the Muslims would put UNHCR on the side of one of the warring parties, at least in the eyes of the Serbs. Thus a decision was made to try to remain as neutral as possible and to provide only limited protection services. From time to time, the matter was reconsidered. Human rights groups constantly pressured UNHCR to take a stronger stand or, at a minimum, to permit them to deploy human rights monitors under the U.N. umbrella. But these measures were discouraged by peace negotiator Lord David Owens, who concluded that such measures would only serve to further complicate his negotiating efforts. As early as January 1993, even before the end of the first year of the conflict, UNHCR had effectively abandoned serious protection efforts in the Bosnian Serb zones.

The deployment of the U.N. Protection Force (UNPROFOR) in Bosnia met with similar results. The Serbs refused to allow peacekeepers to be stationed on Serb territory, so UNPROFOR's ability to protect civilians was almost nonexistent in those areas. Virtually all the displacement that occurred from the summer of 1993 to the winter of 1994–95 occurred in the presence of UNHCR and UNPROFOR deployments.

In early 1993 the situation inside the government-held areas of Bosnia changed. Fighting erupted between Croat and Muslim communities in central Bosnia and in Herzogovina. UNPROFOR troops were stationed and operational there, and in many places, units such as the British, Nordic, and Spanish battalions were able to intervene in local disputes and provide some degree of protection. But overall, the effort fell short. Rules of engagement, designed to protect the United Nations' neutrality, were often rigidly enforced, and UNPROFOR units stood by while some of the worst internecine fighting broke out. U.N. commanders during that period made it clear that the U.N.'s first role was to protect itself and international humanitarian relief efforts, not to intervene in the conflict, nor to protect civilians.

This ambiguity and the contradictory nature of the U.N.'s role in Bosnia were highlighted in the spring of 1993 when the U.N. Security Council, under pressure from the international community, established a series of U.N. safe areas around towns and cities threatened by Serb aggression. In each enclave, the U.N. deployed forces among the civilians, ostensibly with a mandate to protect them. However, the rules of engagement severely limited their protective capacity. The forces could only return fire if *they,* the U.N. forces, were fired upon, but not if the civilian population was attacked.

In February 1994 sixty-eight people were killed and more than 200 wounded by a mortar shell that exploded in Sarajevo's central market. This attack came only two days after another massacre. The international community attempted to strengthen the U.N. safe areas concept, at least around Sarajevo. A total exclusion zone was created, prohibiting both sides from using heavy weapons within a twenty kilometer circle from the center of Sarajevo, and air forces from NATO were assigned to enforce the ban with air power. But the catch was that ultimate responsibility for calling the air strikes resided with the top U.N. civilian on the ground. Time and time again, the U.N. demonstrated a reluctance to use the power that was available, and gradually the protective barrier around Sarajevo frayed.

All of this illustrates the difficulty of providing protection for people caught in conflicts in their own country. UNHCR's Ogata had lobbied for the job of providing assistance to the war victims of Bosnia, but there was no enthusiasm for it among her staff. The subsequent difficulties that the staff encountered only hardened the resistance to engaging in internal operations in other countries. Yet the question remained, if UNHCR didn't take responsibility for displaced persons, who within the U.N. system would?

The Relevance of International Law

International law provides the framework for action on behalf of refugees, it gives legitimacy for protection efforts, and it sets standards for the behavior of nations toward people who have been forced to flee their homelands. By signing an international convention, a country agrees to certain norms of behavior and authorizes the U.N., in the case of refugees, and the ICRC, in the case of war victims, to intercede on their behalf. But is the current body of international law still relevant?

International law is predicated on several assumptions: first, that governments behave rationally or that they can be pressured into behaving in such a manner, and second, that the governments that sign the accords will comply with their provisions. When these laws were formulated, the world was different. The conflicts and crises of concern were largely in Europe, at the interface of East and West. Africa and Asia were still under colonial administration, and the governments in the Northern Hemisphere that were the initial signatories to these conventions were modern democracies with strong legal systems. The wars that were contemplated during those times were international conflicts sparked by great power rivalries, and acceptance of refugees from the other side was a political means for gaining advantage over the other.

The 1960s marked the end of that era. All but a few colonies became independent countries. The great empires of Britain and France dissolved, leaving dozens of unstable, undemocratic, ethnically riven, poor countries in their stead. It took only a short time for those countries to begin to descend into conflict, and by the 1970s, millions of people in Africa and Asia had been forced to flee to neighboring countries for protection. A new operational reality emerged. Conflicts were internal, not between nations. Most were located in extremely poor societies with unsophisticated governments and weak legal systems. The receiving countries, too, were poor, and few were willing to take the refugees, though, in fact, there was little they could do to stop them from coming. In this environment, protection became extremely difficult. Often it was more a matter of keeping people alive in remote areas than of extending them legal services and acting as their advocate. Yet protection and protection methodologies remained highly legalistic. The objective was to encourage countries to adopt the rule of law or accede to international norms of behavior, even when it was obvious that the government concerned gave only lip service to law.

Furthermore, other than the Geneva Conventions, there was little in the way of international law to protect the victims of conflict who remained in their own country. The primary obstacle was national sovereignty. Few countries were willing to propose laws or other measures to try to influence the behavior of a country toward its own citizens. Various measures were proposed, but many international organizations, including the ICRC, sensed that reopening the issue might result in a loss of ground. Thus emphasis remained on protecting those who sought asylum in neighboring countries.

The first major challenge to national sovereignty occurred in 1991 during the Kurdish refugee crisis after the Gulf War. The Kurds, fleeing Saddam Hussein's forces, had been denied entry into Turkey despite the fact that Turkey was a signatory to the International Refugee Conventions. Rather than try to force Turkey to open its borders, the U.N. Security Council passed Resolution 688, which called on Iraq to end the persecution of its own citizens and authorized the international community to take all actions necessary, including military intervention, to rescue those trapped on the border. For the first time, the international community sought to solve a refugee crisis in the country of origin. While human rights experts and international lawyers were outraged that Turkey was not forced to honor its commitments under international law, the fact remains that all the people were successfully reintegrated into their own communities, and they were virtually reempowered to deal politically with their own government. Even while the traditionalists decried what they perceived to be an assault on the principle of asylum, others quickly moved to try to codify the experience and called for establishing a "right to intervene" on behalf of war victims.

Is a new body of law needed, especially one that capitalizes on the experiences of northern Iraq? In the decade after 1985 there were numerous calls for establishing a body of law to guarantee humanitarian access to disaster victims in their own countries. There were many variations. Some proposed a "right to assistance," while others endorsed the right to intervene. Some groups proposed codifying the safe havens concept, essentially authorizing the U.N. Security Council to designate safe areas that would give internally displaced persons a sanctuary in their own country protected by international forces.

Some relief agencies have questioned whether new international laws are needed, and argue that operational approaches recognized under existing provisions of the U.N. Security Council resolutions might be a better alternative. They would like to see such concepts as U.N. safe areas, humanitarian aid corridors, and preventive deployments of United Nations military and police forces developed as a practical alternative.

Another major concern is the advocacy of international law regarding the protection of refugees. Many advocacy groups have pushed to develop laws to protect war victims. The movement was spearheaded by human rights groups that got a boost in the early 1990s when, for the first time since World War II, a war crimes tribunal was empaneled to seek justice for the victims of the conflict in the former Yugoslavia. A similar panel was instituted after the Rwanda crisis in 1994.

On yet another front, the U.N. is being urged to develop a framework for military intervention that will be triggered automatically when certain thresholds, such as mass migration or genocide, have been reached. Proponents argue that the best way to protect people in conflicts is for the U.N. to deploy forces early to prevent, mitigate, or contain a conflict and keep it from exploding. In 1993 a token U.S. force was deployed in Macedonia (as part of UNPROFOR) to keep the war in the former Yugoslavia from spreading southward. Despite initial skepticism, the deployment had a marked impact on reducing tensions in that area.

The view of many of those working on the ground in these complex emergencies is that legal approaches to protection are largely irrelevant. They argue that trying to apply the rule of law in situations that are essentially lawless has little chance of success. In 1993 a group of relief workers in Bosnia called on the U.N. to adopt new, practical measures for protection of minorities and other threatened groups in areas of ethnic tension and strife. Not only did they advocate such measures as increasing the presence of NGOs and human rights monitors, they proposed developing a set of field tactics that could be used by international staff to intervene on behalf of people who were under attack.

Even the normal U.N. methodologies for conducting humanitarian operations were being questioned. The behavior of combatants in Bosnia, Rwanda, and Somalia has challenged many of the fundamental precepts upon which humanitarian operations were based. In Bosnia and Somalia, the U.N. has been criticized for its strict adherence to neutrality and impartiality. The observance of neutrality led the U.N. to treat all sides as if they were equally affected. This enabled the aggressors to exploit the U.N. and undermine its credibility. In Bosnia millions of dollars were wasted on giving aid to the Serbs. While this was done to ensure access to the Bosnian side, it bolstered the Serbs' preposterous claims that they were the principal victims of the conflict. The U.N. even gave them thousands of tons of fuel in contravention of the international embargo, fuel that enabled the Serbs to continue to prosecute the war. The principle of transparency reached an absurd climax when the U.N. force commander in Bosnia, Sir Michael Rose, shared classified information about NATO protective flight schedules with the Serbs in an effort to show them that he was impartial and did not favor the Bosnians.

Relief workers have argued that in situations where one side was clearly the aggressor, attempting to operate under the banner of neutrality could inadvertently favor and give aid to the attacking side. Critics of the traditional approach advocated limiting humanitarian aid in those cases to the side being attacked and abandoning the facade of neutrality and attempts at being transparent. In circumstances where massive human rights abuses and genocide were being carried out, they proposed that national sovereignty be overridden by the international community. While the U.N. does not have the capacity to take over a country, nor are many countries willing to send troops into the midst of a civil war no matter how appalling the human rights situation, there are limited military options such as creating border safe havens and internal safe areas that could provide sanctuary for many victims.

Cross border relief operations into areas controlled by the aggrieved population would be preferable, and in many cases more cost effective, than those operating under the traditional rules.

Another challenge to the existing body of international law also emerged. The present conventions are rooted in Western legal traditions and ethics. Yet as we have seen, the caseload and the countries where crises are occurring are increasingly Islamic. Islam has a different world view of war and justice, and while many of the precepts are the same, the interpretation and the manner in which they are carried out can be quite different. The Holy Koran sets forth humane principles for dealing with captured soldiers and enemies who have surrendered, and many other passages provide the basis for sound international laws to protect civilians and guarantee the right of access. There have been attempts to interpret the Geneva Conventions and refugee laws in the context of the Koran, but these efforts have been resisted by Koranic scholars who argue that law must derive from the Koran, not from other sources.

The implications of this dispute could be far ranging. Some radical Islamic regimes do not feel bound to honor the conventions their predecessors have signed, since they believe the laws originate from other doctrines. Furthermore, the majority of aid comes from the West and is handled by Western agencies whose traditions are rooted in the Judeo-Christian heritage and tradition of helping the disadvantaged. In many Islamic societies poverty is accepted as God's will, and foreign relief agencies are viewed as naive and silly for trying to help the disadvantaged. Thus there is a clash of cultures that extends into the very heart of humanitarian operations.

As the international community considers new refugee law, it would be wise to engage Islamic legal experts and to find ways of developing laws based on Koranic principles as well as Western norms. Furthermore, Islamic states should be encouraged to develop their own conventions and to encourage other Islamic states to ratify them.

The Challenges of Crisis Prevention, Mitigation, and Containment

Perhaps the biggest challenge to the U.N. is not how to improve or expand humanitarian assistance to refugees and displaced persons, but how to prevent conflicts or mitigate and contain them once they have broken out. Ultimately, the best way to reduce the number of refugees is to reduce the number and scale of conflicts. The U.N.'s raison d'etre is the prevention of war, yet its main crisis efforts—humanitarian assistance and peacekeeping—are focused primarily on the consequences of conflict, not prevention.

In the 1980s there was much discussion about the early warning of conflict and refugee flows. Many organizations, including the U.N., set up systems to provide advance warning of potential crises and to allow the humanitarian agencies time to pre-position supplies and personnel to deal with an impending emergency. As it turned out, the problem was not early warning but early response: despite numerous advances in warning methodologies, few agencies were able to take advantage of the warnings or to respond quickly. In some cases, the U.N. was persuaded *not* to respond for fear that preparations for a crisis might exacerbate the situation and trigger an exodus.

While some actions can be taken to speed and improve humanitarian responses, ultimately they will have limited impact on the overall magnitude of the problem. Prevention is clearly a better option. But while it is commonly accepted that prevention costs far less than cure, the practice is otherwise. The breakup of Yugoslavia and its consequences were predicted well in advance, but the will to act decisively was absent. Likewise, Somalia's graveyard spiral into civil strife and famine was evident to the international community, but the fear of intervention was strong enough to block action until hundreds of thousands had died. Information on the probability of ethnic strife in Rwanda was available even before the assassination of its president. Afterward, fear of being embroiled in hostilities prevented robust measures from being taken to protect the Tutsi population. In each of these examples, the humanitarian response was less than perfect; however, the real problem was not one of inadequate humanitarian efforts, but the fact that the world was reluctant to intervene until it was too late. Clearly, mobilizing international will to react with preventive measures is the issue.

The end of the cold war resulted in many new challenges to the U.N.'s humanitarian and peacekeeping agencies. Many conflicts sparked by the collapse of the former Soviet Union and the Eastern bloc power structures were particularly violent because of the high proportion of heavy weapons, such as tanks, large artillery, and aircraft, which have devastating effects when used on civilian populations. Fresh approaches need to be explored and developed to limit the violence and provide a safe operating environment for humanitarian actions. Operation Provide Comfort, in which an allied military force operating under a U.N. resolution intervened in northern Iraq to stop the government from attacking its own citizens, the Kurds, and prevent a refugee exodus, may be a model for new types of action. While a final political situation is still pending, the intervention enabled the Kurds to quickly return home and resume near-normal lives. The continued allied protection, which consists of mainly symbolic overflights by a handful of fighter planes each week, has been called the cheapest peacekeeping mission in history.

Other models and approaches are needed. For example, advanced weapons monitoring technology can be used to restrict the use of certain weapons systems, such as missiles, heavy artillery, and weapons of mass destruction. Tanks, motorized howitzers, and other tracked vehicles are relatively easy to locate: when their engines are on, they are hot and noisy and thus susceptible to detection by infrared and acoustical sensors as well as doppler radars. A monitoring regime using satellites, airborne detection equipment, and ground based sensors could be used to enforce a demarche to the warring factions to park their heavy weapons in an easily observable location; afterward, any weapon caught outside the area would be subject to air attack. With such an approach, the mobility and firepower of an aggressor could be swiftly neutralized, and the levels of violence reduced. Admittedly, this would only be applicable in cases where the major powers had the will to use force, had an overwhelming technological advantage over the warring factions, and were prepared to commit the necessary military assets to the mission. In all likelihood, those would only be conflicts that threatened a region's stability or the West's security. The approach wouldn't end the "machete wars" of the Third World, but it could have a major impact on limiting and containing conflicts on the periphery of the former Soviet Union and the Near East. From a humanitarian perspective, relief operations would be much safer.

In the mid-1990s, the concept of preventive diplomacy began to gain momentum. But the discussions need to be broadened beyond diplomatic measures to include exploration of how specific economic, military, and humanitarian measures can be integrated into the process. Specifically, four categories of action should be developed.

Prevention

Primary emphasis should focus on preventing conflict and humanitarian emergencies through strategic international diplomacy supported by economic, and, if necessary and practical, military deterrence (through preventive deployment of international forces).

Mitigation and Containment

Containing crises and mitigating their impact on civilian populations and neighboring countries require careful understanding of the situation and the efficacy of each available option. Containment strategies such as economic sanctions, military isolation, and arms embargoes must be effective, enforceable, well-targeted, productive, and convincing. In many cases, such measures have proven ineffective, and in some, counterproductive. The sanctions imposed on Serbia served to strengthen popular support for the government's nationalistic policies. If measures are designed to be punitive, they must punish the guilty, not the innocent. In some situations they have harmed the people they were designed to support. The economic blockade of Haiti from 1992–94, for example, resulted in severe economic hardships on the poorest people among the Haitian population, the very people that the government was oppressing.

Mitigation measures that lower the level of violence should be explored. Measures such as no-fly zones have proven effective in lowering the level of casualties and also in reducing damage to critical infrastructure such as water and sanitation lines. In Sarajevo, humanitarian agencies were able to supply emergency pumps and use the existing, undamaged pipes, thereby reducing water shortages and lowering the risk of disease. Containment measures must also be applied in such a way that they do not give one side a disproportionate military or strategic advantage. Situations like Bosnia, where the arms embargo favored the better armed aggressor, must be avoided.

Ameliorating Suffering

Early action is key not only to preventing or containing crises, but also to the efficiency and cost effectiveness of the overall international humanitarian response. Too often, aid is counterproductive and only fuels and prolongs crises. For example, the types of feeding programs used in Somalia drew people out of the rural areas and into the towns where massive, spontaneous refugee camps sprang up. Thus instead of only having to meet food needs, the hard-pressed relief agencies inadvertently generated additional relief requirements that they couldn't meet, and created overcrowded, unsanitary settlements where disease soon became a greater threat than malnutrition. A review of aid strategies in conflicts needs to be undertaken, and measures that can alleviate suffering without exacerbating the strife or increasing the risks to the aid providers and their clients need to be adopted.

Resolution of the Crisis

No conflict is static. Opportunities for resolution can arise at any time, often with startling suddenness. Yet the international community is often unprepared to exploit them or unable to act strategically or decisively. In Bosnia, the imposition of a total exclusion zone for heavy weapons around the besieged capital of Sarajevo in February 1994 had the potential for ending the war. The Serbs were ordered to either withdraw their weapons or place them in designated weapons collection points within the zone. Any heavy weapon firing inside the zone would be subject to air strikes by NATO. The imposition of the zone dramatically altered the strategic picture by denying the Serbs the ability to capture the capital. Had similar zones been placed around other Bosnian cities, the fighting might have ended. Yet the international community, in keeping with conventional views of the noninterventionist role of U.N. peacekeeping forces, reverted to a stance of neutrality and failed to capitalize on the changed circumstances. When the U.N. secretary-general called for member countries to send additional troops to monitor the exclusion zones around Sarajevo, and later Gorazde, the response was minimal. Few countries were willing to station their troops at the weapons collection points deep within hostile territory, where they could easily be taken hostage if the U.N. was forced to use NATO air power to prevent violations. New thinking about how to design measures such as weapons exclusion zones, internal safe areas, and border safe havens is needed. For example, modern surveillance systems could have been employed at the weapons collection points, substantially reducing or even eliminating the need for on-site monitoring. By rethinking the tactics of limited intervention, measures could be formulated that could be employed for humanitarian purposes that would make continued prosecution of a war meaningless and thereby help draw it to a close.

Humanitarian Reforms

If the U.N. is to meet these challenges, major reforms are needed. However, these changes will not happen on their own. The effort will have to be spearheaded by the leading governments. The United States, with its concerns about cost effectiveness of U.N. humanitarian and peacekeeping operations, should take the forefront. What is required is an overhaul of the entire system. But to do that, the U.S. government needs to get its own house in order. First, the government's humanitarian response structure needs to be redesigned so that it is centrally coordinated, covers all victims of humanitarian crises, and eliminates the artificial administrative barriers to assistance. This includes:

- reexamining the operational role of the State Department's Bureau of Population, Refugees and Migration (PRM);

- determining whether to merge the operational functions of PRM with the Agency for International Development's Office of Foreign Disaster Assistance (OFDA) and the newly created Office of Transition Initiatives;
- overhauling the U.S. government's food aid programs and removing barriers to creative uses of food aid;
- reexamining the programs and approaches that the U.S. government encourages NGOs and the U.N. to use in specific emergency situations; and
- demanding more accountability from agencies that receive funding from the United States, especially UNHCR.

Once that is accomplished, the United States should encourage a major overhaul of the relief and peacekeeping system and forge a new U.N. humanitarian architecture that plugs the major gaps, such as aid to internally displaced civilians. The effort needs to go beyond improving coordination; it must address the systemic and mandate problems of the U.N. and other major agencies. At the same time, the U.N. should be encouraged to review the standard approaches its agencies use in responding to humanitarian needs in conflicts. Of special concern are the food aid programs of the World Food Programme and the cost effectiveness of many specialized projects carried out by UNICEF and UNHCR. There is a growing body of statistical data that shows that many of the most popular programs have little effect on saving lives. For example, the U.S. Centers for Disease Control and France's Medecins sans Frontieres carried out studies of supplemental feeding programs in several refugee camps in Africa. The supplemental feeding program was developed to help malnourished women and young children recover from acute malnutrition by giving them prepared, high calorie, balanced meals on a daily basis. Yet the study concluded that there was no significant statistical difference in death and disease rates between those who received supplemental food and those who didn't.

The United States needs to engage the major military powers and the U.N. in a dialogue to develop new models of integrated civil-military operations. The success of Operation Provide Comfort in northern Iraq and the failures of the operations in Yugoslavia and Somalia have left a mixed legacy. These deployments should be carefully reviewed and new doctrines, force structures, and rules of engagement should be put forward. Essentially, a new generation of peacekeeping approaches needs to be developed. The impact of a military deployment and intervention tactics on humanitarian operations also needs to be scrutinized. The arrival of thousands of Western troops in the Somali capital of Mogadishu created a giant economic magnet that attracted thousands of destitute refugees in from the famine zone, further complicating relief efforts in the already overburdened city. When the relief agencies were unable to care for them, the refugees turned to the warlords for work and aid. In return for help, the refugees gave them loyalty and filled their ranks with new recruits.

The United Nations must improve its effectiveness at protecting human rights in conflicts. Protection of refugees, the displaced, ethnic and national minorities, and women has taken a back seat to assistance in recent years. Protection has been approached in a legalistic manner; what is needed is a more activist approach integrated into relief and peacekeeping activities. The United States should promote major reforms in this area. Ultimately, this may prove to be the best way to prevent or mitigate refugee crises.

7

The Role of the Secretary-General

BRIAN URQUHART

The Secretary-General, more than anyone else, will stand for the United Nations as a whole. In the eyes of the world . . . he must embody the principles and ideals of the Charter to which the organization seeks to give effect.—Report of the Preparatory Commission of the UN, 1945, p. 87

T he secretary-general of the United Nations, appointed by the General Assembly on the recommendation of the Security Council, is the only United Nations official mentioned in the Charter. The secretary-general is central to both the political and the administrative life of the organization and is the symbol and

BRIAN URQUHART, currently scholar-in-residence in the International Affairs Program at the Ford Foundation, was one of the first United Nations civil servants, and served in the United Nations Secretariat from 1945 until his retirement in 1986. He worked closely with the first five secretaries-general on peace and security matters, especially peacekeeping, and was under secretary-general for special political affairs from 1974 to 1986. He is the author of *Hammarskjold*, a biography of the second secretary-general, *A Life in Peace and War, Decolonization and World Peace*, and most recently, *Ralph Bunche: An American Life*.

head of the international civil service. The secretary-general also symbolizes the fact that, although the United Nations is an association of independent sovereign states, the organization is also the sum of its membership and represents a collectivity, however tenuous, that has a life and a potential of its own.

In the U.N.'s first fifty years the office of the secretary-general has developed in importance and scope to a greater extent than any other part of the United Nations. It is an essential, and also inevitably controversial, institution, embodying as it does something more than mere international cooperation and sometimes suggesting even a hint of supranational institutions to come—not always a welcome idea to sovereign governments.

At Dumbarton Oaks, in August 1944, the ambivalence of the Allied powers, the future permanent members of the Security Council, about the role of the future secretary-general was already evident. They turned down the idea of a secretary-general directly elected by the General Assembly and insisted that the veto would apply to the selection process. Efforts by smaller governments to change their minds at the Charter conference at San Francisco were unavailing. The appointment has thus always been controlled by the five permanent members of the Security Council, thus imposing, during the cold war at any rate, a lowest common denominator on the selection process. The record of the permanent members in this matter is not a very creditable one.

The Secretary-General's Responsibilities

The founders were also expediently vague about the extent and nature of the secretary-general's responsibilities, which are set out in Articles 97–101 of the Charter. Article 97 establishes the secretary-general as the chief administrative officer of the organization, a full-time job in itself since the secretary-general is the head of the international civil service and is responsible for the worldwide staff of the United Nations.

Article 98 is the first of two articles setting out the political responsibilities of the secretary-general. This is a radical departure from the nonpolitical concept of the secretary-generalship to be found in the Covenant of the League of Nations. Article 98, by

providing that the Security Council, the General Assembly, and
the other main organs may entrust the secretary-general with un-
specified "other functions," has brought him—and the Secretariat—into the arena of political conflict. Even the most apparently
straightforward United Nations resolution often contains ambiguities and compromises; in fact most resolutions on controversial
subjects could not have been passed without such twilight areas.
Thus the secretary-general often finds himself faced with the necessity of taking actions under Article 98 that will be disliked or
contested by one government or another, as he is compelled to
make practical interpretations of the Delphic utterances of the
intergovernmental organ concerned—most often the Security
Council. His only guide here is his judgment as to the intentions of
the majority that voted the resolution, the principles of the Charter
relevant to the situation at hand, a conviction of what is the best
course of action, and the hope that his integrity, objectivity, and
intentions will be respected even if his conclusions are disputed.

Article 99 of the Charter gives the secretary-general explicit
political responsibility in his own right. The Preparatory Commission of the United Nations elaborated on Article 99 in its report as
follows:

> The Secretary-General may have an important role to play as a media-
> tor and as an informal adviser of many Governments, and will undoubt-
> edly be called upon from time to time, in the exercise of his administrative
> duties, to take decisions which may justly be called political. Under Arti-
> cle 99 of the Charter, moreover, he has been given a quite special right
> which goes beyond any power previously accorded to the head of an
> international organization, viz.: to bring to the attention of the Security
> Council any matter (not merely any dispute or situation) which, in his
> opinion, may threaten the maintenance of international peace and secu-
> rity. It is impossible to foresee how this Article will be applied; but the
> responsibility it confers upon the Secretary-General will require the exer-
> cise of the highest qualities of political judgment, tact and integrity.

This anodyne statement is virtually the only official guidance
available to the secretary-general on the implications of Article 99,
which, surprisingly enough, was adopted with very little debate at
San Francisco. The right to bring matters to the attention of the

Security Council implies a watching brief and a broad discretion to conduct inquiries and to engage in informal diplomatic activity in regard to matters relating to the maintenance of international peace and security. Article 33, which enjoins parties to any dispute to seek a solution by peaceful means of their own choice, is also relevant to the secretary-general's duty under Article 99.

Although there is an abiding difference of opinion as to the secretary-general's right to take independent initiatives, Article 99 leaves no doubt that any potential threat to peace and security must be of concern to the secretary-general, who has a duty to do what he can to mitigate it. This has been the basis for the development of the secretary-general's "quiet diplomacy," "good offices," and other intermediary and confidence-building activities over the years. These activities have steadily increased until they fill a very large part of the secretary-general's work program.

Articles 100–101 spell out the international nature of the duties of the secretary-general and the staff, and the arrangements and considerations for the staff's appointment.

Qualifications

When the time came to appoint the first secretary-general, governments were extraordinarily vague regarding the qualifications required of candidates for the post. In September 1945, for example, the U.S. representative on the Preparatory Commission, Adlai Stevenson, told Secretary of State Edward R. Stettinius, "We favor the choice of an outstandingly qualified individual, preferably a figure who has attained some international position and preferably a national of a small or middle power"—not exactly an overwhelming job description. In late December 1945, when the appointment of the first secretary-general was imminent, the State Department mused, "A more common acceptance of the qualifications required for the Secretary-General would be helpful in arriving at a decision." No such luck. (It never seems to have occurred to anyone that the secretary-general could be a woman.)

Probably the most conscientious effort to describe the secretary-general's qualifications was published by a group of former League of Nations officials in 1944.

The qualities which the head of the service should possess are not easy to define. He should be young. Political or diplomatic experience, but not necessarily great fame or eminence, is an advantage. Above all, ability for administration in the broadest sense is important, implying a knowledge of when to be dynamic, to take the initiative and to force an issue; when, at the other extreme, to be content as a purely administrative official; and when, on a middle course, to be a moderator impartially smoothing over difficulties, a catalytic agent in negotiation. . . . In a new organization it may well be that the only qualities which must under all conditions be demanded of the director are those of common sense, courage, integrity and tact.—The International Secretariat of the Future, Royal Institute of International Affairs, London, March 1944

Perhaps the best description of what governments really hope for in a secretary-general can be found in the anodyne words of Max Finger, a former member of the U.S. delegation to the United Nations: "excellence within the parameters of political reality." Not surprisingly, the conduct of the office by its various incumbents has often been controversial.

As things turned out, no detailed statement of qualifications would have been of much avail in January 1946 when the first secretary-general was appointed. After some eminent names— Dwight Eisenhower, Anthony Eden, Lester Pearson—had been bandied about and turned down by the Soviet Union, it became clear that the secretary-general's appointment would be a purely political decision, determined by what the United States and the Soviet Union could agree on—a lowest common denominator if ever there was one. Qualifications, stature, and leadership qualities would all be secondary considerations. The Security Council finally settled on Trygve Lie, the foreign minister of Norway.

The Nature of the Job

The relevant articles of the Charter are a minimal framework for the real work of the secretary-general. Successive incumbents have given their personal impressions of the nature of the job. Trygve Lie referred to it as "the most impossible job on this earth." Dag Hammarskjold said that the secretary-general was "a sort of secular pope, and, for much of the time, a pope without a church." U Thant, a courageous and modest man, said that the secretary-generalship was "the most varied, most interesting, and most challenging political job on earth." To Kurt Waldheim it was "at the same time one of the most fascinating and one of the most frustrating jobs in the world, encompassing as it does the height of human aspiration and the depth of human frailty."

The secretary-general is an international civil servant with 185 masters, who is also periodically expected, especially when everyone else has failed, to be a leader. As U Thant put it, "The Secretary-General's activity will usually seem to some governments too much, and to others too little. He must thread his way through the jungle of conflicting national policies with the UN Charter as his compass, and, if he is lucky, with a directive from one of the main deliberative organs as his guide." When crises arise, the secretary-general may be the world's last hope. He must be prepared to act accordingly, without regard to political reputation and sometimes even to personal safety.

Different secretaries-general have tackled the job in different ways and in varying political climates. All have felt the necessity of a sense of obligation to the human community in its broadest sense, and particularly to its weakest members. All have felt the need to keep a strong sense of justice, of humanity, and of the importance of human dignity, all mixed with an urgent sense of political realism. The secretary-general operates within a world of sovereign states where national interests remain dominant despite technological and other changes and despite the dangers of unbridled nationalism. The secretary-general must work between two poles—at one end the idealism and global objectives of the Charter, and at the other the very pragmatic, and often myopically selfish, nature of national sovereignty. He must try to create a positive mixture from these two incompatible elements.

There is virtually no similarity between the job of a head of government and that of the secretary-general, although the secretary-general is sometimes expected, as a last resort, to take clear-cut and decisive action on problems that have defied the collective wisdom of the member states. Hammarskjold's negotiations to gain the release of the American airmen in China in 1955, or Perez de Cuellar's last minute visit to Saddam Hussein before the launching of Desert Storm, are cases in point. The secretary-general has no sovereign authority, independent power, or even adequate financial resources. No parliament enacts for him the detailed and enforceable legislation that provides a prime minister with precise and continuous directives. He is supported by none of the infrastructure of the great establishments of a state. He travels the world by commercial aircraft. And yet, especially in times of crisis, great things are often expected of the secretary-general.

In this curious and anomalous job, certain qualities are unquestionably required. They include moral stature and integrity, diplomatic skill, fair-mindedness, administrative and managerial ability (or at least the knack of delegating authority effectively), the ability to develop ideas and to communicate them, physical and mental stamina, and a sense of proportion and humor.

The secretary-generalship, at least on paper, is indeed an impossible job. Quite apart from unrealistic public expectations, large responsibilities without significant power or resources, and the contrary attitudes of governments, the job comprises an unmanageable number of major functions. These include:

- managing a worldwide Secretariat and a global organization on a shoestring budget, a sizable part of which is usually overdue (the United Nations is not allowed to borrow);
- implementing the decisions of the Security Council and other organs of the United Nations;
- running peacekeeping and other highly sensitive field operations;
- being the world's mediator in an endless series of "good offices" missions involving quiet diplomacy all over the world;
- providing good offices in human rights and humanitarian situations;
- coordinating the so-called U.N. system of specialized agencies and major economic and social programs;
- representing the United Nations worldwide at conferences and regional meetings and to the media and public;
- maintaining a watch on major developments of all kinds and alerting governments to them;
- generating ideas and strategies on global problems;
- being the world's number one fig leaf and scapegoat.

The Development of the Secretary-Generalship

How far, in practice, have these extremely exigent desiderata been fulfilled? A quick summary of the story of six secretaries-general may give some hint of an answer.

Trygve Lie had to set up the Secretariat, develop the secretary-general's working relationship with governments, preside over the U.N.'s first experiences of international crises—in Palestine and Korea—and find a permanent home for the organization. Except on the latter score, he had nothing but trouble. Over Korea he ran into the dilemma that the cold war presented to each secretary-general—that the secretary-general's position could become impossible when the United States and the Soviet Union disagreed over a decision of the Security Council. He was disavowed over Korea by the Soviet Union, which never recognized him again. He also ran into the problem of the McCarthy period in the United States and its effect on the American members of the Secretariat. He managed, with considerable skill, to get the U.N. settled in New York. He resigned in November 1952 in the hope that all the permanent members of the Security Council could agree on a successor.

The cold war made a nonpartisan third party indispensable to avoiding total paralysis of the Security Council during a dangerous crisis, and this—and the timely arrival of Dag Hammarskjold—gave rise to the activist role of the secretary-general.

After failing to agree on a score of other candidates, the Security Council, in early 1953, appointed Hammarskjold to succeed Lie under the delightful misapprehension that Hammarskjold was a nonpolitical technocrat. Hammarskjold soon showed his mettle. In his first triumph, during one of the cold war's more dangerous moments, he secured the release from China of seventeen U.S. airmen who were prisoners of the Korean War. He subsequently developed the secretary-general's negotiating role, as well as the concept of fielding U.N. peacekeeping forces, first deployed on a large scale in the Suez crisis in 1956. Thus Hammarskjold pioneered a new role for the secretary-general as negotiator, crisis manager, and director of active peace operations.

Hammarskjold paid a heavy price for his activism, which at one time or another alienated various permanent members of the Security Council. He fell out of favor with the United States over Guatemala in 1954, and with the French and the British over the Suez operation in 1956. In the Congo, he infuriated both the Soviets and the French, and he alienated President Charles de Gaulle for good by his actions when the French clashed with newly independent Tunisia over Bizerte. He too was disavowed by the Soviet Union, and also by France.

Hammarskjold believed that the independence, integrity, and activism of the secretary-general and the international Secretariat were vital to the future of the United Nations. In fighting to preserve and develop those attributes, he suffered many setbacks in his final years in office. Hammarskjold was a practical visionary who regarded his task at the United Nations as "working on the edge of human society" to promote the "creative evolution" of human institutions. His aim was the gradual construction of a reliable and just world order through the establishment of international legal precedents and case law, especially in emergency situations. The United Nations would thus be gradually transformed from an institutional and diplomatic mechanism into a constitutional and operational system better equipped to deal with the world's problems.

Hammarskjold was the only secretary-general so far who, through a combination of mystique, charisma, and spectacular performance, became a world-renowned public figure. His death in Africa in September 1961 left the United Nations split down the middle on cold war lines. His successor, U Thant, picked up the pieces and reunited the organization. Of all the secretaries-general, he has been the most unjustly judged. This is perhaps not too surprising. In U Thant's view of his office and responsibilities, moral issues overrode political ones. He was a person of great honesty and courage, and he was not always appreciated in the cynical world of international politics. He brought the U.N. involvement in the Congo to a successful end. (The takeover by Mobutu occurred after the U.N. operation had been withdrawn.) He played an important role in resolving the Cuban missile crisis. He was also instrumental in securing a ceasefire in the ominous war between India and Pakistan in 1965. On his own initiative, he made a prolonged and spirited effort to bring the Vietnam War to an end. But the collapse of the U.N. peacekeeping force in the Middle East in 1967 and the ensuing Six-Day War overshadowed all the positive achievements of his stewardship. He served as a convenient scapegoat on that occasion, although he was the only world leader to go to Cairo to try to persuade Egyptian President Gamal Abdel al-Nasser to reconsider his fatal demand for the withdrawal of the U.N. peacekeepers. Despite a Security Council hopelessly divided along cold war lines, he made valiant efforts to stave off catastrophe.

U Thant's successor, Kurt Waldheim, and his rival, Max Jakobsen of Finland, were the first candidates to campaign actively for the office, setting a disastrous precedent that has been followed ever since. Since that time, self-appointed candidates have lobbied for the post, confusing and monopolizing the already feeble efforts of the Security Council to recommend a suitable candidate to the General Assembly. In practice, the lobbying of self-appointed candidates has, in recent years, replaced any independent search process whatsoever.

Waldheim was neither an inspiring leader nor an original thinker, but he was a hard worker, and he maintained stability throughout the tumultuous 1970s during the uninhibited honeymoon period of the Third World, especially in the U.N. General Assembly. He reestablished peacekeeping as an indispensable diplomatic tool of the United Nations after the 1973 Middle East war. After Waldheim left the United Nations it was discovered that he had misrepresented his war record, and he became the subject of universal opprobrium in the West. It would have been perfectly possible to verify Waldheim's war record *before* he was appointed secretary-general, but nobody bothered. Indeed, but for China's veto, Waldheim would have been elected to a third term with the active support of the United States, France, the United Kingdom, and the Soviet Union. The whole Waldheim episode speaks volumes about the quality and spirit of the appointment process— no open search procedure, no serious vetting of candidates, and a list virtually restricted to those who have declared themselves. In such circumstances, it is something of a miracle that the United Nations has been as well served as it has.

Waldheim's successor, Javier Perez de Cuellar, was a quiet and experienced diplomat who presided skillfully over the transition into the uncertainties of the post–cold war era. He kept on good terms with all governments and was a well-liked but not striking international figure. His strongest suit was quiet diplomacy, which by definition does not gain public acclaim or recognition for its practitioners. After years of frustration, he enjoyed considerable success in the short-lived and illusory renaissance of the United Nations after the end of the cold war.

The present secretary-general, Boutros Boutros-Ghali, has inherited the morning-after hangover from that false renaissance and has had to confront the difficult problems of confronting the tumult of the post–cold war world. Like his predecessors, he is criticized for being both too activist and too passive. Compounding his difficulties, he has also been obliged to reorganize the Secretariat when the organization is more heavily involved than ever in field operations. In a discouraging political climate, he is courageously fighting to keep the organization on course and enhance its effectiveness.

The Present Scope of the Job

In the post–cold war world, the secretary-general is perhaps less essential as a political intermediary than before. As the operational director of the United Nations, however, he (or in the future, let us hope, she) will undoubtedly have a huge and expanding task, with inadequate resources and often with inappropriate mandates. In an age when the media have a commanding position in international life, the secretary-general is also increasingly in demand as a spokesperson for the United Nations and the emergent "international community."

In a period of resurgent nationalism and ethnic strife, growing distrust of international institutions, and diminishing support from governments, the secretary-general is busier—and perhaps lonelier—than ever. The original spirit of international solidarity embodied in the U.N. Charter has weakened in recent years, but the essential institutions of an effective world community, based increasingly on law, are urgently needed. However, the present inclination of U.N. members appears to be a continuation of ad hoc crisis management, which is often too late and sometimes inappropriate, ineffective, and expensive. A crisis of credibility has resulted. For this failure to adapt, the secretary-general will continue, unjustly, to be held accountable.

The United Nations now deals less with conflicts between states, for which it was established, than with civil and ethnic conflicts, for which it was very definitely not designed. Most of the critical situations in which the United Nations is now involved do not impinge on the national security concerns of the major powers. They concern, in the main, humanitarian issues within the borders of states or failed states. Altruism is a far weaker catalyst for international action than the threats to international peace and security that demanded U.N. action during the cold war. This does not mean that the United Nations will not continue to be in demand when governments need a dumping ground for an urgent yet unwelcome problem, but it makes the secretary-general's capacity for effective action more uncertain than ever.

Fifty years hence, the current failures of the U.N. will probably not be seen as Bosnia or Somalia. Rather, unless there is a radical improvement, historians will probably focus on the failure of the world organization to come to effective grips with the great global problems that are even now inexorably shaping the future. At the present time there is an extraordinary dearth of international leadership, either at the national or the international level, whether on immediate security problems or on long-term global problems. Without such inspiring leadership, the best drafted resolutions or agendas or action plans will in most cases remain little more than well-intentioned words and phrases. Only the resolutions of the Security Council are mandatory. The decisions of the other organs are recommendations, to which only leadership and hard work can give meaning and reality.

Future secretaries-general will face their greatest challenge in the economic and social area. If they are to succeed, they will have to pull together the so-called United Nations system of specialized agencies and programs, to imbue it with new and powerful ideas, and to rally the support of governments and the private and nongovernmental sectors. They will have to lead a serious and concerted campaign to contain and resolve the great global problems that increasingly threaten human society—population, poverty, environmental damage, more equitable economic, fiscal and trade arrangements, responsible governance, crime, to name only a few. The steady development of a system of international law in vital fields of human activity will be indispensable to this effort. Short of a new generation of national leaders devoted to international causes, such as existed in the immediate post–World War II period, the lead will have to be taken by international officials led by a respected, authoritative, and sufficiently charismatic secretary-general. Do governments want such a figure? And if so, how will they set about finding him or her?

The United States Interest

Assuming that the United States has a strong interest in an effective United Nations, what sort of secretary-general should the United States be looking for? Short-term interests might indicate a preference for a secretary-general significantly biased in favor of the United States, and strongly influenced by the United States. Longer-term considerations indicate that this is not a good idea. A secretary-general obviously controlled by the United States will inevitably lose the confidence of the rest of the membership and will therefore lack the constituency and support needed either to function effectively in critical times or to administer and manage the organization with authority. Such an arrangement, incidentally, would be out of line with both the letter and the spirit of the Charter.

Experience has shown that a strong and independent secretary-general is in the best interest of *all* the member states. The experience of the Eisenhower administration is relevant in this respect. Dag Hammarskjold's early efforts to deal with the disruptions of the Secretariat caused by the Joseph McCarthy phenomenon were initially a considerable problem for the administration in Washington. Furthermore, Hammarskjold's first major clash with a member state occurred when he disagreed strongly with the United States government over its actions in Guatemala in 1954. Hammarskjold's firm handling of these two issues, however, impressed other governments with his independence and objectivity.

This reputation stood him in good stead in the following year when he successfully negotiated the release by the People's Republic of China of the seventeen United States airmen whom the Chinese courts had convicted of espionage. Eisenhower, Dulles, and Henry Cabot Lodge evidently concluded from this experience that an independent, able, and enterprising secretary-general was on balance far more in the interest of the United States than a lackey, and they enthusiastically supported Hammarskjold for the rest of his time at the U.N., not without disagreeing with him from time to time.

During the Bush administration the then permanent representative of the United States to the United Nations, Thomas Pickering, took the lead among his fellow members of the Security Council in discussing improvements in the Council's approach to the recommendation of a new secretary-general. He put forward the idea of a more effective and widespread search procedure and the possibility of a single seven-year term. These explorations appear to have died out when Ambassador Pickering was transferred to another post.

In considering the appointment of the secretary-general, there will inevitably be self-declared candidates, and there will be those who insist that the secretary-generalship is basically a political appointment with all the limitations that that entails, rather than the world's most important civil service appointment. The truth is that the secretary-generalship has elements of both concepts. He or she, however, is required to perform an infinitely important, demanding, and difficult job. The secretary-general will play a potentially vital role in making a success of the future. The primary considerations, therefore, must be ability, authority, judgment, integrity, and the appropriate qualities of leadership. The secretary-general does not necessarily have to be a diplomat or a politician. The job is sufficiently challenging and important that the whole world should be searched for the best possible candidate.

It is surely in the best interests of the United States, a great power with worldwide responsibilities, to do all it can to help in finding such a person.

Investing in the Future—
Revitalizing the Appointment Process

The present secretary-general's term expires at the end of 1996. It remains to be seen whether U.N. members have any interest in improving the process of selecting the secretary-general. Miraculously, the present approach has thus far produced no outright disasters, but it would be rejected as a bad joke by any serious institution in the private sector. It requires neither a wide-ranging search procedure covering the world at large and both genders, nor a serious effort to establish in advance the credentials and intentions of the appointee. At a minimum, the Security Council and the General Assembly should discuss and define the essential qualifications necessary in determining the best person for the job. Ability, authority, and leadership capacity, rather than political convenience, must take priority if the United Nations is to shoulder its increasingly vital responsibilities and make the necessary transition to the very different world of the twenty-first century.

A few obvious changes would substantially improve the selection process. Besides initiating a more thorough, stringent, and wide-ranging search procedure, individual campaigning should be barred. The Security Council should take the initiative in searching for the best possible candidates. The veto should not apply to the Security Council's recommendation of a candidate, and the unwritten ban on candidates from the five permanent members of the Security Council should also be lifted.

The temptation to run for a second five-year term can only disrupt the performance of an incumbent secretary-general, and, in any case, the job is a uniquely exhausting one. A single seven-year term would allow plenty of time to carry through serious policies without the pressure and distraction of a time-consuming reelection campaign or the cumulative exhaustion of two five-year terms. It should become the rule.

Conclusion

The approach of the member governments to the appointment of the next secretary-general will be an interesting measure of their real attitude toward the United Nations and to the future of international organization. It may also give some indication of their views as to how the United Nations itself should develop in the years leading up to the twenty-first century. The universal recognition that we live in an increasingly interdependent world, the challenge of great global problems, and the incessant use by politicians of the phrase "international community" might lead one to suppose that member governments would wish the U.N. to develop progressively into the public service sector of that "international community," moving on from the association of independent sovereign states that was founded in 1945 to a system better equipped to manage the multiple problems of the modern world. Such a development would mean that the U.N. would steadily move from its current ad hoc, improvisational efforts to an approach that was more systematic, more proactive, better equipped for operations, more in touch with the forces that are shaping the future, more democratic and participatory, and increasingly constitutional in its nature. This would be very much in line with Hammarskjold's idea of the "creative evolution" of human institutions. The secretary-general, as the executive head of a world organization serving all governments, will have a unique responsibility both for fostering this development and for making new arrangements work.

At present there is little indication that governments are thinking along these lines. On the contrary, there seems to be a general determination to stick to the status quo, or even to cut back on already overburdened international institutions. This negative state of mind does not, of course, inhibit governments, or the media and the public for that matter, from complaining of the inadequacies and shortcomings of the United Nations, and sometimes of the secretary-general as well, in dealing with current problems. Especially in recent years, the secretary-general and the United Nations have often served as a very convenient screen to conceal the gulf that exists between the moral high ground that national politicians love to take rhetorically on international matters and the increasingly limited willingness of the most influential governments actually to get involved in difficult or long-term international enterprises.

This prevailing mood makes the work of the secretary-general even more difficult than usual. Nonetheless the secretary-general's office and efforts are vital to the preservation and growth of the delicate plant of international responsibility and cooperation that first germinated in 1919, withered and died in the 1930s, and was revived, much stronger than before, in 1945. The secretary-general of the United Nations is, and will remain, a central element in what is human society's best long-term hope: the gradual development of a global society based on law, justice, and peace.

8

Reforming the United Nations or Going Beyond?

DONALD J. PUCHALA

U nited Nations reform is like the weather: everyone talks about it, but no one can do very much. The last several years have seen an outpouring of writing on the United Nations and its reform, of which *Renewing the United Nations System* by Erskine Childers and Brian Urquhart is a most thoughtful example. This book, and many others, are replete with countless constructive recommendations concerning policies, programs, staffing, funding, and coordination that would, if taken seriously, make the United Nations much more effective in today's world.[1] Yet the sad

---

DONALD J. PUCHALA has been Charles L. Jacobson Professor of Public Affairs at the University of South Carolina since 1981, and serves also as the director of the university's Institute of International Studies. From 1966 to 1981 he was a professor of political science at Columbia University, where he was also associate dean of the School of International and Public Affairs and director of the Institute on Western Europe. Professor Puchala has authored or edited twelve books, including *Issues Before the United Nations General Assembly* and *The Challenge of Relevance: The United Nations in a Changing World Environment.* He is also the author or coauthor of more than sixty journal articles.

fact is that the reformers' recommendations for the United Nations are being taken no more seriously today than they ever were in the past, and, as students of the United Nations well know, the organization's past is strewn with the corpses of dead reform proposals.[2] The prognosis for U.N. reform is therefore not encouraging. But, as explained below, this may not be such a bad thing in the context of contemporary international relations, because it is not altogether clear that the United Nations fits into this context.

The Agenda for Reform

Why is the United Nations in need of reform? The simple answer is that the organization does not work as well as it should, or indeed as well as it could. It does not keep the peace very well, or foster economic and social development very well, or promote human rights very well, or relieve disasters very well, or work as efficiently or effectively toward any of its goals as well as it should and could. Notwithstanding the many episodes over the last fifty years where the United Nations unquestionably influenced the course of human history for the better, as well as the several instances over the last decade where it helped to cushion the world's transition to the post–cold war era, the world organization has not functioned to its members' satisfaction. Both critics and reformers have directed their attentions mainly to four realms of U.N. affairs: peacekeeping, development, finance, and management. Recently, the question of restructuring the Security Council has also become an important reformer's theme.

Shortcomings in Peacekeeping

The kinds of conflict situations in which the United Nations is typically being asked to intervene nowadays fall into operational "gray areas" between traditional impositions to separate warring parties and full-scale military enforcement against aggressors. For such situations the United Nations has not yet produced appropriate doctrines, procedures, rules of engagement, or exit plans, and this is costing lives and money as well as undermining U.N. credibility. Interventions today are also much more complex than those of the past: they often have humanitarian as well as military dimensions; they require civilian as well as military personnel; and they involve delicate balancings between military measures aimed at halting or deterring hostilities and diplomatic measures aimed at resolving conflicts. Reformers point out that the U.N.'s failure to fully understand and doctrinally adjust to the new circumstances surrounding peacekeeping guaranteed the failures in Yugoslavia and Somalia and the confusion in Rwanda.

Most analysts agree that the United Nations will be called upon to engage in peacekeeping in the future, and that the organization should answer many of these calls. But it must be better equipped both doctrinally and materially to accomplish its missions. Practical recommendations for improving the quality and efficiency of U.N. peacekeeping abound. These include formulating common military doctrines and rules of engagement, engaging in contingency planning, improving communications between U.N. headquarters and the field, setting up training facilities and programs, pre-positioning equipment, improving logistics and command and control, and establishing financial reserves on which to draw so that U.N. interventions need not be delayed for want of start-up funding. Some recommendations go even further and call for the establishment of a U.N. rapid-reaction force that could be quickly injected into conflict zones, and/or the earmarking and training of national contingents that would be held constantly ready for U.N. service.

Enhancing the United Nations' capabilities to engage in *preventive diplomacy* is yet another object of reformers' attentions. Preventive diplomacy encompasses the panoply of means and measures by which the United Nations may step into, and work to resolve, international disputes before they reach crisis proportions. Preventive diplomacy is the stuff of Chapter VI of the Charter. It has been frequently engaged in by the United Nations, but always in an ad hoc manner, often too late, usually without adequate background knowledge, operational information, or backup from headquarters, and almost always on budgetary shoestrings. Good sense suggests that trying to prevent crises and resolve disputes before they escalate is in all ways more economical than intervening in battles. Therefore, improving the U.N.'s abilities under

Chapter VI has become an important reformers' cause.

Giving the United Nations access to more plentiful, timely, and accurate information is one important way to equip the organization to act early and effectively. Recommendations for enhancing the intelligence capacities of the U.N. Secretariat range from establishing in-house analytical units, to electronically integrating data bases throughout the U.N. system, to creating a network of U.N. "embassies" in world regions, where Secretariat political officers would monitor and report upon emergent conflicts.[3] The notion of "U.N. embassies" finds favor in both academic and official circles in the United States, though there is presently strong opposition from other U.N. member states who deem political monitoring from U.N. posts to be an infringement of sovereignty. Some modest steps have already been taken to enhance the U.N.'s early warning and information-gathering capacities, though the organization is still largely beholden to its member states for vital information.

Problems in the Development Area

As with peacekeeping, U.N. shortcomings concerning the promotion of economic and social development have been both intellectual and material. Though mandated by its Charter "to employ international machinery for the promotion of the economic and social advancement of all peoples," the United Nations has not been able to ameliorate the plight of the world's poor, thus leading Childers and Urquhart to note that "it may well be that history will judge this to have been the greatest failure of the world organization in its first fifty years." Poverty abounds worldwide, wealth remains concentrated in a small number of countries, and standards and qualities of life in the poor and rich countries respectively remain eons apart.

Explaining the failure of the last fifty years of efforts at economic development is more involved than explaining the specific failures of the United Nations. But even if many factors have to be considered in explaining economic development's failures, it is still the case that the United Nations has not performed well. It has failed to formulate macroeconomic strategies for the world that would have created conditions conducive to the uplifting of the poorer peoples. In the same way, it has failed to formulate coherent, consistent, long-term development strategies, and has instead fallen upon promoting a succession of development slogans— "take-off," "import substitution," "trickle down," "basic human needs," etc.—that have lacked sound analytical foundations, consistent application, or practical usefulness. "Sustainable development" is only the most recent of these development slogans, and it too is probably headed for history's dustbin. The United Nations' intellectual failures are due largely to the political-ideologically charged atmosphere that has perennially stymied the organization's attempts to formulate development policies or even to set priorities. These North-South differences persist and could well intensify in the future.

The United Nations has also failed organizationally in the development field. Existing economic and social capacities are fractured. Countless agencies, organs, and suborgans are charged with development tasks, and there is relatively little communication and coordination among them, either at U.N. headquarters or in the field, even though their mandates overlap and their instrumentalities are similar. While technically agents of the United Nations, the specialized agencies operate autonomously, and even more the Bretton Woods institutions, which typically shun cooperation with other U.N. bodies. In the field, different agencies sometimes operate at cross-purposes, as, for example, when the United Nations Development Programme (UNDP) succeeds at helping a given country establish a social service capacity and the International Monetary Fund (IMF), imposing austerity, compels the country to tear this capacity down. The sheer number of development-promoting, assistance-giving U.N. bodies also forces the dispersion of development monies, redundant, costly overhead expenses, and confusion and endless paper work for recipients. Even when bureaucracy is weathered and development assistance flows, chances tend to be about one in three that no tangible economic or social results will ever come of any given U.N. assisted project.

The bulk of reformers' proposals directed toward improving the U.N.'s development performance calls for somehow improving coordination among U.N. developers. Some propose, for exam-

ple, establishing an Economic Security Council that would direct
the social and economic affairs of the United Nations in a way
similar to that of the Security Council operating in the realm of
peacekeeping. Others would opt for a revitalization of the Economic and Social Council (ECOSOC) that would enhance its policy-making and coordinating capabilities and place it authoritatively at the hub of U.N. development activities. Here especially,
some say, would be an opportunity to rein in the specialized agencies, to subordinate them to the United Nations per se, and to
coordinate their activities with each other and with U.N. headquarters and field bodies. Still others would opt for an economic
and social "czar," or director-general for development, appointed
at a very high level within the U.N. Secretariat and charged with
coordinating development policies and activities for the U.N. system on behalf of the secretary-general. Such an official would also
oversee macroeconomic policy making at the global level. Many
proposals call for the consolidation of available U.N. development
funds into a single pot, which might evolve into a development
bank with a humanistic orientation to counteract the World
Bank's commercial orientation. By contrast, proposals generated
by The Nordic U.N. Project called for upping the operational
capacities of the World Bank so that it would need to depend less
upon the UNDP and other U.N. development bodies to implement its projects in the field.[4]

Global Governance on a Fraying Shoestring

Upon his retirement in 1993, Under-Secretary-General Dick
Thornburgh submitted to Boutros Boutros-Ghali a critical report
on the management of the United Nations in which he characterized the budgeting process as "almost surreal."[5] The fundamental
problem regarding the financing of the United Nations is that the
organization's members do not allot the U.N. enough money to
accomplish the tasks that they assign. Practically speaking, a world
organization simultaneously conducting eighteen peacekeeping
operations, and concurrently involved in servicing dozens of deliberative organs, extending disaster relief, promoting economic and
social development, caring for millions of refugees, and gearing up

for a major effort against the destruction of the earth's natural environment cannot succeed on a budget smaller than that of New York City.

More immediately, the financial problem of the United Nations is that remittances by member states are irregular, unpredictable, and sometimes withheld, thus creating the surreal situation of which Thornburgh spoke. Because member states pay their dues late, sometimes partially, and sometimes not at all, U.N. financial officers are constantly forced to borrow across accounts, draw down reserves, postpone payments and commitments, go hat in hand to national capitals, or engage in opaque or otherwise creative bookkeeping.

With regard to the financing of peacekeeping, monies are raised by special assessments for each operation, and because funds reserved to finance the start-up costs of missions are invariably exhausted (because they have been shifted to make up shortfalls elsewhere), operations cannot be launched until new funding is approved.

Few peacekeeping missions can begin in earnest immediately after the Security Council approves them. The Secretariat must first prepare a mission budget, which can take several weeks. It then submits this budget to the Advisory Committee on Administrative and Budgetary Questions (ACABQ) for approval. Meanwhile the U.N. cannot contract for equipment or services above a $3 million annual limit, for each operation, on the Secretary-General's "unforeseen and extraordinary" spending authority. This makes it difficult to mobilize troops and to move them to operational areas speedily.

The ACBAQ normally takes less than a week to approve a mission budget. . . . When the budget is formally approved by the General Assembly's Fifth Committee, and then by the General Assembly, an assessment letter is sent to member states and the U.N. can begin spending up to the full cost of the mission.

This system has many disadvantages.[6]

The debilitating financial plight of the United Nations actually has little to do with any profligate handling of resources. The major finding of the Independent Advisory Group on U.N. Financing is that delinquency on the part of member states is at the root of the U.N.'s financial troubles. Consequently, the foremost recommendation for reforming the financing of the United Nations is that member governments must pay their assessments in full and on time. Secondly, member governments whose payments are in arrears must clear their debts to the United Nations with all due dispatch, and the United Nations should be allowed to charge interest on outstanding balances. Beyond calling for responsible behavior on the part of member states, reformers also recommend higher levels for the U.N.'s various reserve and working capital funds. In addition, the assessment formulas need to be rethought and revised to more realistically reflect different countries' capacities to pay, and peacekeeping payments should be lumped into a single assessment rather than separately called in for each operation. The United Nations should be allowed to borrow money.[7] Most importantly, the United Nations is going to have to be granted additional resources if it is to operate effectively in the post–cold war environment.

Bureaucracy Run Rampant

Issues of bureaucratic mismanagement cross-cut all other reform questions. Making an efficient, expeditious, purposeful, professional organization out of a congeries of persons, talents, cultures, languages, tasks, roles, and missions was already a most daunting challenge in the days of the League of Nations. In the case of the United Nations, critics contend, "international civil service" has almost become an oxymoron. The United Nations bureaucracy grinds along notoriously slowly, and the ratio of expectation to outcome is frequently disappointing. Coordination across departments and programs in the Secretariat is sporadic, since coordinating committees have not proven effective, and across agencies in the U.N. system coordination is frequently not even attempted.[8] Redundancies, duplications of effort, contradictory efforts on the parts of different agencies, avoidances of responsibility, accountability, and evaluation, as well as occasional fraud and professional misconduct are ready grist for critics' mills. Further afflicting the international civil service are the bureaucratic politics, the fief building, and the paranoia, egomania, interpersonal skulduggery, and backstabbing that tend to be endemic in most large human organizations. In the United Nations such antics are extraordinarily in evidence. The Secretariat appears to be undergoing perpetual reorganization, which typically produces little by way of improved efficiency and much by way of depressed morale among the staff.

Reasons for the bureaucratic shortcomings of the U.N.'s international civil service are manifold. Starting from the top, it is not unfair to say that individuals appointed to the office of secretary-general are usually chosen for reasons other than their reputations as skilled administrators, and the last several CEOs of the United Nations have surely proven themselves to be other than skilled administrators. Starting from the bottom, there are many people of questionable competence working for the United Nations, and the average talent level has been most adversely affected by the fact that nowadays almost every appointment to the Secretariat is a political appointment effected by some national ambassador's successful lobbying. Another way of looking at the personnel question is to observe that there are too few genuinely competent people in the Secretariat, and the result is that a small corps of truly outstanding and remarkably dedicated people tends normally to be overworked well past the point of diminishing returns.

Coordination is the casualty of a constitutional structure that makes the United Nations a horizontal organization with diffused authority instead of a vertical one where authority can be enforced hierarchically. Coordination is also hampered by the perennial political predicament wherein lack of consensus among member states (sometimes even within member states) sends different departments and agencies marching in different directions. Lack of resources also hampers bureaucratic efficiency at the United Nations because the Secretariat is asked constantly to do too much with too little, and in such circumstances there is a good deal that simply does not get done well or done at all.

Recommending bureaucratic reform at the United Nations has become a cottage industry for pundits. It has also become a near obsession for the U.S. government. Most recommendations call for "leaning," "meaning," "streamlining," and "downsizing." The idea that the United Nations ought to be able to do even more with even less appears to have widespread appeal, although, after nearly a decade of bureaucratic downsizing, it is difficult to imagine the United Nations doing any more with any less. Other recommendations call for the appointment of a deputy secretary-general for administration, who would relieve the secretary-general of management responsibilities, an inspector-general who would press for transparency and accountability and sniff out fraud, and an ombudsman who would hear complaints from the staff and bring biases and nepotisms to the surface. There exists a veritable atlas of reorganization charts, many of them replete with imaginative transbureaucratic coordinating councils, commissions, committees, and the like. There are also reasonable recommendations for raising professional salaries so that persons of greatest ability, including a goodly number of women, can be recruited, promoted, and retained. Some rather blunt proposals point to the need for backbone in resisting pressures for political appointments.

Restructuring the Security Council

Finding a way to make the array of permanent seats in the Security Council less reminiscent of the allied coalition that fought World War II and more representative of today's distribution of power and influence gains importance as the Security Council becomes increasingly active. To be effective the Security Council must remain credible and legitimate, which is the reason that the Council has to structurally symbolize a distribution of international status that most of the world community can accept. Admitting Japan to permanent membership on the Security Council has long been the official policy of the U.S. government, and seating Japan also has the support of a large number of other U.N. members, although Asian backing for Japan is lukewarm. The admission of Germany is also widely acceptable, but some would prefer instead a rotating representation from the European Union. Of course, admitting Japan and Germany, *and doing nothing else* to the Security Council finds almost no favor. How to admit other regional powers, who to admit, how to allocate veto powers, how to balance permanent and non-permanent members, how to amend the Charter without devaluing it, and how to emerge from all of this and still have a workable Security Council remain unanswered questions.

The Prognosis for Reform

If the post–cold war world were really as George Bush imagined when he told the 45th U.N. General Assembly that

we have a vision of a new partnership of nations that transcends the Cold War. . . . a partnership united by principle and the rule of law. . . . a partnership whose goals are to increase democracy, increase prosperity, increase the peace, and reduce arms. . . . a world of open borders, open trade, and most importantly, open minds,[9]

then there could be reason to be optimistic about reforming the United Nations. But this is not our world. Dissensus among the member states stemming from power-political rivalries and ideological antagonisms has been the fundamental obstacle not only to U.N. reform but to the organization's total usefulness throughout the second half of the twentieth century. Dissensus continues today, and the United Nations is likely to be its continuing victim.

While it is true that power-political rivalry has abated as a result of the collapse of the Soviet Union, and that no new global confrontation of armed giants will occur as long as the preponderance of the United States lasts, it is also true that new ideological antagonisms are brewing. As the grand debate between East and West lapsed into obsolescence, the even grander debate between North and South came into clearer focus. In part, the new debate is a continuation of the destructive dialogue between the rich and the poor that shook the United Nations during the 1970s and gnawed away at international cooperation in economic and social issue areas in the ensuing decades. It has to do with differing conceptions of justice and equity, with differing understandings of the history of the nineteenth and twentieth centuries, with differing assignments of responsibility for the plight of the disadvantaged, with differing images of an acceptable status quo, and with differing prescriptions for the goals and instrumentalities of international public policy. Even a cursory review of the plenary documents of the 49th General Assembly should suffice to convince one that none of these differences has disappeared from the ideological discourses of today.

But the brewing ideological confrontation is more complex, and ultimately more incendiary, because it interweaves North-South themes with West–non-West ones. This brings very fundamental values into irreconcilable conflict. For many of the elites of what was once termed the "Third World," the hegemony of the West is as political-philosophically objectionable as the hegemony of the North is economic-philosophically objectionable. Differences between West and non-West are about the respective values of individualism and collectivism, the definition of human rights, the definition of human well-being, the respective desirability of democracy and authoritarianism, the means and ends of government, the meaning and function of law, and, even more basically, the origins of knowledge and the meaning of truth. In contention are the values of the West embodied in the themes of the eighteenth century Enlightenment, and the values of other great and newly resurgent human civilizations such as the Islamic, the Persian, the Chinese, and possibly the Russian. Ideological debate has already begun in U.N. organs concerned with human rights. Chances are that the entire United Nations will again become a main forum for contending world views.[10] A new cold war hardly promises the consensus necessary to reform the United Nations.

There are also some more practical reasons why reforming the United Nations remains unpromising. First, the U.S. government is not especially interested in reforming the United Nations, or at least Washington is not very interested in reforming it in ways that would notably improve the organization's effectiveness.[11] The U.S. Congress harbors a deeply negative image of the United Nations; many members of Congress question the relationship between U.N. membership and U.S. national interests; and even those sympathetic to the United Nations are unsympathetic to allocating any new resources to the world organization. For its part, the Clinton administration all but prohibited future U.S. physical participation in U.N. peacekeeping, and its reform agenda emphasizes the old saw of "leaning" and "meaning" the U.N. bureaucracy, sniffing out fraud, deemphasizing develop-

ment, and shifting priorities in the direction of human rights, the promotion of economic privatization, and political democracy. Most consequential in the current American attitude toward the United Nations is a rather distinct unwillingness to exercise leadership in the reform effort. Without active American leadership the United Nations probably cannot be reformed!

Nor, save for the Scandinavians, Canadians, New Zealanders, and Australians, do most other member states show much real interest in reforming the United Nations. Many in the Third World have become disenchanted with the institution because their high hopes that the United Nations would be an instrument for world economic and social revolution were dashed in the exhausting North-South debates of the 1970s. They have really gotten very little from the organization and view it as a Western tool. Some Third World elites also fear that a reformed United Nations, and especially a Western dominated one, could readily become more aggressively interventionist to the detriment of their sovereignty.

It should also be noted that enthusiasm for reform is rather unevenly distributed within the United Nations itself. For many of those Secretariat officials who have been "reforming" for the last fifteen years, the possibility of genuine change is greeted with cynicism. "Plus ça change, plus c'est la même chose" readily translates into countless languages spoken in the international civil service. For others in the bureaucracy, the prospect of change is threatening, and the tendency to delay or derail reform via resistance from the inside is quite real.

Moving Beyond Reform

Realistically speaking, the long record of failed attempts at U.N. reform is discouraging, and obstacles to improving U.N. capabilities and performance in the future loom frustratingly large. Hence the paradox: the reformers' analyses are sound, their criticisms of the United Nations are constructive, and their recommendation for change are reasonable to the point of rendering change imperative. Yet there is only the remotest of possibilities that real reform of the United Nations, beyond perhaps the restructuring of th

Security Council, will happen. This leaves the world with a limp-
ing organization that does not work very well, cannot be improved
very much, and will probably remain the subject of reformers'
recommendations, and the source of their frustrations, up to the
millennium and beyond. Because the United Nations has inspired
intense normative attachments, especially among those of us who
have been battling the organization's destructive critics for so
many years, there has naturally been great reluctance on the part
of serious students of the United Nations to entertain the notion
that the multilateral needs of contemporary international relations
might be better served by an alternative institution. But because it
is now reasonably clear that the United Nations either cannot or
will not be effectively reformed, the time has come to think anew.

What is key to new thinking about world organization is that
whatever the structure contemplated, it must fit usefully into the
real international political and economic environment that will
surround it for the foreseeable future. What this means is that
multilateral institutions relevant for the early twenty-first century
must be able to function productively in an environment characterized by: 1) a highly skewed distribution of military power that
will favor the United States possibly for several decades; 2) an
unequal and stratified distribution of the world's wealth that advantages industrialized countries located mainly, though not exclusively, within the Western cultural domain, but which are not
hostile to economic development in the poorer regions of the
world; 3) a zone of enduring peace encompassing the trilateral
world of North America, Western Europe, and most of the industrialized and newly industrializing Pacific Rim; 4) cultural plural-
ism that has political-ideological import, particularly in diver-
gences in values among Western, Chinese, Islamic, and Russian
cultures; 5) a zone of intermittent, and largely domestic, violent
conflict encompassing much of what was formerly called the Third
World, but that probably also includes the former Soviet Union;
and 6) impending limits on the carrying capacity of the earth's
natural environment that will be more in evidence in some geographic regions than in others, but will likely have implications
everywhere. Within this projected environment, international relations will take place both within and between the different eco-

nomic and cultural zones. Within and between the zones there will also be strong imperatives for multilateral rule making and continuing needs for, and rewards from, collective action. Among the poorer countries there will be continuing needs for internationally delivered welfare services. Since the quality of relations will differ greatly depending upon the zones within which or across which they take place, it is most unlikely that a single universal international organization like the United Nations can accommodate the multilateral needs of the emergent world.

Functionalism Revisited

The functional approach to international governance evolved in a spate of innovative thinking at London's Royal Institute of International Affairs during the 1940s.[12] The functionalists imagined that the world could be ordered functional sector by functional sector—e.g., trade, finance, food and agriculture, health, social affairs, disarmament, and the like—through the work of specialized international organizations, technically staffed and closely linked to kindred staffs within member states. Heaping all of the world's problems upon a single, central, multipurposed organization, the functionalists reasoned, was unfeasible primarily because no organization could conceivably be constructed to simultaneously undertake the manifold tasks. In addition, there was the concern, proven meaningful by hindsight, that in a centralized, all-purpose organization, political deadlock anywhere would cause gridlock everywhere.

The founders of the United Nations deferred slightly to the functionalist blueprint by keeping intact a number of preexisting specialized international organizations, like the International Labor Organization, the World Health Organization, and the Universal Postal Union, and by establishing several new ones. However, the main thrust of the Charter and the preference of most charter members were to push toward centralization, with the result that many of the functions of the specialized agencies were duplicated in the United Nations Organization, and the specialized agencies were peripheralized in the U.N. system. The United Nations was thus bifurcated into a United Nations Organization at its center, and a United Nations System of smaller agencies arranged in outlying functional space. Eventually, the specialized agencies chose to increasingly distance themselves from the United Nations Organization, largely to avoid control over their activities and resources by central authorities in whom, for a variety of reasons, they had decreasing confidence.

There is something to suggest that the world's multilateral affairs might be better attended today and in the future by dismantling much of the U.N.'s center and individually strengthening the specialized agencies that now constitute the periphery. It is, after all, the center—the peace and security mechanisms, the development mechanisms, the budget and finance mechanisms, the management practices, the coordination committees, the super-bureaucratized channels, and the New York and Geneva Secretariats most generally—that are not working very well, and that are frustrating reform efforts. Why not rationalize the world's division of multilateral labor and spin off tasks to specialized agencies that are specifically mandated, staffed, and budgeted to execute them?

A Reconstituted United Nations System

Any number of designs for a world system of functional cooperation are conceivable, and this is not the place to discuss detailed blueprints. Generally speaking, a workable design for an alternative multilateral system would need to preserve the United Nations General Assembly because it performs a most useful function in international relations. The General Assembly is a meeting place for the governments of the world and a debating forum where ideas and ideologies confront, contend, and sometimes converge. It is one of the few places where humankind enters into dialogue, and the General Assembly is therefore most necessary as long as no one has any illusions about endowing it with global legislative authority.

The other forum for world debate, particularly concerning questions of values and culture, is in the deliberative organs of the United Nations Educational, Scientific, and Cultural Organization. UNESCO therefore ought also to be preserved, though it should be limited to its world forum role, and accordingly stripped of its operational programs, which today make it more of a controversial development agency than a useful center for the exchange of ideas. If a new cold war is to be fought, let it be fought in the General Assembly and in a reconstituted UNESCO. However, when global consensus can be attained in these deliberative organs, it can and should be a source of policy guidance for other international agencies. The General Assembly will continue to require a modest staff to service its meetings and a modest budget to cover expenses.

A world peacekeeping agency needs to be established. Its constitution would reproduce Chapters VI and VII of the U.N. Charter, plus the good offices role of the secretary-general and whatever fact-finding, early warning, or other intelligence functions the secretary-general's office and the Secretariat's Department of Political Affairs presently perform. The Security Council, reconstituted in some manner to make it more representative, would become the policy-making organ of the agency, and elements of the current Secretariat's Departments of Political Affairs and Peacekeeping would constitute the staff. Conceivably, some of the recommendations that are circulating today for enhancing the U.N.'s peacekeeping capacities would be taken to heart and built into the new world peacekeeping agency.

Other innovations might include folding the human rights activities of the United Nations into the functioning of the World Court, and also integrating there the functioning of the international criminal court. Steps ought to be taken to make it possible for private individuals as well as corporate persons to appear before the court, and the court should be generally upgraded as a center for the interpretation, and possibly the enforcement of international law. Additionally, the United Nations Environment Programme will need to be upgraded to the status of a specialized agency, and likewise the Disarmament Commission and its subsidiary organs, which might be integrated into the International Atomic Energy Agency. The United Nations Disaster Relief Organization should be elevated to the status of a specialized agency, and the activities of the High Commissioner for Refugees, the U.N. International Children's Emergency Fund (UNICEF), and

several of the U.N.'s special funds could be consolidated within a
world humanitarian relief agency. This new agency might mod-
estly augment its staff with experts currently working in the Secretariat's Department of Humanitarian Affairs.

The United Nations Industrial Development Organization
should be abolished because its present functioning reproduces
efforts in fields of economic development that are already the ken
of several other agencies. Otherwise, much of the world's multilateral efforts in development can and should be located in the several specialized agencies already mandated to perform such tasks.
These would include the Food and Agriculture Organization,
which would take over the World Food Programme and the International Fund for Agricultural Development, the World Health
Organization, which would focus more specifically on improving
health conditions in the poorer countries, and the International
Labor Organization, which would focus on improving social conditions in poorer countries. Each of these agencies would need to
augment its operational activities to replace the United Nations
Development Programme and the existing array of trust funds
earmarked for development. Financing economic development
would be the mission of the World Bank and the regional banks,
and integrating the developing countries into the world economy
would be one of the tasks of the International Monetary Fund and
the World Trade Organization.

Setting global standards and monitoring compliance would
continue to be the already useful and generally well-performed
functions of the International Civil Aviation Agency, the World
Intellectual Property Organization, the International Telecommunications Union, and the International Maritime Organization. The newly constituted World Environmental Protection
Agency would also be primarily a standard-setting organization
and not a development agency. Many of the other specialized
agencies would also have standard-setting assignments. The Universal Postal Union and the World Meteorological Organization
would surely need to continue performing their valuable services.
What would disappear from the new United Nations system would
be the United Nations Organization as we know it today.

There should be no expectation that a newly constituted multilateral system built as a lattice of functionally specialized agencies would eliminate all of the problems that chronically plague the United Nations Organization. Bureaucratic inertias and bureaucratic politics are endemic to bureaucracies, and bureaucratic ills certainly infect functional agencies too.[13] It is also difficult to imagine that a prevailing ideological dissensus in the world would not hamper international cooperation even in a functionally structured multilateral system. If coordination among departments, programs, and agencies is a problem today, decentralizing the system is unlikely to improve this situation. Practically speaking, if resource scarcities are brakes on the effectiveness of today's United Nations, there is surely no guarantee that resources will be any more abundant in a functionally organized system.

Still, reorganizing international cooperation along functional lines would be a distinct improvement over the present system. The obvious advantage of transforming the present centralized system into a decentralized functional one is that the restructuring would eliminate much that is dysfunctional in the present system—the cumbersome and frequently chaotic departments of the U.N. Secretariat, the moribund Economic and Social Council and its many wheel-spinning commissions, centers, councils, conferences, and institutes, the questionably useful U.N. Regional Commissions, the operationally overloaded Office of the Secretary-General, and much more. More important, transparency, responsibility, and accountability would all be enhanced in the decentralized system, as it would become less difficult to identify where, how, when, and by whom tasks are to be performed. It would also become less difficult to monitor and evaluate performance. Redundancy in missions and operations could also be reduced, and resources might possibly be saved as a result. Under the functionally decentralized system, the coordination of international services in complex situations would be, as it should be, the responsibility of the governments who receive the services. Interagency coordination could be enhanced by locating the headquarters of all of the specialized agencies in the same place (which would also rather markedly reduce the costs of conducting diplomacy).

In a decentralized, functionally focused, multilateral system, the entire organization would not necessarily come into jeopardy when one of its parts fails. For one thing, such a decentralized system would be less vulnerable to political assaults from disgruntled governments, because it would be harder to indict, and politically or economically punish, the entire system where the source of the unease turns out to be the performance of a particular agency. Institutional reform in such a system also might be less difficult because reformers' attentions could be concentrated on the poorly performing agencies, while others were left to continue their useful functioning. The reshaping of UNESCO over the last several years under Federico Mayore is an example of how such reform can be accomplished. Not least important is the fact that such a system of specialized agencies is a good deal more acceptable to the United States Congress than the existing structure, and, realistically speaking, Washington's willingness to allocate resources to the United Nations still impinges dramatically upon multilateralism's future.

Notes

[1] See in particular, United States Commission on Improving the Effectiveness of the United Nations (1993); Rochester (1993), pp. 109–232; United Nations Association of the United States of America (1987); Independent Commission on the Future of the United Nations (1993); Righter (1995), pp. 245–376; Coate (1994), pp. 3–66.

[2] The Childers and Urquhart report charts this cemetery of dead reform proposals in rather comprehensive fashion.

[3] Peck (1993), pp. 6–13.

[4] The Nordic U.N. Development Project (1991), pp. 68–73.

[5] Thornburgh (1993), p. 26.

[6] Independent Advisory Group (1993), p. 17.

[7] The Independent Advisory Group on U.N. Financing did not endorse the idea of giving the United Nations borrowing authority because it concluded that this would encourage member states to avoid their responsibility to finance the U.N. See Independent Advisory Group (1993), pp. 12–13.

[8] Childers and Urquhart (1994), pp. 74–84.

[9] Bush (1990), p. 152.

[10] Harries (1994).

[11] Puchala (1994).

[12] This thinking was eloquently captured in David Mitrany's two essays, "A Working Peace System" (1943) and "The Functional Approach to World Organization" (1945). See Mitrany (1966), pp. 25–102, 149–166.

[13] McKnight (1975), p. 169.

9

Preparing for a
Better U.N. Future

CHARLES WILLIAM MAYNES
AND RICHARD S. WILLIAMSON

O rdinarily, an anniversary is an occasion for celebration, but the fiftieth anniversary of the United Nations must be an occasion for examination. Support for international institutions in political circles in Washington is perhaps at the lowest reached in the postwar period. Only a few years after George Bush announced that the United Nations was poised to play a growing role in world affairs with the end of the cold war, international institutions have almost no champions in Washington. Although public opinion surveys do not reveal any growing public disillusionment with the United Nations—on the contrary, support is high and growing—the political class in Washington is increasingly hostile or indifferent.

Some might conclude that this new development is the result of the political revolution that took place in the November 1994 elections, which brought a Republican majority to both houses of Congress. It is true that opposition to the U.N. is particularly intense in the Republican party. The *National Journal* on November 12, 1994, pointed out that in that year "ninety per cent of the GOP's 178 House Members either voted against the United Nations every time (112) or all but once (49). Of the 55 Republican senators, more than two-thirds opposed pro-UN positions all of the time (20) or all but once (11)." And the Contract with America of the Republican majority in the Congress contains provisions that would limit U.S. support for U.N. peacekeeping.

But the assault on international institutions is not coming from one party or point of view. A concentration on recent voting records or campaign strategies may convey a false impression. Much of the difficulty in which the U.N. finds itself in terms of U.S. attitudes is a recent phenomenon. For example, at least sixty-five Republicans, including Speaker of the House Newt Gingrich, supported the U.N. at least 25 percent more often in the last Republican administration than in the Clinton administration. Key Republican congressional leaders like James Leach and Nancy Kassebaum have been congressional leaders in the effort to support the U.N.

Congress often tends to take its lead from the administration in the field of foreign policy, and the Clinton administration's attitude toward the U.N. has been uncertain to say the least. It is often forgotten that the hardening of the Clinton administration toward the U.N. took place prior to the tragic loss of eighteen U.S. soldiers in Somalia. It was some weeks *before* the setback in Somalia that President Clinton announced to the General Assembly that the United States would be adopting a more critical attitude toward U.N. peacekeeping. "If the US is to say 'yes,' the UN is going to have to learn to say 'no' " [to new peacekeeping operations].

Relations between the secretary-general and the Secretariat on the one hand and the Clinton administration on the other have also been strained at best. It was thirteen months into the Clinton administration before the secretary-general was invited to visit the White House. This is the first administration in postwar history to attack Secretariat officials repeatedly in public fora. When the incumbent suggested that he might run for reelection, officials at the U.S. Mission to the United Nations stated anonymously to the press that his chances were those of a "snowball in hell."

The administration's December 1994 decision not to reenter the U.N. Educational, Scientific, and Cultural Organization (UNESCO), notwithstanding the important reforms completed in that body, was not taken under pressure from the Republican opposition. Indeed, as the *New York Times* reported on January 1, 1995, "Congressional staff members who follow American relations with the United Nations said that there was no certainty that UNESCO would have been made an issue by Republicans, a number of whom support membership."

Perhaps one reason for the rising bipartisan criticism of the United Nations is a widespread tendency in the post–cold war period to address the U.N. as an independent actor rather than to consider it a possible tool. During the cold war commentators were much less likely to do this since the key actors in almost every crisis were the superpowers themselves. But with the end of the cold war and with the great powers often concluding that events in remote parts of the world have little effect on their national interest, there is a growing tendency to look to the U.N. as almost a supranational actor able to carry out the functions of a major state.

In fact, the United Nations even in the altered circumstances is a tool, not an actor. It is the sum of its members, especially the determinative permanent five. It is true that the Secretariat, both for good and bad, has a life of its own as does every bureaucracy. And it must be addressed and managed in that light. But the Secretariat possesses no independent resources and can move ahead only when the major states acquiesce in its actions. On virtually every critical issue, the permanent five dominate. And among those five, the United States, as the world's most important state, has enormous capacity to drive the consensus on issues of importance to it.

As different as the two operations were, the U.N. approved coalition against Iraq and the U.N. force in Haiti probably would not have been approved in a secret Security Council vote. But a decisive majority could be mobilized in a public vote because the United States was determined to receive approval. In this light, the current criticism of the United Nations is in large part a criticism of the member states and, in particular, the inconsistent and often ineffectual participation of the United States in the organization.

Over its first fifty years the United States has had a checkered relationship with the United Nations. In the 1940s and 1950s the West had an overwhelming majority within the organization, and its policy toward the United Nations reflected this advantage. Despite frustrations during the early years with our cold war rivals and their efforts to use it as an arena for propaganda, generally the United Nations served in the late 1940s and 1950s as a natural extension of the policy of the United States and its Western allies.

However, by the late 1950s and into the 1960s the United Nations changed dramatically. It became the midwife for the new nations emerging from European colonies in Africa and Asia. These new nations were militarily weak and irrelevant and economically poor and aggrieved. The United Nations was one of the few venues in which they could express their frustrations. They spoke out to the discomfort of their former colonial rulers and their allies, which included the United States. During this period American engagement in the United Nations became less central to U.S. foreign policy, and to some it was a hostile forum. But because of the cold war, it always remained an important forum. Few serious leaders in the United States wanted to leave the floor clear for the Soviet Union to seize advantage.

Within the United Nations the Soviet Union worked studiously to develop new alliances of convenience with both the East and the South. It exploited the issues of Israel and South Africa. By 1974 the Arabs and Africans had joined together to pass a resolution labeling "Zionism as racism," which caused American support for the United Nations to plummet. Many in the United States came to see the United Nations as an environment hostile to U.S. interests.

Ironically, 1974 was the high water mark of this Third World effort to use U.N. organs to stigmatize the United States and its allies. Coming shortly after the 1973 war in the Middle East and the subsequent oil embargo, Third World extremism reflected temporally a sense of historical destiny, a moment when the power of Third World solidarity and the oil weapon would force the North to the bargaining table on a number of critical issues. Beginning in the last year of the Ford administration and continuing in the Carter administration, the United States and its allies began to reestablish a sense of proportion in the United Nations and were able to defeat efforts to continue the "Zionism is racism" canard and to begin work on the seminal resolutions that brought independence to Zimbabwe and Namibia. In 1978, under U.S. leadership, the U.N. Security Council created a U.N. peacekeeping mission in southern Lebanon, which in turn helped to preserve the environment that made Sadat's historic mission to Jerusalem possible.

Then in 1979 the Iranian revolution again seemed to bring another cycle of Third World extremism, and although United Nations members generally supported the American position throughout the painful hostage crisis with Iran, the general perception in America grew that the United Nations was an institution subsidized by Americans to permit others to denounce America. The moment for a "cold shower" had arrived.

During the 1980s the environment at the U.N. General Assembly became one of confrontation and rhetorical brinkmanship. Congress exacerbated this by withholding the U.S. contribution pending significant budgetary and administrative reforms. But this "cold shower" set the stage for a major improvement in U.S. relations with the U.N. toward the end of the Reagan administration and throughout the Bush administration. A foundation was laid for the Bush administration to go to the U.N. for support in the effort to force Saddam Hussein to disgorge Kuwait.

Now a new cycle at the United Nations has begun. With the collapse of the Soviet Union and the elimination of the Communist system as an alternative model, the United Nations has become a forum of consensus on the issues of free markets, democracy, and the rule of law. That is not to say that all members adopt these desirable practices, but there is no longer any sustained ideological challenge to them. As the secretary-general recently pointed out, more than sixty members have recently requested assistance in carrying out democratic elections. Regrettably, since the Gulf War, neither Republicans nor Democrats have adopted a U.N. policy responsive to the new conditions. American policy has vacillated wildly from moments of benign neglect to moments of unrealistically high expectations as we attempted to off-load problems on the world body.

One might ask whether it matters. According to one view, it does not. Those who hold this view might argue that the United Nations has always been at the margin of U.S. foreign policy concerns. There has always been a wide disparity between what prominent U.S. statesmen said before the General Assembly and what they said in closed policy councils. Secretary of State Dean Acheson's view of the United Nations was scarcely less hostile than that of General de Gaulle, who was legendary in his dismissal of international institutions, including the U.N.

A more extreme version of this suspicious approach holds that the U.N. remains a positive danger to American interests. Proponents of this view contend that the U.N. is a "dangerous place" and that it propagates values and supports programs inimical to American interests. This position, however, had more adherents during the cold war than after.

Our own belief is that the United Nations is a vital institution that is in great need of improvement. We would like to see that improvement take place. We would like to see both parties support it and the institution at large. We believe that a serious reform effort deserves our support because the United Nations does matter for at least the following reasons.

1) The United States is a global power with security and commercial interests on every continent. By its very nature, such a power must remain concerned with international rules, norms, and regimes that are relevant to American interests. It must be vigilant in their defense or amendment. Establishing and maintaining international rules, norms, and regimes is one of the principal functions of the United Nations and its specialized agencies.

2) The United States sees itself as an international leader. Every administration aspires to this role. But it is hard to be a leader if one is absent from international fora or constantly on the defensive there. It is also hard to be a leader if the United States is always saying no. It is hard to be a leader if the United States threatens not to do its fair share. It is not possible to be a leader if the United States does not take into account the concerns of its closest allies, which are anxious for the United States to play a constructive role in the United Nations.

The bipolar ballast of the cold war is gone. Whereas during the cold war, governments were forced because of ideology, geography, or self-interest to pick sides either with the East or West, now there is a far greater margin for maneuver within the community of nations. There is a dispersal of power centers. One result of this is that the unipolar world imagined by some is already gone and we now live in a more precarious and varied world, in which the need for multilateral problem solving is heightened.

3) We are *not* members of a global village and are unlikely to reach that position for decades, if not centuries, to come. But the world's politics and economics are increasingly globalized. It is hard to believe that the world's business can be globalized and adequately managed if there are not also global institutions that assist nation states in managing the new international reality. There are many multilateral fora that can be used to advance U.S. interests. Among them are the North Atlantic Treaty Organization (NATO), the Organization of American States, the Group of Seven (G-7) bringing together at the summit the world's major economic powers, the Organization for Security and Cooperation in Europe (OSCE), and others. Each has its special characteristics, but the United Nations itself offers many advantages. Thus the record of the U.N., while it should be better, is one of considerable benefit to humanity in general and Americans in particular. Many U.N. critics overlook such contributions as the following.

- The U.N. promotes peace. Through the office of the secretary-general the U.N. has helped to negotiate an end to the Iran-Iraq war, to persuade the Soviet Union to withdraw its troops from Afghanistan, and to end the civil war in El Salvador.
- The U.N. buys needed time for diplomacy and accommodation. U.N. peacekeepers at a cost of 1,000 dead and thousands wounded have monitored ceasefires in South Asia, the Middle East, and Cyprus for decades, providing states in conflict with the assurance that agreements were being respected and that actions by their rivals were not placing them in danger. Though the U.N.'s thirty-five peacekeeping operations have not been cheap over the years, their cost is only a small fraction of the cost to the international community of continued wars in such volatile areas of the world as South Asia and the eastern Mediterranean.
- The U.N. heals nations. Through peacekeeping and peace-building efforts the U.N. has been able to restore a degree of civil society to Cambodia, El Salvador, Mozambique, Namibia,

and Nicaragua, where hundreds of thousands of people have
died in civil wars.

- The U.N. promotes democracy. U.N. missions have provided
electoral assistance and advice to more than forty-five countries,
including the organization and conduct of elections in Cambodia, the supervision of the electoral process in Namibia, the
observation and verification of elections of referenda in Angola,
El Salvador, Eritrea, Haiti, Mozambique, Nicaragua, and
South Africa. As mentioned, the number requesting assistance is
constantly growing.
- The U.N. has provided legitimacy to several critical U.S. foreign policy concerns—the American led intervention in the Korean War, the American led intervention in the Gulf, the Nonproliferation Treaty, and most recently the American led
intervention in Haiti.
- U.N. agencies provide the indispensable institutional underpin-
ning for a number of international regimes that are of enormous
value to the United States and other major participants in the
international economy. Examples are the International Atomic
Energy Agency's safeguards program, which is central to America's nonproliferation effort; World Weather Watch, which
saves U.N. members billions each year because of early warning
of changes in the weather; the World Meteorological Organization's program, which brings order to the world's airwaves; the
Food and Agriculture Organization's Codex Alimentarius,
which protects the health and safety standards of foods traded
internationally; the World Health Organization's (WHO) campaigns to limit the spread of communicable diseases, which is
critical in an age of international travel; the International Civil
Aviation Organization's safety standards at world airports,
which ensure the safety of traveling Americans; and several
regimes for the protection of international property rights,
which is of critical importance to U.S. industry.
- The U.N. promotes sound economic policy: U.N. development
agencies, including the U.N. Development Programme
(UNDP), the World Bank, and the International Monetary
Fund, have promoted the kind of market oriented economic
policies that the United States believes are most suitable for

democratic societies. This trend has been particularly pronounced since the late 1970s when the evidence that state directed economic activity was providing diminishing returns became overwhelming.

- The U.N. saves lives. Agencies like the World Health Organization, the U.N. International Children's Emergency Fund (UNICEF), and the UNDP have saved millions of people from sickness and disease. It is estimated that in recent years 20 million people would have died from smallpox had WHO not eradicated it in 1981. Three million children a year live because WHO and UNICEF have cooperated on a program that has immunized 80 percent of the world's children against the six killer diseases—polio, tetanus, measles, whooping cough, diphtheria, and tuberculosis. The WHO program against river blindness saves the sight of some 7 million children a year. Since 1960 death rates of children in developing countries have been halved through innovative techniques of oral rehydration therapy and improved water supplies pioneered by U.N. agencies. The percentage of rural people with access to safe water has grown from less than 10 percent in 1945 to nearly 65 percent today.

- The U.N. promotes human rights. Despite the many tempestuous ideological disputes that have raged in the U.N., which were particularly dominant in the 1970s and part of the 1980s, overall the organization has promoted the ideas of democracy and human rights on which the American experiment is based. The end of the cold war has made the U.N.'s efforts to promote democracy and human rights less controversial and contested.

This recitation of the strengths of the United Nations is not to suggest that the organization lacks its weaknesses. It has many that have troubled several administrations, Republican and Democratic, in recent years. U.N. members have used the U.N. as a propaganda forum, jeopardizing its technical work to score political points. The United States itself was not entirely innocent of this behavior, especially during the height of the cold war. But particularly in the manner in which a majority of U.N. members addressed the issues surrounding apartheid and the Middle East question, great damage, as already discussed, was done to the technical work of the U.N.

Too much of the work of the U.N. General Assembly and the Security Council is conducted at the level of the lowest common denominator. Too much of this work reflects political posturing rather than serious analysis of the issues. In recent years the Security Council, in particular, has edged toward irresponsibility in the way that it has passed resolutions without an adequate regard for the reality on the ground. One U.N. commander in Bosnia publicly announced that he no longer read Security Council pronouncements because they bore so little relationship to the reality he was confronting.

The U.N. Secretariat, despite recent reforms, is still not properly organized to deal with the worldwide peacekeeping responsibilities it has assumed. Problems of command and control need to be resolved. Procurement procedures need to be improved. Accountability must be increased. Under U.S. leadership, progress has been made, but more needs to be accomplished.

The role of the U.N. in the field of economic development is in need of radical restructuring. The decisions of the Economic and Social Council (ECOSOC) have little relationship to reality. Coordination among the specialized agencies is inadequate. Too much of the scarce development funds available are wasted because U.N. agencies tend to allocate money to countries according to political formula rather than according to project merit.

The personnel policies of the U.N., though recently improved somewhat, remain an institutional scandal. Governments have prevented the institution from establishing a professional selection and career process that would help raise the quality of Secretariat personnel.

The financing of the U.N. is grossly unfair. Under current provisions, the budget of the U.N. can be adopted by a two-thirds vote by states whose total contribution to the U.N. budget is only a few percent. One permanent member of the U.N. Security Council, the People's Republic of China, which is poised to be the world's largest economy, contributes less than 1 percent of the U.N. budget although it enjoys a veto power. Japan, which contributes 12 percent, is not a member of the Council. To be sure, recent budgets have been adopted by consensus so that a constitutional crisis has been avoided. But this system of financing limits sharply the effectiveness of the U.N. Major donors like the United States will not permit the U.N. to assume new responsibilities so long as the financing arrangements are so inequitable.

Personal accountability in the U.N. is not high enough. In all government bureaucracies, there are employee protections that do not exist in private industry. Nonetheless, in the U.N. it is too difficult to dismiss an employee for cause. There is no effective way to convict an employee who has committed a criminal offense.

What can be done to reform the United Nations? Following is a possible action program.

The U.N. cannot gain the overall support it needs within the United States unless it benefits from what we might call tough official love. Public opinion polls demonstrate that there is general good will toward the U.N. in the United States, but the president and secretary of state occupy key leadership positions. The fact is that for many years the American people have not heard their leaders say many good things about the U.N. There has been a tendency in all administrations to criticize the U.N. for failures that are more those of the member states than of the institution itself. There has been little effort made at the highest levels to couple with their criticism an articulation of the considerable advantages the United States derives from its membership in the U.N. at the same time that we are calling for reform. In short, recent administrations have failed in their educational responsibilities toward the American people.

The Clinton administration in its first year oversold the U.N. Its critics may now be underselling the organization. It was never possible for the U.N. to shoulder responsibilities that even many major states have difficulty undertaking. To suggest otherwise did great harm to the U.N. But it is also not in U.S. interests to suggest that the United States can, without harm to its own interests, totally disregard international opinion as expressed in international bodies like the United Nations and unilaterally take whatever measure happens to enjoy majority support in the Congress or the administration. There is a critical need for balance in the U.S. approach to the U.N.

The United States needs a fresh look at the issue of peacekeeping that would include the leadership of the Congress as well as the administration. Presidential Decision Directive 25 (PDD-25), the administration's statement on U.N. peacekeeping, which reflects the disaster in Somalia, presents too crabbed a view of U.S. interests in this important area. It never makes it clear that the United States, like all major powers, has a national interest in the management and reduction of conflict. It is certainly true that this or any other administration cannot treat U.S. forces like mercenaries to be dispatched wherever an administration may decide without regard to pressing U.S. national interests. It is true that the U.S. military consists of volunteers, but these men and women volunteered to defend the United States of America. They did not necessarily volunteer to participate in whatever U.N. peacekeeping operation may be endorsed by the U.N. Security Council, even if the United States votes for it. A decision to participate should therefore be made in close consultation with the leadership of the Congress. In addition, the United States probably should create a special unit within the American military for individuals willing to volunteer for U.N. peacekeeping duty. This unit could be earmarked for U.N. service. The creation of such units would enable the United Nations to move with much greater dispatch in a crisis. Now often months are lost along with the opportunity to have a positive impact as the secretary-general attempts to find the troops necessary to carry out the Security Council mandate.

The United States should make it clear that its participation in U.N. peacekeeping under any foreign command must take place only within the limits of traditional peacekeeping, that is to say, when the parties to the conflict agree on the introduction of U.N. forces. If U.N. troops are to engage in any enforcement action, the U.S. position should be that U.S. participation in any U.N. blessed operation entails U.S. command as was the case in the Korean and Gulf Wars.

The United States needs to take a broader view of Security Council reform. The issue is not simply the inclusion of influential states like Germany and Japan, but also adherence to the Charter to ensure that those who are elected to the Council meet the stipulations of Article 23, which states that the nonpermanent members of the Security Council should be elected with "due regard being specially paid, in the first instance to the contribution of Members of the United Nations to the maintenance of international peace and security and to the other purposes of the Organization, and also to equitable geographic distribution." The United States should press the view that no new state should be accorded permanent status on the Security Council unless it was willing to make an exceptional contribution to international peace and security. One way to do this would be through extra financial contributions from the non–veto-wielding members of the Security Council. Another would be to insist that no state be elected to the Security Council unless it had established an earmarked unit for U.N. duty. Admittedly, some might argue that current permanent members do not meet this standard, but the establishment of such a standard for the new permanent members would put more pressure on countries like China to do their fair share. Regarding the nonpermanent members, the United States should insist that part of Security Council reform include a requirement for those seeking election to the Security Council to take steps demonstrating their "contribution . . . to the maintenance of international peace and security."

A critical issue for the United Nations is adequate financing. The reforms suggested above for the Security Council should help to meet part of this problem. But for the United Nations to carry out its mission, member states must pay their dues in full and on time. All recent presidents—Ronald Reagan, George Bush, and Bill Clinton—agree that the United States should meet its international obligations and should pay its U.N. dues in full. We appeal to the U.S. Congress to follow this bipartisan example.

But we also believe that we must begin preparing for the time when the financial requirements for conducting the world's business in such areas as peacekeeping, refugee relief, and economic and political development will greatly exceed current funding possibilities. As the chapters prepared for this American Assembly volume underscore, the responsibilities of international organizations are exploding as the funding is declining. The number of refugees in the world is soaring. Peacekeeping is grotesquely underfunded. A serious commitment to human rights would require a significant increase in funds for monitoring and investigation.

The costs of arms control compliance are certain to increase as the international community takes new steps to control nuclear and chemical weapons. It may be impossible for many countries in the Third World to survive unless they do more for themselves, but it is also difficult to believe that they will not need significant help from the outside.

How will the international community pay for these expenses? It is inconceivable that the current funding arrangements will suffice. We believe that the international community should begin a serious exploration of alternative methods of funding. We wish to be clear in our position. The United Nations is not today in a position to become the beneficiary of autonomous sources of revenue. Adequate accountability is lacking. The effects of developing new sources of revenue are unknown. But over the years, there have been several proposals for international taxation that deserve deeper study. The day is approaching when the international community will have to tap these new sources or allow a growing volume of international business to remain unfinished or inadequately managed.

Meanwhile, to bring greater rationality to U.N. finances, we support a policy that would require future peacekeeping operations to be funded more equitably. There is not Charter barrier, for example, to the members of the Security Council seeking exceptional contributions from the region that would most benefit from a U.N. operation. Thus Gulf states might be required to provide the bulk of the financing for the continuing U.N. operation in Kuwait. European states ought to bear the bulk of the financing for U.N. operations in Europe. Africa might not be able to shoulder this new responsibility, but it is probably the only region in the world unable to accept a larger share of the burden.

In the context of U.N. reform of the Security Council, we also believe that the United States should explore the principle of equal financial contributions from all permanent members. In theory, they all have an equal interest in their stewardship of the system. They should therefore contribute equally.

The end of the cold war has also changed the rationale for U.S. participation in the U.N. In the past, whatever might be said publicly, the United States was anxious to be a member of every international organization because of fear that if the United States were absent, the Soviet Union might seize a leadership position. With the cold war over, the United States should look at every U.N. institution from the standpoint of whether membership really serves U.S. interests. Those interests, as we have indicated, are broader than those of most states because of the unique position of the United States as a world leader and the world's remaining superpower. But there may be U.N. organizations whose mandate is not sufficiently relevant to U.S. interests to justify U.S. membership. An example may be the United Nations Industrial Development Organization.

Over the years there has been a proliferation of U.N. development funds. Yet the UNDP is supposed to be the queen of the U.N. system. The United States should support the concept of a merger of the central U.N. funds and programs (specifically the UNDP, the U.N. Fund for Population Activities, and UNICEF) together with the International Fund for Agricultural Development and many of the separate technical trust funds of the specialized agencies into a single U.N. development fund so that the system would be better poised to carry out the coordination function most outside studies of its programs have recommended. With the change in the international environment, we also support the reallocation of funds to program areas like human rights and democracy promotion that are now underfunded.

The role of the secretary-general is critical. The United States has developed a very testy relationship with the current incumbent, who is likely to go down in history, however, as among the most influential secretaries-general in U.N. history, rivaled only by Dag Hammarskjold. It is imperative that we develop a better relationship with his successor if the U.N. is to undertake the kinds of reforms most American specialists would like to see. The United States should begin to promote the idea that no one should be elected to the position of secretary-general who has not presented to the Security Council and General Assembly his or her program for U.N. reform and his or her conception of the job he or she is seeking. The United States should threaten to veto candidates who fail to provide such a program.

As the United Nations turns fifty, the world is in need of more multilateral solutions. The United States for its part must become more serious about multilateral diplomacy. Today the foreign service is composed, as it always has been, of men and women of unusually high intelligence and analytical ability. However, today as in the past, it is populated and structured in a manner to reward bilateral diplomatic skills.

We suggest that a multilateral cone be created within the foreign service. This should involve greater training in multilateral diplomacy. Young, talented foreign service officers (FSOs) should not be shunted to the political cone as the most ready avenue for advancement, but rather rotated in various multilateral fora to develop the necessary experience and skills in multilateral diplomacy such as coalition building and the limitations of precedential analysis. And the multilateral cone should have some ambassadorships with which it could reward promising senior FSOs. There should also be rewards for FSOs doing tours on Capitol Hill and in state legislatures where they could hone legislative skills readily transferable to multilateral diplomacy in the U.N. There should be a premium placed on circulating young entry and midlevel FSOs through a variety of multilateral venues: NATO, OSCE, U.N. Offices in Vienna, and the U.S. Mission to the U.N.

In brief, the U.N. should be accepted for what it is—an institution with unique and valuable characteristics, in particular universality. It should be accepted that the United States cannot on the one hand fail to show aggressive leadership in the selection of the secretary-general, and then wash its hands when the new incumbent does not respond fully to the concerns and priorities of the United States. But most fundamentally it must be understood that the United Nations requires sustained and hard work by the United States at all levels if the tool is to be well used and is to be effective in advancing important U.S. interests.

Bibliography

Bair, Andrew. 1994. "Yugoslav Lessons for Future Peacekeepers." *European Security* 3:2.

Bertrand, Maurice. 1985. *Some Reflections on Reform of the United Nations.* Geneva: United Nations Joint Inspection Unit, No. 91.

Berdal, Mats. 1993. *Whither UN Peacekeeping? Adelphi Paper 281.* London: International Institute for Strategic Studies.

Bush, George. 1990. "The UN: World Parliament of Peace." *Dispatch* 1:152–154.

Childers, Erskine, with Brian Urquhart. 1994. *Renewing the United Nations System.* Uppsala, Sweden: The Dag Hammarskjold Foundation.

Clark, Jeffrey. 1993. "Debacle in Somalia: The Failure of Collective Response." In Damrosch 1993.

von Clausewitz, Carl. 1976. *On War.* edited and translated by Peter Paret. Princeton: Princeton University Press.

Coate, Roger A. ed. 1994. *U.S. Policy and the Future of the United Nations.* New York: The Twentieth Century Fund Press.

Dadzie, Kenneth. 1993. *Report of the Special Advisor and Delegate of the Secretary-General on Reform of the Economic and Social Sectors.* New York: United Nations.

Damrosch, Lori. ed. 1993. *Enforcing Restraint.* New York: Council on Foreign Relations.

Danida Study. 1991. *Effectiveness of Multilateral Agencies at the Country Level.* Copenhagen: Government of Denmark.

Doll, William, and Steven Metz. 1993. *The Army and Multinational Peace Operations: Problems and Solutions.* Carlisle Barracks, PA: U.S. Army War College.

Doyle, Michael W. 1986. *Empires.* Ithaca: Cornell University Press.

Durch, William. ed. 1993. *The Evolution of UN Peacekeeping.* New York: St. Martins Press.

Fetherston, A.B. 1994. "Putting the Peace Back into Peacekeeping." *International Peacekeeping* 1:2.

Franck, Thomas M. 1985. *Nation Against Nation.* New York: Oxford University Press.

Glenny, Misha. 1995. "Yugoslavia: The Great Fall." *New York Review of Books,* March 23, 1995.

Goulding, Marrack. 1993. "The Evolution of United Nations Peacekeeping." *International Affairs* 69:3.

Groom, A.J.R., and Paul Taylor. eds. 1975. *Functionalism: Theory and Practice in International Relations.* London: University of London Press.

Harries, Owen. 1994. "The Next Cold War?" *National Review,* August 1, 1994, pp. 28–37.

Higgins, Rosalynn. 1993. "The New United Nations and the Former Yugoslavia." *International Affairs* 69:3.

Independent Advisory Group on U.N. Financing. 1993. *Financing an Effective United Nations.* New York: Ford Foundation.

Independent Commission on the Future of the United Nations. 1993. *Toward Common Goals.* Ottawa, Canada.

Kenney, George. 1995. "Bloody Bosnia." *Washington Monthly,* March 1995, pp. 49–52.

Mackinlay, John. 1993. "Problems for US Forces in Operations beyond Peacekeeping." In *Peacekeeping: The Way Ahead?* McNair Paper 25, Institute for National Strategic Studies. Washington, D.C.: National Defense University.

Mackinlay, John, and Jarat Chopra. 1993. *A Draft Concept of Second Generation Multinational Operations 1993.* Providence: Watson Institute.

Maynes, Charles William. 1993–94. "A Workable Clinton Doctrine." *Foreign Policy* 93.

McKnight, Allan. 1975. "Functionalism and the Specialized Agencies." In Groom and Taylor 1975.

Mitrany, David. 1966. *A Working Peace System: An Argument for Functional Development of International Organization.* Chicago: Quadrangle Books.

Nordic U.N. Development Project. 1991. *The United Nations in Develop-*

ment—Reform Issues in the Economic and Social Fields. Stockholm: Almqvist & Wiksell International.

Netherlands Ministry of Foreign Affairs. 1991. *A World of Difference—New Framework for Development Cooperation.* The Hague.

North South Roundtable. 1989. *Reforming the United Nations for the 1990s.* Rome: Society for International Development.

Peck, Connie. 1993. "Preventive Diplomacy: A Perspective for the 1990s." *Occasional Papers Series, Number XIII.* New York: The Ralph Bunche Institute on the United Nations.

Picco, Giandommenico. 1994. "The U.N. and the Use of Force." *Foreign Affairs* 73:5.

Puchala, Donald. 1994. "Outsiders, Insiders, and U.N. Reform." *The Washington Quarterly* 17:161–173.

Ramet, Sabrina. 1992. "War in the Balkans." *Foreign Affairs* 71:4, pp. 79–98.

Rieff, David. 1995. *Slaughterhouse: Bosnia and the Failure of the West.* New York: Simon and Schuster.

Righter, Rosemary. 1995. *Utopia Lost: The United Nations and World Order.* New York: The Twentieth Century Fund Press.

Roberts, Adam. 1993. "The United Nations and International Security." *Survival* 35:2.

Rochester, J. Martin. 1993. *Waiting for the Millennium: The United Nations and the Future of World Order.* Columbia, S.C.: University of South Carolina Press.

Ruggie, John. 1993. "The United Nations: Stuck in a Fog between Peacekeeping and Enforcement." In *Peacekeeping: The Way Ahead?* McNair Paper 25, Institute for National Strategic Studies. Washington, D.C.: National Defense University.

Sahnoun, Mohammed. 1994. *The Missed Opportunities.* Washington, D.C.: USIP.

South Commission. 1990. *The Challenge to the South.* Geneva.

de Soto, Alvaro, and Graciana del Castillo. 1994. "Obstacles to Peacebuilding." *Foreign Policy* 94.

Steinberg, James B. 1993. "International Involvement in the Yugoslav Conflict." In Damrosch 1993.

Stevenson, Jonathan. 1993. "Hope Restored in Somalia." *Foreign Policy* 13:154.

Thompson, Kenneth. 1980. *Masters of International Thought.* Baton Rouge: Louisiana State University Press.

Thornburgh, Dick. 1993. *Report to the Secretary-General of the United Nations.* New York: The United Nations.

Touval, Saadia. 1994. "Why the UN Fails." *Foreign Affairs* 73:5.

United Nations Association of the United States of America. 1987. *A Successor Vision: The United Nations of Tomorrow.* New York: UNA-USA.

United Nations Secretary-General. 1994. *An Agenda for Development: Recommendations.* New York: United Nations A/49/655.

United States Commission on Improving the Effectiveness of the United Nations. 1993. *Defining Purpose: The U.N. and the Health of Nations.* Washington, D.C.

Urquhart, Brian. 1993. *Ralph Bunche, An American Life.* New York: W.W. Norton.

Weiss, Thomas. 1993. "New Challenges for UN Military Operations." *The Washington Quarterly* 16:1.

Final Report of the Eighty-Seventh American Assembly

At the close of their discussions, the participants in the Eighty-seventh American Assembly, on "U.S. Foreign Policy and the United Nations System," at Arden House, Harriman, New York, April 20–23, 1995, reviewed as a group the following statement. This statement represents general agreement; however, no one was asked to sign it. Furthermore, it should be understood that not everyone agreed with all of it.

U.S. policy toward the United Nations is in crisis. The United States has started on a course that could turn out to be as fateful as the Senate's decision after the First World War not to join the League of Nations. The United States is, in fact, in danger of drifting out of the United Nations. Before this decade is over, the United States may have ended its contributions to several U.N. agencies, lost its vote in the General Assembly, and begun the dismantlement of a structure that Republican and Democratic administrations have spent fifty years creating.

Yet these dramatic developments are taking place without a serious national debate that would permit the American people to consider the consequences of current trends. U.S. policy toward the United Nations, a combination of executive and legislative actions, suffers from an ad hoc, incoherent character that threatens to cause permanent damage to U.S. global interests.

As in other areas of foreign policy, budgetary considerations are now driving substance. The United Nations cannot and should not be shielded from careful budgetary examination. But instead of a rational debate about which U.N. activities and institutions are most in U.S. interests and therefore should be defended, and, moreover, which are essential to the U.N.'s long-term effectiveness, U.S. foreign policy is being unhelpfully debated as a choice between multilateralism and unilateralism, with the administration identified with the former and Congress identified with the latter. It is a false debate.

To be effective, any international policy must combine unilateral with multilateral efforts. In the field of nonproliferation, for example, the five permanent members of the Security Council have relied on multilateral instruments to establish and defend an international regime against the proliferation of nuclear, chemical, and biological weapons. But few believe that the regime could survive without parallel, unilateral efforts by the major powers, in particular the United States, to defend the nonproliferation norm. The United Nations has helped to bring peace to Cambodia, El Salvador, and Namibia, but it was unilateral efforts by the United States and others that made the U.N. success possible.

With the end of the cold war and the end of the ideological struggle between East and West, there is general acceptance within the U.N. system of the norms of democracy, free markets, environmental protection, and human rights. But this acceptance is not an accident. It is the result of U.S. leadership, often expressed through unilateral actions that subsequently found multilateral acceptance. Yet U.S. defense of these norms alone would be less effective if it did not have the United Nations as a forum in which to secure their broad legitimation. Moreover, in some cases unilateral action would prove ineffective, and to rely on it in every case would be beyond the capacity of the United States.

The United Nations is therefore not a cause to be pursued for its own sake, but a tool that previous administrations and Congresses have found useful in defending U.S. interests. They did not always pick up this tool because its use was not always appropriate. And sometimes they tried to use it and, as in Bosnia or Somalia today or the Congo earlier, found that the dangers were greater than anticipated. Nonetheless, all postwar administrations, Democratic and Republican, took care to see that this important foreign policy instrument was maintained because they knew it might again be needed.

Now a U.S. fiscal hammer is poised to damage or even smash that tool.

This Assembly found significant retrenchments in some U.N. operations necessary and unavoidable. The task is to approach the pruning process rationally and to ensure that the activities of the United Nations that most serve U.S. interests are not lost. A goal of this report is to help in this effort.

At the same time we wish to prepare for the future. This current crisis should be seized as an opportunity to join with others to streamline the United Nations and to push it to concentrate on programs that can enjoy widespread political support among the citizens of its most powerful member.

A fundamental rupture in the U.S. relationship with the United Nations may be approaching. Now is not a moment for drift or business as usual.

Peace and Security

Working for peace is what the world most wants and expects of the United Nations. Its first obligation is to seek to forestall the outbreak of conflict through traditional diplomatic means such as mediation.

Nonproliferation

One of the clearest vital interests the United States has in an uncertain and dangerous world is to prevent the spread of nuclear and other weapons of mass destruction. This interest has been pursued through the United Nations effectively and at rather low cost. Multilateral action is even more important now than during the cold war era, when the superpowers were sentries of nonprolif-eration and the technology for such weapons was less widely available.

Preventing the spread of weapons of mass destruction demands intensified actions by the United States and other countries, working in concert with the United Nations, to provide a climate where member states feel secure enough not to seek these weapons. Indefinite extension of the Nuclear Non-Proliferation Treaty can further enhance that sense of security. The United Nations has done a good job of creating a climate where the acquisition of such weapons is considered illegitimate. In general, the United Nations, through the International Atomic Energy Agency (IAEA), has done well in providing confidence that nations are honoring their nonproliferation commitments. But the problems in Iraq and North Korea are a warning that the world must do even better.

IAEA's resources must be strengthened with, for example, new detection technologies and broader rights for surprise inspections. The major powers must ensure that the IAEA has the information needed to do its job. The Security Council must also be better prepared to back up the IAEA with sanctions, if additional states embark on the road toward nuclear weapons capability.

The norm against acquiring such weapons can be strengthened. The Security Council should endorse through a resolution the 1992 Security Council Summit declaration that proliferation constitutes a threat to international peace. The Council should designate a senior official who would follow developments and report regularly, ensuring sustained attention to the issue. Steps should be taken through the United Nations to strengthen enforcement against nonstate actors engaged in the illegal transfer and production of proscribed nuclear material.

Peacekeeping and Enforcement

Peacekeeping has been the biggest, most rapidly expanding part of the U.N. budget. This spending will inevitably decline due to hard experience and lowered expectations. The United Nations wants no more unfunded peacekeeping mandates from the member states. We agree.

It should be remembered, however, that traditional peacekeeping has prevented the resumption of wars in places like Cyprus and the Middle East that had the potential of necessitating U.S. involvement and could have resulted in the vast loss of life and treasure.

Traditional peacekeeping is a method for containing conflict where the United Nations places lightly armed troops between warring parties who have agreed to their presence as part of a peace process. By their presence, such soldiers create a climate where the resort to violence is illegitimate. They also offer assurances to previously warring parties that ceasefires will be maintained. The United States should support these activities, not necessarily with its own troops, but with its unique military capabilities ranging from logistics to command, control, communications, and intelligence (C^3I).

In recent years the United Nations has proven to be useful in the settlement of a new kind of conflict involving not interstate aggression, but civil war and internal strife. Provided that the parties to the conflict agree, the United Nations has helped bring an end to conflict in such different countries as Cambodia, El Salvador, Mozambique, and Namibia.

In these cases, the United Nations has added to the more traditional approach of peacekeeping such innovative approaches as supporting human rights, supervising demobilization, and monitoring elections. In such cases, however, the United Nations must be wary of moving toward measures that erode its impartiality.

The United Nations has encountered its greatest difficulties in conflicts where the various parties do not accept U.N. involvement or renege on their earlier acceptance of it. In these cases force must be used to implement the mandate. This Assembly concluded that when force is necessary, it is most effective for major military powers to lead. But a U.N. endorsement should almost always be obtained. It will generally be desirable for the United Nations to monitor the performance of the forces legitimated by the U.N. endorsement. If U.S. forces are to participate, a U.N. endorsement should be sought to legitimize the action and help rally public support.

To rebuild support for U.N. peace operations, it is necessary before embarking on any of the three categories discussed to apply rigorous criteria for success. What is the nature of the conflict? What are the expectations of intervention? What actions are contemplated? What are the rules of engagement? What is the anticipated cost, who will pay for it, and how are we ensuring it will be cost-effective? What is the degree of consent among the warring parties for U.N. intervention? When is the mission over? What is success, and what is the exit strategy for failure? What are the measures crucial to achieving lasting peace in the aftermath?

Unless there are satisfactory answers to these questions, the mission probably should not be undertaken. The international community may have to restrict its response. It may wish to apply political pressure or economic sanctions. At the same time, the United States should not approach these questions too narrowly. Arguing over who will pay for U.S. armored personnel carriers, which delayed a U.N. deployment in Rwanda, is an odious response to genocide. Looking to the future, the United Nations should not abandon efforts to develop methods for implementing the peace enforcement role that is embodied in its Charter and principles.

Human Rights

The promotion of human rights has been one of the greatest U.N. successes. The principles embodied in the Universal Declaration of Human Rights, which are consistent with the United States' own values and principles, are now universally accepted. Momentum to expand human rights and democracy is, however, potentially threatened by U.S. disengagement from the United Nations. Of special concern would be the impact on the U.N.'s effectiveness to monitor workers' rights violations through the International Labor Organization (ILO) and to protect the human rights of women.

Over time the pace of the worldwide revolution toward freedom and democracy could substantially slow. A world of states that respects human rights is not only in U.S. moral interests, but in its security interest as well. States that adhere to the U.N.'s principles of human rights historically have been more likely to be peaceful and stable than those states that flout human rights.

The United States now has the opportunity to close the gap between the establishment of human rights norms and actual compliance with those norms. It is one thing to set standards, it is another to develop the instruments to promote and enforce those standards. The United States should continue to lead in developing machinery to monitor and report publicly on human rights abuses and to hold the abusers accountable. In this regard, the United States was the leading advocate for the creation of a High Commissioner for Human Rights and for strengthening the investigative capacity of the Centre for Human Rights. Without the active and sustained efforts of the United States to strengthen these instruments and promote their effectiveness, however, they will continue to be watchdogs with no teeth, and their potential role in building democratic institutions and in conflict prevention will not be realized. Without the United States, they will be unable to advance the foreign policy vision of human rights and democracy, a vision that enjoys widespread support in the United States. If U.S. foreign policy practice is to accord with U.S. foreign policy rhetoric, the United States must give its strong moral, political, and financial support to these vital instruments.

For the United Nations to advance the cause of human rights effectively, fundamental reform is essential. To cite only one example, the U.N. Human Rights Commission contains some of the world's worst human rights violators and thus invites charges of hypocrisy, which renders it far less effective than it should be. If the commission decides to investigate alleged human rights abuses by one of its members, but that member refuses to admit to its territory a commission fact finder, it should be required to withdraw from the commission.

War crimes tribunals for the former Yugoslavia and Rwanda are a breakthrough means to hold egregious abusers of human rights accountable. These instruments deserve strong endorsement and financial support from a fully engaged U.S. government. The recent ratification of the International Convention on Civil and Political Rights should be followed by ratification of other major human rights treaties.

Refugees and the Growing Challenge of Complex Emergencies

One consequence of the end of the cold war has been an explosive increase in the number of refugees and displaced persons. According to the U.S. government's own best intelligence esti-

mates, released to the public in January 1995, more than 40 million
people—nearly 1 percent of the world's population—are in need
of or dependent on international aid to avoid large-scale malnutrition and death. In the past, due to the cold war competition and
claims of sovereignty, international relief agencies responded to a
limited range of humanitarian emergencies and refugee flows.
This trend changed with the U.S. led humanitarian intervention
in northern Iraq in the spring of 1991. Since then, demands on
several key U.N. agencies have been unprecedented and show no
signs of diminishing. The budget of the U.N. High Commissioner
for Refugees has doubled since 1989, and comparable pressures
are being felt by UNICEF, the World Food Programme, and the
many American and other nongovernmental humanitarian organizations that work closely with the United Nations.

The United Nations, while not always successful in adapting to
these harsh new realities, will continue to have a vital comparative
advantage and a unique mandate to address the humanitarian
imperative to help refugees and internally displaced people.
UNHCR's work and that of its operational partners have been
critical components of many peacekeeping operations. The
United Nations' coordination and response capacity in this area
must be strengthened. In an era of resource constraints, the efforts
by the U.N. Secretariat to integrate better the planning and joint
efforts of the Departments of Peacekeeping, Political, and Humanitarian Affairs deserve U.S. support. But U.S. influence in improving the early warning and rapid response capabilities of the United
Nations to reduce the eventual high costs of complex emergencies
is at risk if the United States refuses to make the necessary investments in preventive action.

Humanitarian Relief and Development

Support for development helps increase national self-reliance
and encourage an international culture of cooperation vital for
maintaining peace, protecting the environment, safeguarding
human rights, reducing poverty, and tackling shared global problems. This Assembly believes, however, that the United Nations'
development efforts must be concentrated, restructured, and re-

formed. At a time when the world faces an upsurge in humanitarian emergencies and refugee flows, the United Nations' limited development resources are going to be severely strained. The financial squeeze that the United Nations will be experiencing forces a reexamination of its role in international development, requiring it to concentrate on those functions it does well—including technical cooperation, humanitarian relief, and refugee assistance—while leaving to others those functions that it performs less effectively. The U.N. development agencies are not as well placed as the Bretton Woods institutions to promote long-term economic growth and sustainable development in less developed countries. The U.N. development agencies should be reorganized and pared down to focus only on those activities that cannot be performed more effectively by other multilateral or bilateral agencies, nongovernmental organizations, and private enterprise. Other than those programs proven to be effective in providing health, nutrition, and family and community services to vulnerable populations, primarily women and children, aid and development assistance delivered by U.N. agencies should concentrate on ameliorating immediate problems.

However, currently these assistance efforts are carried out by a host of overlapping agencies. With the United Nations' looming financial crisis and with support in the United States for the United Nations suffering because of many Americans' perceptions that it is a wasteful and inefficient organization, it is imperative that the United Nations consolidate and streamline its agencies and activities designed to promote human well-being. The United States should actively engage with other U.N. members to design and support such reforms.

Environment

The United States has a major interest in the work of the United Nations in the international field. The United Nations has midwifed important environmental conventions that have established a framework for multilateral cooperation on ozone depletion, climate change, transport of hazardous waste, ocean dumping, and biological diversity. The United Nations has a continuing role in supporting the development of common environmental standards and assisting the self-policing mechanisms established in the conventions. But to make further progress, the United Nations must now look at ways to consolidate the expert secretariats set up to support the work of the conventions. It must integrate the environmental monitoring activities carried out through various U.N. agencies (e.g., the U.N. Environment Programme, the World Meteorological Organization, the Food and Agriculture Organization) into their support functions.

The United Nations Conference on Environment and Development capped a decade-long effort to integrate the principles of environmental protection into the broader context of development. With the adoption by consensus of Agenda 21, more than 170 member states recognized that sound environmental protection policies are essential for sustainable economic development.

For effective implementation of Agenda 21, the United States must work with other countries to strengthen the capacity of the Commission on Sustainable Development to monitor national sustainable development action plans. Although the United Nations has less capacity to fund major environmental programs in the developing countries, given its monitoring and convention support activities, closer and more effective collaboration with the International Bank for Reconstruction and Development (IBRD) and other regional development banks is imperative.

Funding Realities and Options

This Assembly believes that the U.S. government is legally obligated to pay its annual assessment, and it supports the position of the last three presidents that the United States should pay its legally obligated arrearages. Given the current political and budgetary climate in the United States, however, it seems likely that the U.S. government will not pay its remaining legally obligated arrearages to the United Nations, or all of its current assessed obligations, or its previous level of voluntary contributions to U.N. agencies. The expected cuts are likely to be much larger than in any previous similar period of retrenchment.

Principles

In undertaking this painful budget cutting exercise, the U.S. government should be guided by four fundamental principles. First, if the United Nations is to remain a vital instrument of U.S. foreign policy, any review of U.S. contributions to peacekeeping and other U.N. activities must be carried out within the total context of U.S. national security planning to determine whether, in the post–cold war era, more cost-effective alternative reductions in less vital items of the much larger national defense budget are possible. Second, across-the-board cuts should be avoided in favor of differentiating among U.N. agencies and functions. Identical percentage reductions will not reflect true U.S. priorities and could unduly penalize elements of the system that are of particular value to us. This implies a readiness to sharply reduce or even eliminate funds for programs or agencies determined to be of relatively low priority. Third, if assessed obligations are not to be fully honored, the United States should renegotiate them rather than act unilaterally, which would clearly undermine a principle of international law that the United States values extremely highly, namely, that states must honor international obligations that states have chosen to assume. Initially, then, the United States should concentrate budget cuts on the voluntary programs, while embarking on immediate negotiations to reduce U.S. contributions to the assessed budgets. Finally, as part of this exercise, the United States should go beyond posturing rhetoric and systematically engage other countries in a serious multilateral process of reform of the U.N. system.

Criteria

The differentiation process among agencies and programs should be carefully grounded. Agencies and functions that promote U.S. interests and values should be maintained and, if necessary, enhanced: e.g., human rights, nuclear nonproliferation, refugees, the environment, and low-intensity peacekeeping operations. U.N. programs that have a proven track record, such as the U.N.

Population Fund, should get preference. Cost effectiveness, including both good management and leverage of U.S. funds, is
another important criterion. Finally, many U.N. functions that
have a comparative advantage in addressing issues of global scope
should receive priority. Illustrative of the many U.N. programs
that meet these criteria are promotion of human rights, nuclear
nonproliferation, refugee protection, environmental monitoring
and norm setting, combating epidemics, and addressing maternal
and child mortality.

Consequences

The impact of these cuts will be varied. It is possible that the
United States will lose some influence in multilateral decision
making and that programs of particular value to the United States
could be adversely affected. While it is conceivable that other
countries might increase U.N. contributions to make up for the
U.S. shortfall, they might, conversely, be tempted to make their
own cuts. Other major donors might also pick and choose their
own priorities within the U.N. system, thus undermining the principle of universality that has been a pillar of the multilateral system. This, in turn, could lead to a serious diminution of the U.N.'s
ability to carry out essential functions. These are all very serious
costs that decision makers should consider carefully.

U.N. Reform

Although reform measures will not forestall U.S. funding cuts in
the short run, such reform is, nevertheless, indispensable to ensure
strong future support of U.N. activities by both the United States
and other major donor countries.

It is almost universally recognized that the United Nations is in
need of serious administrative and management reform. Mandates must be clear and realistic. Overheads need to be evaluated
and cut. Flexibility to move human and material resources in response to emergency situations needs to be enhanced. Personnel
policies need to be overhauled. The principle of geographical representation should be clearly subordinated to the merit principle in

hiring, with the aim of significantly raising the quality of staff. Gender discrimination should be eliminated and more women candidates proposed for senior positions.

Better coordination within the U.N. system should be more than a slogan: it should be a carefully researched process that results in the elimination of duplication and overlap, streamlining, and, if necessary, the transfer of functions among agencies.

The U.N. budget should be developed and presented in a manner that would more clearly reflect actual program expenditures. Given the likelihood of increasing U.N. budgetary needs, combined with the budgetary constraints of member states, serious study should be given to supplementary funding sources, such as fees for services and public/private partnerships.

In light of these far-reaching changes and challenges ahead, selection of the next secretary-general becomes critically important. In place of the custom of political and geographical horse-trading, the Security Council should launch a formal search process to identify the best possible candidates, regardless of geographic region: internationally respected men and women who combine strong character, exceptional management and administrative skills, political savoir-faire, and who, as leaders, can personify a sense of universal moral solidarity.

In advancing all or any of these or other reforms, U.S. leadership is essential. The price of effective leadership is a willingness to shoulder its burdens as well as its privileges.

Conclusion

This report has been conditioned by the harsh fiscal realities facing the U.S. government and the real need for reform in the U.N. system. It has been informed by considerations that we believe can be building blocks for a sound bipartisan U.S. policy toward the U.N. system.

If the U.S. political climate is not favorable and if budget pressures are fierce, they should not be supreme. Any durable bipartisan policy must be driven by U.S. interests. In this post–cold war era, many vital U.S. interests are best advanced through multilateral means, and some, in particular, through parts of the U.N.

system. This report has highlighted many of these areas.

Given the continuing value of the U.N. system to advancing many U.S. interests, decisions resulting from the U.S. fiscal crisis should neither cripple this important foreign policy tool, nor cause us to withdraw from the United Nations, nor breach U.S. treaty obligations. The administration and Congress also must soberly review the fateful course on which we are now embarked, since it could well lead to the complete dismantlement of the U.N. system.

By a realistic assessment of ways and means through which U.S. interests are advanced through the United Nations and a willingness to focus U.S. financial support and activities on those parts of the U.N. system most vital to U.S. interests, we believe this report lays the foundation for the restoration of a bipartisan U.S. policy toward the United Nations. To build on this foundation, the United States must work with other member states to advance meaningful reforms such as those outlined herein.

Partisan attacks on the United Nations aside, no country has a greater interest than the United States in international respect for the web of international law and norms that the United Nations and its members have so carefully built up over several decades. Without this web the United States would be forced to defend unilaterally, and at great cost, its citizens and businesses at various points around the globe. Before the administration and Congress, collectively and separately, tear at that web, they should, soberly and with full awareness of our interests and commitments, consider the course on which we are moving, since it seems to be pushing us toward a fateful withdrawal from the postwar multilateral system.

We believe that whatever current passions may be, the United States will again wish to turn to the United Nations as a cost-effective tool to seek solutions to world problems that bear fundamentally on U.S. interests and values. For this reason, we appeal to the administration and Congress to proceed with caution, and to the United Nations to embark on a serious program of reform with dispatch.

The excessive, often unfounded, political attacks on the United Nations should cease. We call on the president to provide leadership at this crucial time by consulting with Congress and convening in the summer of 1995 a White House conference on the United Nations where a bipartisan group can work for a broad consensus for a revitalized U.N. agenda consistent with the value of this institution to us and to the world.

The tough decisions discussed in this report are not happy choices. But compelled by the harsh fiscal realities, perhaps they can become the basis for a more durable bipartisan U.S. policy toward the United Nations in this new world.

Participants
The Eighty-Seventh American Assembly

KRISTINA A. ARRIAGA DE
BUCHOLZ
Executive Director
Valladares Foundation
Alexandria, VA

*RICHARD E. BENEDICK
Senior Fellow
World Wildlife Fund
Washington, DC

J. KENNETH BLACKWELL
Treasurer of the State of Ohio
Columbus, OH

SAMUEL L. BROOKFIELD
President
Business Council for the
    United Nations
New York, NY

JANET WELSH BROWN
Senior Fellow
World Resources Institute
Washington, DC

MICHAEL CAHILL
U.N. Correspondent
Monitor Radio
New York, NY

MICHAEL W. DOYLE
Professor of Politics and
    International Affairs
Center of International Studies
Princeton University
Woodrow Wilson School of
    International Affairs
Princeton, NJ

LEWIS DUNN
Vice President
Science Applications
    International Corporation
McLean, VA

CHRISTINA EGUIZÁBAL
Program Officer
The Ford Foundation
New York, NY

TOM FARER
School of International Service
The American University
Washington, DC

THOMAS M. FRANCK
Murry and Ida Becker
    Professor of Law
Director
Center for International
    Studies
New York University School of
    Law
New York, NY

JESSE FRIEDMAN
Deputy Executive Director
American Institute for Free
    Labor Development
Washington, DC

FELICE D. GAER
Director
Jacob Blaustein Institute for
    the Advancement of Human
    Rights
American Jewish Committee
New York, NY

INGE GEDO
Department of Political
  Science
U.S. Air Force Academy
U.S. Air Force Academy, CO

†MARRACK GOULDING
Under-Secretary-General for
  Political Affairs
United Nations
New York, NY

WALTER GRAZER
Director
Environmental Justice
  Program
U.S. Catholic Conference
Washington, DC

CATHERINE GWIN
Vice President for Studies
Overseas Development
  Council
Washington, DC

JOHN LAWRENCE
  HARGROVE
The American Society of
  International Law
Washington, DC

RUTH J. HINERFELD
Vice Chair
United Nations Association of
  the U.S.A.
Larchmont, NY

KEIR JORGENSEN
Research Director
Amalgamated Clothing and
  Textile Workers Union
New York, NY

‡ALAN F. KAY
President
Americans Talk Issues
  Foundation
Commissioner of "The Global
  Commission to Fund the
  U.N."
St. Augustine, FL

‡MELINDA KIMBLE
Deputy Assistant Secretary for
  Global Issues
Bureau of International
  Organization Affairs
U.S. Department of State
Washington, DC

**JIM LANDERS
Dallas Morning News
Washington, DC

*JAMES F. LEONARD
Former Deputy Permanent
  Representative to the United
  Nations
Arlington, VA

HERBERT LEVIN
Executive Director
America-China Society
New York, NY

EDWARD C. LUCK
President Emeritus
United Nations Association of
  the U.S.A.
New York, NY

BRYCE NELSON
School of Journalism
University of Southern
  California
Los Angeles, CA

‡DIANA OHLBAUM
Professional Staff Member
United States Senate
Committee on Foreign
  Relations
Washington, DC

DONALD J. PUCHALA
Director
Institute of International
  Studies
University of South Carolina
Columbia, SC

KENNETH M. QUINN
U.S. Department of State
Washington, DC

DONALD H. RIVKIN
Schnader, Harrison, Segal &
  Lewis
New York, NY

TRUDY RUBIN
Philadelphia Inquirer
Philadelphia, PA

OSCAR SCHACHTER
Professor Emeritus of
  International Law and
  Diplomacy
Columbia University Law
  School
New York, NY

**BENJAMIN SCHWARZ
The RAND Corporation
Santa Monica, CA

RICH SIMPSON
Department of Political
  Science
U.S. Air Force Academy
U.S. Air Force Academy, CO

†GILLIAN MARTIN
  SORENSEN
Under Secretary/Special
  Advisor to the
  Secretary-General for Public
  Policy
United Nations
New York, NY

‡JOHN J. STREMLAU
Carnegie Commission on
  Preventing Deadly Conflict
Carnegie Corporation of New
  York
Washington, DC

JAMES S. SUTTERLIN
Yale University International
  Security Studies
New Haven, CT

JOANNA WESCHLER
United Nations Representative
Human Rights Watch
New York, NY

MAURICE WILLIAMS
Senior Associate
Overseas Development
  Council
Chevy Chase, MD

*Discussion Leader
**Rapporteur
†Delivered Formal Address
‡Panelist

About The American Assembly

The American Assembly was established by Dwight D. Eisenhower at Columbia University in 1950. It holds nonpartisan meetings and publishes authoritative books to illuminate issues of United States policy.

An affiliate of Columbia, the Assembly is a national, educational institution incorporated in the state of New York.

The Assembly seeks to provide information, stimulate discussion, and evoke independent conclusions on matters of vital public interest.

American Assembly Sessions

At least two national programs are initiated each year. Authorities are retained to write background papers presenting essential data and defining the main issues of each subject.

A group of men and women representing a broad range of experience, competence, and American leadership meet for several days to discuss the Assembly topic and consider alternatives for national policy.

All Assemblies follow the same procedure. The background papers are sent to participants in advance of the Assembly. The Assembly meets in small groups for four or five lengthy periods. All groups use the same agenda. At the close of these informal sessions participants adopt in plenary session a final report of findings and recommendations.

Regional, state, and local Assemblies are held following the national session at Arden House. Assemblies have also been held in England, Switzerland, Malaysia, Canada, the Caribbean, South America, Central America, the Philippines, and Japan. Over one hundred sixty institutions have cosponsored one or more Assemblies.

Arden House

The home of The American Assembly and the scene of the national sessions is Arden House, which was given to Columbia

University in 1950 by W. Averell Harriman. E. Roland Harriman joined his brother in contributing toward adaptation of the property for conference purposes. The buildings and surrounding land, known as the Harriman Campus of Columbia University, are fifty miles north of New York City.

Arden House is a distinguished conference center. It is self-supporting and operates throughout the year for use by organizations with educational objectives. The American Assembly is a tenant of this Columbia University facility only during Assembly sessions.

About the United Nations Association of the United States of America

The United Nations Association of the United States of America is a national organization dedicated to enhancing U.S. participation in the United Nations system and to strengthening that system as it seeks to define and carry out its mission. UNA-USA's action agenda uniquely combines education and public outreach, substantive policy analysis, and ongoing U.S.-U.N. dialogue.

UNA-USA is a leading center of policy research on the United Nations and global issues, such as environment, security, narcotics, development, and human rights. It carries out high-level dialogues with scholars and government officials from many parts of the world in order to identify fresh ideas and areas of potential cooperation. Through a series of programs, UNA-USA brings together leaders of business, Congress, academia, and the U.N. community for discussions of pressing problems on the international agenda.

With a growing nationwide network of Chapters, Divisions, and affiliated organizations, UNA-USA reaches a broad cross-section of the American public. The Association provides information and educational services on the work of the U.N. and on other global issues for students, scholars, Congress, business leaders, and the media. Each year it coordinates the observance of U.N. Day (October 24) in hundreds of communities across the nation and Model U.N. programs for tens of thousands of high school and college students.

Index